Ways of Enspiriting:
Transformative Practices for the Twenty-First Century

Cover design, book design, and photographs by Susan Tyler

First Edition, 1995

Library of Congress Catalog Card Number 94-090563

ISBN 0-9643701-0-7

Printed in the United States of America

WAYS OF
ENSPIRITING

Transformative Practices for the Twenty-First Century

warren ziegler

FIA INTERNATIONAL LLC
Denver

Contents

CONTENTS

Introduction

One of the virtues of "after-the-fact" reflection is that it helps make sense of events and actions which, when they occurred, issued forth under a different light. As I think about its origins, that is the case with *Ways of Enspiriting*. Though I began writing it in the summer of 1989, it has been in the making since my childhood when I first became aware of the presence of spirit in my life but *didn't know what to do about it or with it*. Since that will be the case with many readers of the book, that is a major reason for my writing it: *what to do with your spirit? What is its call to you? Why respond to it?*

Spirit has been palpable in all of the important events of my life, private, personal, public. From the very beginning of my conscious memory, I felt called...but for what and by whom I did not know. As with many of us brought up to live and work in a world which gives spirit so little space to flourish, it took decades before I realized that much of my own quest had been not a search for God—for that was never a problem for me—but for the *practices which would release my spirit and enable us to enter into partnership.*

That story—spirit's seeking a place in my life—would be quite ordinary and uninteresting were if not for the fact that 25 years ago, in my early forties, I left a life of action and returned to a university setting to study the future...and to begin the reflection which, ultimately, led to this book.[1] Most of the futurists sought a "scientific" or "predictive" approach to the work. Few of our methods invited the active participation of any but so-called experts, thus leaving billions of ordinary people out of the action. But I soon began to sense that all of us—not only futurists but all people everywhere—were entering into a time of

---

[1] I joined the Educational Policy Research Center at Syracuse in 1969. That was one of two centers established by the U.S. Office of Education to investigate the future of education and make policy recommendations to the U.S. Government.

transformation. We called it "social change," thereby relieving it of both its promise and its mystery, and our responsibility in bringing it about.

My spirit pushed at me—I can give it no other explanation—compelling me to design an approach that would open up the mysterious domain of the future to the hopes, the fears, and the intentions of citizens from all walks of life. Over the years, as I worked with my fellow-citizens, I discovered that when they envisioned the future of their lives, their communities, and their organizations, they were tapping into a reservoir of spirit that most were unprepared to acknowledge, much less handle with skill.

Understand that 25 years ago, we had no ready language for this discovery, and certainly not in the futures field whose advocates were bent on legitimating their work in planning, policy formation, and social science generally. They fought the truth—and most still do—that the future is a metaphor for the human imagination which, in principle, is as universal a human capacity as breathing.

In 1980, after ten years of conducting envisioning workshops using the futures-invention methods I had developed, my dear colleague Elise Boulding and I inaugurated a project entitled "Imaging a World Without Weapons." We—and the facilitators we trained—worked with hundreds of people around the globe, in academic, government, religious and community settings. That was a grand project. It is as pertinent now, given the state of the world, as it was then. It deserves its own story. But for *this* introduction, let me make the point that with that project, for the first time in public and in my writing, I stated that the *source* of our envisioning was our spirit in its *active* voice which I call the *enspiriting* mode.

I did that with great trepidation, for I had been trained as a social scientist and in philosophy as a skeptic, with neither a theological tradition nor a religious upbringing on which to stand. In naming *spirit* as the source of true envisioning, here's what I learned:

People—i.e., participants—were not put off by calling them to their spirit. To the contrary, in communities, in corporations, in schools and universities, in governments, in professional groups, they acknowledged, sometimes reluctantly, sometimes eagerly, that spirit was at work in envisioning the future of their lives, their communities, and their worlds. That reciprocity, that welcome, gave me courage to say that envisioning the future and taking action in the present to bring it about were acts of the human spirit. So let that spirit speak out—I invited—to help us configure a future which is worthy of us and of which we are worthy.

All well and good. But I couldn't stop there. To acknowledge the presence of spirit in this participatory, envisioning approach to the future did not relieve me of the need and the responsibility to *discern its action with rigor and discipline coupled with a loving invitation.* My own training and, no doubt, the disposition of my own spirit, led me, inexorably, to ask of spirit not "What is it?" but "What have we to do with it?" and "What has it to do with us?"

I examined 20 years of the practices of envisioning—its art, its craft, its techniques—in order to uncover *a path to our spirit and, at least as accurately, a path spirit could travel to become once again active in our lives.*

One result of that "research and development" are the enspiriting practices set forth in this book.

Through these practices, my spirit has re-entered my life. It was always there. Now it is active, its potential involvement always present, working in partnership with my social biography, always inviting me to its adventures, both separate from me and deeply a part of my being. It hasn't made me a "better person." My "self-esteem" has not risen. Nor have I constructed a new religion, a new cult, a new ethic. These are practices for entering into **dialogue** with your spirit and thereby with the great spirit of the universe of which yours is a part. I have uncovered some access points, some swinging gates, by virtue of experiencing my spirit and of working with many persons who were likewise engaged.

Why do that...the *enspiriting*? Why read this book? Why initiate these practices in your own life, family, community, work, politics? Because we have entered into a time of transformation on this planet, transformation at the most private and the most worldly levels, in all domains of human endeavor and in all cultures. Our spirit calls us to that transformation and challenges us to accompany it on its great adventures into our futures as well as our pasts. This is a unique time on this planet...not the first, not the last, but *now*. Seize it, as I try to. Let your spirit speak in you, to you, and through you. Participate in our transformation. Look to your spirit for the guidance and the courage to do that.

None of us make this journey alone. Spirit is of us all and joins us together through *its sociability*. I could not have written this book without the help of hundreds of participants, fellow envisioners on the path to their spirit, without the help of a dozen or so dear colleagues who have been, each in her or his way, a fellow-enspiritor. Writing this book has been a great wrestling with my spirit as it has sought to get beyond those aspects of my social biography that have continually sought to deny it voice. Doubts, frustrations, wanting to give it up have surfaced with each page. But good people have encouraged me and pushed me, and *all* of them are senior enspiritors: Donna Cardinal and Susan Sharpe in Canada; Gordon Dveirin, Marnee Harding, Grace Healy, Bob Luton and Paul McIsaac stateside; and numerous others too many to name with whom I have entered into **dialogue** about spirit in its many manifestations not once but often.

Roberta Bhasin did a superb job of editing my writing to render it more intelligible without interfering with my ideas. So any argument you may have about the enspiriting disciplines and practices is with me, not her. I welcome that and thank her.

Many questions arose about the *publication* of this book, both technical and substantive. They were addressed and resolved into the publication you now have in your hands by virtue of the collegial, professional, and financial support of Susan Anderson, May Maury Harding, George Koustas, Susan and Max Tyler, the former of whom designed this publication to meet both her and our high standards, and my dear brother, Jerome M. Ziegler, whose faith in my work has been matched only by our affection for each other.

The most creative *natural* enspiritor I have ever known was my good friend and fellow-enspiritor, David Fendrik, whose untimely death severed a comradely bond that spirit heals. His spirit never ceased its loving challenge to mine, so I dedicate this work to him. My wife, Mandy, let me write this book despite the many personal and work sacrifices it has entailed. My youngest son, Zachariah, age five when I began, pushed me to it by the prophecy of my spirit: Unless we enter into transformation *now*, through the ways of enspiriting, though it may take a second or a thousand years, his century—the Twenty-First—will be no place for decent human beings to live.

Warren Ziegler
Denver, Colorado
October, 1994

1

A Literacy of Enspiriting™

What Is Going On Here?

The words "spirit," "spiritual," and "spirituality" are on everybody's lips these days. After centuries of absence from the language of getting things done, references to the spiritual have re-entered the popular mind. Leaders proclaim the need for a spiritual approach to everything from employee motivation to health-care reform and the inability of our schools to educate many of our children. Editorials announce the need to bring spiritual values back into quality-of-life decisions. The breakdown of the family and the high divorce rate are now blamed on the absence of a spiritual element in our most intimate settings.

For some, the new spirituality is like a psychological aspirin. Finding a real or make-believe spiritual path assuages the guilts, fears and pains that come from living in a world of social disintegration and personal upset. For others, the new spirituality is a rallying cry, bolstering their unwillingness to listen to any but their own version of God's call.

What is going on here? Like a desert longing for rain, the need for a spiritual presence in our lives overwhelms us, and we thirst for any thing or person that enters in the name of spirituality.

The "New spirituality" is a fad, captured by coffee-table conversation, late-night talk shows and management training. Typically, Americans are responding at a surface level, acting out of ingrained cultural patterns. If our problem is the lack of something we need, let's go out and get it, buy it, make it, market it, sell it, consume it...and eventually throw it away as the next chimera appears on our empty horizon.

But beneath these surface responses, a sea change is taking place. At the depths of our humanity, our culture, our civilization, our very presence on this planet, something authentic and transformative is at work. But no amount of intoning, proclaiming, advertising, marketing or generally publicizing will uncover it. We must learn to experience it at a depth unknown and untried by most of us. We must seek the right starting points of what may well turn out to be a new journey along an ancient path.

That is what this book is about: Discovering the right starting points so that each of us in our own way can participate in a renaissance of the spirit at a core level, sweeping our lives clean of the effluvia of three centuries of denying our spirit, denigrating others and dehumanizing our planet.

From the Spiritual to Enspiriting

The way the "New spirituality" is usually introduced tends to make it into a thing, an idea whose time has come, an object that we might manipulate to fit our ideology or religious beliefs and make serve our commands. For centuries, we have tried to do that with God. To no avail. Walter Brueggemann, an eminently practical theologian, in *The Prophetic Imagination* (1978) points out that God is free, unchurched, not just there hiding behind the alter, not "on call" like a surgeon sleeping on a cot in the emergency room, ready to bind up our wounds and address our grievances. Much to our dismay, God is free. So is spirit. We can not capture our spirit and simply add it to our arsenal of problem-solving weapons, training protocols, or therapeutic techniques.

What then is spirit? At its most elemental, spirit is an active voice within us. Spirit is born into us when we are enfleshed, leaves us when our body dies. Spirit pervades everything in the universe. Each of us gets a piece of it. I know it not by seeking to define it, not by building a theology around it, but by sensing and watching and hearing it at work in us.

In the early 1980s, I sought a language for this voice that was emerging from so many people with whom I had been doing envisioning for over a decade. The first were Syracuse University graduate students. But over time, they included government executives, business people, school teachers and administrators, professionals, citizens, experts and persons old and young, rich and poor. As they imaged the future of their lives, their institutions, their worlds, it came increasingly clear that they were doing something more than making wishlists, formulating goals, or strategizing for the future. Indeed, the active voice of their envisioning was quite different: Deep, true, enduring, surprising, energizing, critical of the status quo, loving and nurturing, communal, sometimes quite painful and, when invited to its adventures, joyous and even ecstatic.

Seeking to name this active voice, I came to the notion of *enspiriting*. Rather than being a passive entity which, like a joker, gives us a win in life's poker game if we're lucky enough to draw it, *spirit enspirits. And those who learn to enspirit are enspiritors.*

By its enspiriting, spirit calls us, pushes us, entices us. It hides from us when not welcomed. It interacts with and even negotiates with our social biography so that it can find room to breathe. It takes us on great adventures of love and daring, risk and danger, creativity and birthing; and it loves, warms, nurtures and cares for us if we will let it *and if we will, in turn, love and nurture it.* It takes us to new spaces, to that which is possible, desirable, foundational, crucial in our lives, our work, our politics, our being with others in our families and schools, our culture and our whole way of life.

In short, *enspiriting is transformative.* It brings into being that which was not and never has been.

Now, once again in humanity's troubled history, when injustice and civil strife, deprivation and starvation, over-population and loneliness, mammon and environmental devastation rear their beastly heads, the spirit in us calls us to transformative tasks.

How to begin?

Start with Yourself

My own experience with enspiriting began quite early, in my pre-adolescent years. As with most of us, the play of spirit in my life and work took place far beneath my conscious awareness. Spirit—untamed, undisciplined, effervescent—sought many ways to express itself, as I believe it does with all of us. But my upbringing as a creature of our 20th-century culture gave me no guide to the enspiriting experience—what it is, how it lives and works in us, why now, at the end of this century, its nurturing, endisciplining and emancipating must take precedence over everything else in our lives.

An early personal anecdote may reveal how spirit emerges unintended but consequential. When I was 10, I came upon a youngster threatening a group of kids with a rusty bayonet he had found somewhere. He shoved the bayonet at the circle of kids that surrounded him, trying to break out while they jumped back and forth, jeering, laughing, taunting. I don't know how the episode began, but I walked up to the circle and gentled him with words and gestures long forgotten. I remember a feeling of great calm which, somehow, transferred to him as if he were a nervous horse on whose nose I had placed a warm and loving hand. He laid the bayonet in my outstretched hand.

What was that about? I ask myself five decades later.

Where do we find starting points for the work of enspiriting?

Look to your own life. The search is both inward-seeking and outward-looking. *That interplay between the inner and the outer is the key to enspiriting*. That means that this is not a self-help book for those whose concerns start and end with their own salvation. Nor is it for those who seek to save the world but lose sight of their inner lives. The invitation to enspiriting that this book offers is, in principle, for everybody, indeed for the entire world. But the right starting points for enspiriting, uncovering its disciplines and learning their competence begin with you, not someone else.

For some of you, the starting point will have been a happening—such as my own—at an early age, something that caught you up short, that came out of nowhere, for which you can give no account. You began on the path of *deep questioning* or perhaps *deep listening* (two of the seven ways of enspiriting treated in this book) about who and what you are, about what brought you to this planet, about your life and loves and work; for even at that early age, your spirit sought to create a space in your future life.

For others of you, starting points early in your life may not have been joyfully propitious. Happenings at an early age have been emotionally or physically traumatic. In many countries, including the United States, there are those who experience the pain and denigration of being marginalized in a de-humanizing culture rife with prejudice against folks with a different skin color, different ethnic heritage or religious persuasion, different gender or age, or with physical handicap. For them, a starting point for enspiriting may involve penetrating that extraordinary dynamic interplay of self-denigration caused by others. That entry point, however, goes far deeper than the intellectual parameters of psychological or sociological analysis. It must reach into the seedbed of spirit wherein is found the courage (in the Greek sense of *Thumos*, spirit as courage or will) to move through and beyond the grasp of social biography and cultural determinants to the adventures of your spirit.

The location of right starting points (for there are *wrong* ones!) is as varied as the totality of humanity into whose flesh and culture spirit has entered. For some, the events come from the larger outer world, even one far-distanced from their personal lives. Such events in the world may tear at you like a mighty monster sinking its claws into your consciousness and never letting go. Is it a Nazi-bred holocaust, religious cleansing in the Balkans, the killing fields of Cambodia, death squads in Central America, starvation in the Sahel, apartheid in South Africa, gang warfare in America's inner cities? Why these touch one person's spirit and not another's is a question whose response demands a great deal of inner work of the kind described in this book.

Negative events all too common in everyday life may also serve as starting points for your enspiriting. Not having—or losing—a job is certainly one for those imbued with a work ethic. Where earning a living goes hand-in-hand with God, Motherhood and Apple Pie, loss of job and work can be devastating and not only because the monthly mortgage or rent can't be paid. Some blame themselves for being down-sized, can you believe it? Or are blamed by others.

Self-denigration, family stress, despair: These, too, can be turned into creative starting points. Their trauma is immediate, sometimes private, sometimes public. So too with abuse, victimization, injustice, death of a loved one, environmental rape: Any of these may serve as starting point on the path to recourse, restitution and re-affirmation. Enspiriting is one such path. But it is also many paths, for enspiriting speaks in many different tongues. *Each person's spirit is unique, unpredictable, non-linear, a piece of a universal fractal.* Among the disciplines of the spirit described in this book, you will find a starting point for healing in at least one of them.

Do these different starting points share a common spark? All of our experience suggests so. With the many who have done enspiriting, that spark has been ignited by what I call *disharmony, inner tension, imbalance in the interior spaces.*

The Loss of Inner Harmony

In our day and age, an invitation to the enspiriting path often commences with a sense of a loss of harmony and balance in one's life. That is not surprising. The old sanctuaries of family, work, community and church are lost to many of us by virtue of the immense social changes in this century. We long to go deeply into a space out of which new societies and new cultures, new myths and new celebrations, new self-definitions and new roles are generated. That is an envisioning space for self-empowerment and of healing. That space I call spirit, that which lies within us and without. It is the source of our creativity, our ecstasy, our vision of the future, our courage and our capacity to nurture one another.

How do I know this? Over two decades of work in envisioning with thousands of people have provided an enormously rich experience in seeing them respond in just these ways. That experience constitutes the evidence upon which the enspiriting disciplines are based.

What This Book Is About

It's about three things.

First, what enspiriting is and what its disciplines are.

Second, a description of how and why to engage in enspiriting, learning, rehearsing, and testing out the competence of each of seven enspiriting disciplines.

Third, the application of the enspiriting disciplines to personal, organizational, and community life.

What are these seven disciplines of the spirit?

1. Deep Listening™ the Empty Vessel Way

I first wrote about *deep listening* over ten years ago.[1] In deep listening, you learn to become silent. Perhaps the most difficult art in the world to learn. Without silence, deep listening is impossible. It is from a space of silence that often spirit first learns to speak.

You also learn to put your social biography aside. You learn to empty of everything so that, quite literally, all that is left is spirit. So I speak of *being silence, a way of being that permeates* your entire self rather than *being silent;* for deep listening is not a task or a thing to do.

This amounts to a supreme *yielding. It is exactly the opposite of an active posture.* Spirit then receives and welcomes the other. It attends to other's words, spoken and unspoken, without judgment, without demanding credentials, without requiring substantiation or proof. As you empty yourself of all but spirit, often and for the first time, the other may hear her own "words" and may listen to *her* spirit.

Chapter Two sets forth the first three modes of deep listening. It describes how and why to be a deep listener and how to start. Chapter Six picks up on deep listening again, setting forth three additional modes, including the *empty vessel way* in which one's spirit listens to another's, sometimes without talk between them.

---

[1] *Deep Listening the Empty Vessel Way,* The Futures-Invention Associates, Denver, 1984

2. Deep Questioning™

Deep questioning penetrates to the heart of the matter. It peels off the layers of propriety, obfuscation and subterfuge that obscure or deny what is going on in the world and in your life. This is an intellectual way of enspiriting.

Chapters Three through Five set forth the How and the Why of deep questioning. They bring you face-to-face with the serious consequences of its application in your life and your world. Deep questioning and deep listening work closely together, like the forefinger and the thumb, opposable. By their ability to face each other, together they are extraordinarily tenacious in coming to grips with the issues of your spirit.

3. Deep Learning™

This is the pivotal enspiriting discipline. It is not easy to learn.

In *deep learning,* you seek to engage with your spirit unencumbered by your body, your beliefs, your upbringing, even by who you think you are. You seek to dispense with and get beyond the stories of your life that no longer serve you, stories of put-down, of self-denigration, of rivalry and jealousy, sometimes false tales that poorly or even wrongly describe your world. Violence on television and pornography, for example, are such false tales. So too are the stories that lead to religious, ethnic, or racial bigotry. Such stories hide us from our spirit. They lead us away from the quest of our spirit and put us on the path of evil.

Thus is deep learning surely transformative. It puts you into that inner space where, as in outer space, all is new, all is fresh, and all is engaged in the act of creating.

In Chapter Seven, I invite you to the initial work of deep learning. In Chapters Eight through Ten, I introduce three start-up exercises that help you discern the tension between your life and your spirit, a piece of inner work already begun in deep questioning. Chapter Eleven presents the *unlearning* mode of deep learning, followed by two key chapters on *unpeeling* and *unfreezing,* where you dispense with social biography and enter the space your spirit inhabits. That is the space of deep imaging.

4. Deep Imaging™

Twenty-five years ago at Syracuse University, I began "Futures-Invention," a play on the title of a book by a scientist and early futurist, Dennis Gabor, called *Inventing the Future* (1964). Ten years into it, my mentor and colleague, Elise Boulding, taught me that imaging was at the heart of the transformative work of envisioning. Later still, I came to realize that the source of *deep imaging* is spirit.

Deep imaging moves you directly into the space in which your spirit adventures forth to tell you the stories (past, present and future) that your social biography and culture have either denied or not permitted to be told.

Practitioners of deep imaging enter into an imaginal space where they discover the "might be's," the "could be's," and the "should be's" in their lives and their worlds. Mary Watkins (1984) has called this the life of the imaginal, where spirit feels very much at home.

In Chapters Fourteen and Fifteen, I set forth the literacy and the practices of deep imaging; and in Chapter Sixteen, I extend an invitation to your spirit to tell its story through deep imaging.

The Meta-Disciplines

Of the seven, three disciplines can be termed "practical": *Deep listening, deep questioning,* and *deep imaging.* You can apply these competences to "real-world" situations almost immediately. Their results become visible to others who have not yet begun the enspiriting. In one national church, for example, where we did an envisioning project on the future of religious community and ministry, lay partici-pants from many congregations applied some of the deep listening, deep question-ing, and deep imaging competences to their experiencing of each other, to their forming themselves into a community of learners, and even to their covenanting together. These disciplines received a practical application in addressing that which troubled their spirit. The national church hierarchy and administration had difficulty containing that reaffirming and regrounding of spirit. Participants were covenanting directly with God and with each other, bypassing the institutional apparatus. The results were highly visible. The project began to challenge the church's structure of powers and principalities, particularly at the hierarchical management levels. Shades of the catacombs and the bishops! Too much for the hierarchy. The project was abandoned.

What of the fourth discipline, *deep learning*? It is the fulcrum on which rest the levers of transformation.

The last three I call the meta-disciplines. *Intentioning* is the first. *Discerning* and *dialogue* are the other two. These three meta-disciplines reach beyond the operational disciplines for a territory of enspiriting that is more complex in both its inner and its outer workings. Their competences are more sophisticated and require substantially more practice.

5. Intentioning™

For most of us, *intentioning* (the act of coming to your intentions) has been learned and practiced through goal-setting. Through the language of goals, we seek to give direction to our lives and careers, our organizations and our communities. Intentioning, however, is a far cry from goal-setting. As a discipline of the spirit, intentioning enters into conscious awareness through the form of a *compelling image* that describes that which you cannot *not* be and cannot *not* do.

This apparently awkward double negative is central to intentioning. In Chapters Seventeen and Eighteen, I describe enspiriting activities that help you discover your mode of intentioning. Each person finds her own mode through a rich combination of inner and outer work. In the outer work, spirit is tested in the crucible of its interaction with others. Living the consequences of these interactions is an important way your spirit becomes present to others.

6. Discerning™

Discerning is a special kind of enspiriting that may take some time to learn, perhaps a lifetime. But you may also come to it quickly as you learn to feel, acknowledge, read and act on your intuitions. In discerning, spirit turns back on itself to distinguish true from false images, right from wrong actions and good from bad intentions.

Turning back on itself is a *reflexive* act, much like spirit viewing itself in its own internal mirror. Spirit learns to use an internal feedback spiral, learns to listen to itself, enters into its own internal dialogue. You will recognize this as talking to yourself at a level much deeper than usual. I call this *strong self-talk;* it is not a matter of airing grievances, recriminations, or even wishlists. It is your spirit in intimate dialogue with itself.

In Chapters Nineteen through Twenty-One, the inner acts of discerning are described so that you can move as swiftly along a discerning path as you need to. Some discerning needs a lifetime. That's okay. But cloudy or ambiguous judgments are often of the moment. They call upon an immediate, no-nonsense, deep probe into "What's going on here?"

7. Dialogue™

This is the final and penultimate discipline of the spirit. It is discourse among enspiritors into which your spirit enters along with the spirit of others. It is not chit-chat or idle conversation. It is not always even verbal. More than anything, *dialogue* is becoming present to each other in that special way that enspiritors have when they enter into community.

People who think that enspiriting is solely an individual act miss half the point. While each of us is of the spirit, its taming, endisciplining and emancipation occur most naturally *in dialogue with others.* Deep listening and deep questioning, for example, are learned with others who are engaged in the same act. Together, they form themselves into a community of learners.

Dialogue is the most joyful, poignant, insightful, and fulfilling quality of what we call human relationships. Martin Buber talked about it as an "I-Thou" to which I add an "I-We." It is found in love—and sometimes even in making love—in politics in a strong democracy, in teaching and learning—sometimes even in schools—and in community-building in a society whose churches, work places, cities, neighborhoods, even family life are too often bereft of community.

Chapter Twenty-Three depicts the three occasions for dialogue: With God, with others and with yourself. In this last chapter, I invite you to begin the formation of and participation in a community of learners which is a vehicle for entering into the transformation of ourselves-in-the-world.

The Centrality of Deep Learning

Why call *deep learning* pivotal?

As you will shortly discover, the seven disciplines of the spirit are truly one. I separate them out to talk about them and to teach them. An analogy may be helpful. The enspiriting disciplines are like fingers, brother and sister to each other, born to work together but still having to learn how to do that, taking each other's place when needed. All, they are joined together as fingers to the hand.

Deep learning is the hand. It gives strength and direction to the other disciplines. It receives their input and feedback and invites out their responses.

Of one thing be sure: Without this deepest engagement with your spirit through deep learning, transformation of yourself-in-the-world and ourselves-in-the-world is nigh impossible. The violence toward and the waste of human beings, the pillage of our planet, the millions of unfulfilled and disempowered human beings in all cultures and in all countries will never cease on this planet—and in your own life—until and unless we all become deep learners.

Taming the Spirit

Have you got a sense, yet, of why I make this distinction between "spirituality" and *enspiriting*? Why I talk about a *discipline* of the spirit and about *endisciplining*? Why I call us enspiritors rather than members of a religious denomination, sect, group, or cult? Why I emphasize the enspiriting ways of being and doing rather than setting down a theology or philosophy of the spirit? Why, finally, I invite you to discover, to emancipate, to nurture and warm, to provide breathing space for your own spirit?

Spirit is palpable. It's there, always was and always will be. The problem is that in entering into the "real world" of flesh and blood, it is easily led astray. In what Joel Kovel has called our de-spiritualized world (1991), spirit runs and hides, a child fearful of an adult world where it is avoided, where it is not invited into and celebrated in everyday life, where it is not allowed to participate in the great debates of parliaments, corporation boards, high-technology decisions, scientific inquiry and, more importantly, all the little parts of daily living and loving and working that make up our lives. When a great consumer paean is offered up to Jacuzzis, VCRs, Hondas and vacations away from the drudgery of job so many experience rather than to celebrate spirit, what would you expect it to do? One of spirit's aspects is its fragility in the face of a world where it's not wanted except under the hidebound settings of the religious enterprise.

Despite its reticence when not welcomed, spirit's energy is enormous. It is a true example of Einstein's energy-mass equation, $E=mc^2$. Though spirit may lie dormant if not lovingly invited and carefully nurtured—that is what *parenting* should be all about—it may also burst forth as undisciplined raw energy, subject to the command and control of hurtful persons and harmful missions as well as spontaneously creative acts which are a blessing.

What is this "taming"? It consists of one part *yielding* to spirit and one part *endisciplining* spirit. Yielding means getting out of its way, providing it breathing room so that it can venture forth like a fledgling eagle, spread its wings, begin to soar. Endisciplining means providing it a safe habitat for its learning of itself so that it can harness its energy, focus its spontaneity and enter into our enormous task of self-reconstruction and the transformation of ourselves-in-the-world.

The seven disciplines of the spirit are all literally about taming in a loving way. Persons who are enspiritors and who facilitate the emergence of spirit in others—be they corporate executives, government leaders, citizens bent on building a new civitas, farmers, parents, school teachers, etc.—are engaged in acts of great loving. Their caring about the spirit of others and the unambiguous sharing of *their* spirit calls out the spirit of others in good ways.

How do I know this? I have seen it happen too many times to discount the enspiriting events and relationships as phantasms. Some years ago, I conducted a workshop with 30 teachers and school administrators as part of a project on the future of education in their school districts. We did a lot of enspiriting together in the disciplines of *deep imaging* and *deep questioning*. Among the participants was one person of unusual sensitivity to and perspicacity about her own spirit though she rarely revealed it to others *until* we had all worked together for three days.

She drove home the evening of the third day. Her husband greeted her at the door with the announcement out of the blue—and some documents to prove it beyond discussion—that he was divorcing her. She was an extraordinary intellect with a doctorate in a highly refined science, kept in the back of her husband's cave so that he, a professor at a highly-respected liberal arts college, would not have to acknowledge her personhood, her competence and her potential as a senior knowledge professional who might very well outshine him.

She called and her spirit responded. That very evening, after her daughter went to bed and the professor-husband had left the premises, she sat by the stream of her spirit and deep imaged her path, her future, a new social biography she would invent. Literally, *she moved inside herself to new spaces*. Within a few months, she had translated her inner work into outer action and was well along a path to become a senior scientist with a national organization, recognized in her field, living with her loving daughter and discovering the freshness of relationships with others who celebrated rather than feared who she was.

The New Literacy

Like everything else that's new and untried or long forgotten, the seven disciplines of the spirit amount to a literacy for enspiriting. To become literate in anything requires the acquisition of competence in the language of that metier. Computer literacy, for example, means to understand and be able to give to the computer commands, use its multiple offerings, its protocols and rules and, ultimately, at least some of its programming capabilities. How are these acquired? Not much by lecturing or proclaiming or theorizing; but rather, by lots of practice and trial, error and correction at the keyboard. As one achieves competence, the computer becomes a source of important work, bringing to a given task *to which it is relevant* its enormous power.

So too with enspiriting. It is a grand offering, one that it would be foolish to refuse. Enspiriting has protocols and rules that can be learned through practice, through trial, error and correction. Enspiriting's disciplines constitute a literacy by which spirit too becomes a source of great and grand achievement.

But here the analogy ends. Until switched on, the computer is inert. *Spirit is never inert.* It is the most alive entity around, much more than the human body. Spirit never dies. It exists at the essence of us. It can bring to each of us, and to all of us in concert, a quality of life and living that no social or economic indicators of material well-being can begin to touch.

This means that once invited to be visibly and palpably present, spirit is always in action. Do we want to subject it to the safeguards of command and control, to the rules and regulations by which we humans seek to make social life safe, behavior predictable, culture unchallenging and ordinary living uninteresting? Not at all. But we must understand that spirit too joins in the circuses to escape from itself, those that are merely entertaining and those that are despicable—holocausts, wars, civil strife.

Spirit has its own life. Rarely is it the same as the life scripted into your social biography, your career, your relationships, your status and roles. That which you invite it to be and do become *its* tasks, too. Once your invitation is accepted, that becomes its *self-invitation*. The ball is no longer exclusively in your court.

In short, there is no structure of command and control in the literacy of enspiriting. The administration of shrines, temples, mosques and churches tried to silence the Christian Meister Eckhardt in the 12th century and the Zen Bhuddist Master Ikkyu in the 14th. Is it surprising that their spirit still breathes life into ours today? Had the confining structures of command and control been successful, there would be no art or artists, no inventors and no voyages of discovery and absolutely no transformation.

A new comparison takes over. The literacy of enspiriting is of the kind that we would attribute to loving if it had a literacy beyond its poetry which most of us neither know nor read. Are we born to love? Are we born to it as a baby to sucking at a woman's breast? Scarcely. That we can all learn the multiple acts of loving and being loved is certainly true. Many of us don't learn them. So too with enspiriting. That each and all of us has a piece of spirit I have no doubt. But this book is not about "spirits," but about *that spirit which is universal and all-encompassing of which each of us has a piece.* So I write the singular word *spirit* even when its reference is to each of us as well as to _all_ of us. Spirit manifests itself in so many ways for which science can give no account, not because scientific inquiry is inadequate or unsound but because spirit's domain, its habitat, and its meaning lie outside the universe of scientific discourse.

But loving is another matter. Though the words for loving are in short supply, its acts are multiple, dynamic, complex, everywhere, unpredictable, of great energy, joyful and painful. So too with enspiriting.

Entering your child's room at 2:00 AM to put back over him the covers kicked off, adjust the window, exit with the touch of a kiss on the ear or your hand lightly brushing his cheek.

Learning that a colleague has lost a loved one or suffered some setback, walking over and giving a hug or laying a hand on the shoulder, eyes touching eyes just for a moment as you open that window for your spirits to join.

Watching the taunting or other emotional violence inflicted on a friend, perhaps a classmate or gangmate and putting your own body between and in front, at risk, so as to absorb the hurtful blows of negative energy before your friend's spirit goes even further into hiding.

In making love, shifting your presence from an inward expectancy to an outward seeking as you live your lover's unique ecstasy of the spirit. A technical word for that is empathy. The empathic mode is central to deep listening as is the nurturing mode. Being empathic and nurturing extend throughout loving acts, both the intimate kind and the fellow-feeling kind that tighten the stomach and make spirit weep as the killing fields and the decimation of our children sweep across the planet like a latter-day bubonic plague.

And doing the dishes as from your mate's tired eyes comes an unspoken thanks, as much a loving act as talking your mate through his death watch so that as spirit is reborn, it is warmed and caressed by yours.

All of these are spontaneous, yes, and yet learned, too. That combination, true of loving, is the key to the literacy of enspiriting: To enable spirit to reach out to the rest of you —your social biography, as I call it, and your body and mind—with its spontaneity intact, its adventures still before you and its vast energy focused on the tasks you negotiate.

Your literacy is to learn to yield, not to censor, not to judge, but to invite and tease out so that your spirit can respond.

Can this be done?

Start with _deep listening_ and discover for yourself.

2

The Way of Deep Listening, Part One:
Silence, Attention, Empathy

We start the enspiriting with deep listening. One goes very far inside, to the inner reaches, to the silence where spirit resides, awaiting a call from another.

Until now, your spirit has rested easily, moving about slowly and flowingly in the *tant'ien*. The *tant'ien* is the Chinese word for the center of your vital life force or energy, your *chi*. It is located just above and behind the pubic bone, in what is referred to as the pit of your stomach. It is the space where your spirit waits in silence, listening for the first cry of another's spirit through words that are spoken and unspoken.

The First Mode: Being Silence

This is the first mode of deep listening. It is the universal way into it, the beginning of it and also the ending.

Many of us have a profound aversion to silence. We want to fill the void with chatter and noise, with the restless energy that means we are not at peace. Silence runs counter to the modern styles of communication that bombard us with information we don't know what to do with and the academic research that makes the bombardment so effective.

The invitation to deep listening is to *yourself* to make an inner silence whence busy thoughts are stopped and feelings cease. It's an invitation to be like a rock emerging from the sea, silent, impenetrable, lasting, solid, untouched by the waves that wash over and around. Or to be a swaying tree rooted so deeply in its soil that when the breeze stops and the leaves cease their whispering, all is still as if waiting in silence for that which only silence brings.

Find your own metaphor as you begin this inner work of deep listening, of silence.

As you do so, forget enspiriting for a moment and just be silence.

Do you know what that means?

Being silence is not quite the same as being silent. The latter is a task, a thing to do, an activity. But *being silence* is a state that moves through and permeates our body, our mind, our feelings, our spirit. *We become silence.*

Here are some outward signs. There is no fidgeting. There is no body language. A speaker who is sharing with you waits for your response *but there is none.* You may even look away, sitting or standing at right angles to each other rather than face-to-face.

What? No eye contact? We grow up being taught to look one another in the eye. "How am I to build trust?" you might ask. "If I look away, they'll think I have something to hide! I can't talk with somebody," you might add, "without looking them in the face."

But deep listening is not about talking. It is about *listening.* In deep listening, silence reigns.

The Practice: Be Silence

How be silence? You don't "do" silence. You are silence. Being silence is non-action, waiting, patience. In an age where we frantically seek to fill the void, deep listening through the open gate of silence presents practical difficulties. The following exercises are designed to help.

An Exercise in Being Silence (No. 1)

In this exercise, be by yourself. Perhaps outdoors, in your garden, in your city park or village green; on a dirt road or path through fields of wheat, alfalfa, cassava, apple trees, whatever is growing there. Stand or be still. Breathe deeply. Quiet your thoughts. Open your hands, palms up, as a welcome.

Now be silence. Listen to the sounds of your own breathing. Move inside your body to your toes, then ankles, then knees, then legs, up and through your body. Quiet your thoughts.

Is this a meditation? Is this a centering? Is this a yielding? Is this an inner quieting? The naming matters little, so long as you are being silence, so long as the silence pervades you.

Be silence for 30 seconds. For two minutes. For half-an-hour. As you learn it and practice it, silence becomes another way of inner life and inner work.

A Joint Exercise in Being Silence (No. 2)

This exercise is for two persons.

Here, you will need to prepare your partner for your *deep listening*. She must be ready for your being silence, because for most of us in the West, being silence is both strange and difficult. So you seek silence first by yourself, and later when partnering you prepare each other.

"I will be silence," you say. "I will look away," you say. "But I will be listening deeply."

You see, then, the "trick"? *You must give yourself permission to be silence. And you must ask for your partner's permission.*

What happens next? You have a partner. She talks. She says something that is real to her, by which I mean important though not necessarily earth-shaking. Deep listening is not psychotherapy. Your partner does not have to reveal a "secret" part of herself or talk about a "problem" and await your solution.

Deep listening is not giving advice, counseling, helping the other person work her way through her own tangle. It is being silence. Sometimes, the tangle does unravel, like your hair — or your emotions — coming unknotted not by a comb, not by a word of wisdom, but by being silence.

Healing often begins in silence.

Is being silence all there is to deep listening? Not at all. There are five other modes. But none can be entered except through the gate of silence.

For how long should we be silence?

There are no rules.

Some years ago I did a deep listening with 40 or 50 farmers from Alberta Province in Canada. We began with the first mode, being silence. One farmer talked about something important while the partner listened in this way of silence. They had 10 minutes each, then switched roles.

"How many," I asked after 20 minutes in their groups of two, "were able to maintain silence for a minute?"

Most hands went up.

"How many for two minutes?"

Less than half.

"How many for three minutes?"

A few hands tentatively reach upward like fledgling birds trying their wings.

"How many for five?"

Silence reigned.

Is that all there is to deep listening? No. But it is quite a lot.

The Second Mode of Deep Listening: Giving Attention

Being silence and giving attention go hand in hand. Giving attention is the active side of being silence. Ingrid Alderson, a colleague in Vancouver, said to me, "Attention is something you give, not pay."

Deep listening is a gift of the spirit: To give attention to the other so that *nothing else exists in the universe but this unique, singular focus of attention in being silence.* As you listen, your thoughts, your feelings, your images have been shunted aside. You have emptied yourself so that in the silence you can give attention unequivocally to the other. Yet you have turned away at the surface, looking away, seated or standing at right angles or walking together with face averted. How can you be giving the gift of attention?

In fact, giving attention in silence and being and doing nothing else are a rare kind of presence. It is not analysis. It is not active listening. It is not an intellectual task. (Sometimes these come after, through *deep questioning.* Hold off on that.)

So what *is* it?

Two stories may help, one from the modern era, one a bit older. First, the contemporary.

In a small town in Ohio, I worked with a few hundred people on envisioning the future of their human resources. Afterward, we broke into groups of 30 or so. One group practiced deep listening: In pairs, one person spoke of his concerns, issues, dissatisfactions, while the other sought to deep listen for only 10 minutes practicing the modes of being silence and giving attention.

After the practice session, we gathered for *praxis,* a reflection by all in that group on what it's like to deep listen. Several persons talked a bit and then the mayor of the community spoke up. He hemmed and hawed. He slowly shook his head, up, down, sideways. "Never," he said, "Never in my entire life has anybody ever listened to me that way. She gave me her full attention. I know I had it. I felt it, even though for five or six minutes she was silent."

"What was that like?" I asked.

Silence. Inner reflection. Softly, then: "I *was* somebody. I counted. It was the first time I ever felt that way."

Giving attention is certainly not my discovery. As I spent years working with deep listening, discovering how this way of enspiriting worked, I uncovered this mode of giving attention.[2] Listen, now, to the words of Ikkyu, the Zen iconoclast, the master of the cloud gathering and cloud journeying:

> One day, a man of the people said to the Zen Master Ikkyu: "Master, will you please write me the maxims of highest wisdom?"
>
> Ikkyu immediately took his brush and wrote the word, "Attention."
>
> "Is that all?" asked the man. "Will you not add something more?"
>
> Ikkyu then wrote twice running: "Attention. Attention."
>
> "Well," remarked the man rather irritably. "I really don't see much depth or subtlety in what you have just written."
>
> Then Ikkyu wrote the same word three times running: "Attention. Attention. Attention."
>
> Half angered, the man demanded: "What does the word attention mean, anyway?"
>
> And Ikkyu answered gently: "Attention means ATTENTION."

Sometimes, as we begin this journey into the way of enspiriting, people would like to be given an intellectual account of it. What should I expect? What is it like? Why this way and not that? How do you know?

This book, of course, takes up those questions. But not too much. Do not substitute the book or the words for the practice. Reread Ikkyu's koan. His method, as the method of all koans for the Western mentality, is transparent. *Become* an attention focus. Feel it in your bones as your eyes turn inward and your mind empties of its thoughts. This is an action of the spirit. When it happens, you will know it far more deeply than any intellectual explanation can possibly provide.

These beginning exercises are simple in their offering, perhaps not so simple in their taking up.

---

[2] The *koan* was shared with me by Katherine Shamballa when we were working together at Syracuse University in the 1970s in the early days of the envisioning project.

The Third Mode of Deep Listening: Being Empathic

In *Star Trek, the Next Generation,* Counselor Troy portrays a certain quality we call, in this earlier century, being empathic. For those who are not aficionados of the popular TV series, empathy is nevertheless the bridge your spirit crosses to enter onto another's path.

Being empathic is a foundational mode of enspiriting, though I offer it to you through *deep listening.* At the everyday level of human interaction, empathy is the most *fully human* of our traits just because it is so close to the world of enspiriting. Often, we confuse being empathic with sympathy. But being empathic goes beyond feeling another's bereavement or loss and expressing the sorrow or fellow feeling. Rather, being empathic is an exploration through which your spirit joins with another's. In being empathic, you move yourself into the other's space and live it as if it were your own. You become her. You live her trials and tribulations, her pain, her joy, her ecstasy, her biography. In short, *merge your spirit with hers.* Her words, as she talks, become yours. Her images become yours. Her deepest feelings become yours. Her deepest thoughts become yours.

Some deny this possibility. Once, I did a project with 40 to 50 black and white persons in which we envisioned a community without prejudice and racism. After days of intense sharing, speaking truth to power, we let our bigotry and reverse prejudice hang out for all to see. As each discovered the common humanity of all, I heard a black person say to a white person: "But in the end, you can't feel my pain. You can't share my pain. You can't know, white man, what it's like to grow up black in America *because you didn't and I did."*

I thought to myself: "If I can't feel and share in your pain, right smack in you and you right smack in me, no Constitutional provision, Supreme Court decision, or legislative enactment is going to provide the space in this society—or any other— for you to discover and be yourself in all the ways you choose." But I did not say it. As she cried her anger I felt her tearing in me.

A few years later, I worked with a group of 20 souls for a long weekend of envisioning, enspiriting and empowering. In their deep listening, they worked in pairs. I watched as the silence moved like a mist through the room in which the pairs sat, each in their own space protected from any incursions by the attention they were giving each other.

Afterwards, in the praxis, as we reflected together on what this was like, a male member of the group told his tale as his partner, a woman, listened with the rest of us. This man was in his 60s; retired; a successful entrepreneur who had built up a chain of stores throughout the Mid-South; a "can-do," "no-nonsense," albeit quietly attentive person who had successfully trekked the jungles and deserts of the business culture; tall, thin, spare, and graying with a hidden dimension of his being about to emerge.

He stared into the center of the circle we had formed.

"I listened," he said, addressing us all but clearly speaking through us to his partner. "I caught your words, was silent, gave attention. I heard her speak her thoughts, her concerns, her images." Silence. Would he tell us what she had shared in those intimate moments of *deep listening*? Not directly, not quoting. Then he continued: "But I got more." Silence. We stirred in our chairs. What was going on here? He turned then directly to his partner, a woman in her 40s, pretty in a plain way, her kids now out of the nest, seeking her own path, not the next steps but new steps, tentatively dancing with her own empowerment, what that might mean, the dangers, the risks, the adventures her spirit was about to offer her biography.

"I received a sense of great pain. You didn't speak it. But I got it. I got a sense of great turmoil in you, wrenching and pulling and tearing. It hurts. I don't mean, *You hurt*. I mean, *I hurt*. I don't mean, *I hurt for you*. I mean, *I hurt*."

Anglo, male, Protestant, successful businessman, retired, all those nonsense sub-cultural indicators that tell us absolutely nothing about anything important when we enter the way of enspiriting: He had listened in that way I call being empathic. His spirit had joined hers.

She wept, then, but only a little. She gave a public acknowledgment. "You felt me," she said. "I said nothing about what's going on inside. Yet you caught it. You were there. You were me, just for those moments."

They looked at each other in awe. Silence. The group moved on to the next piece of business.

Can Empathy be Taught?

Can empathy be taught? Can empathy be learned? Like so many of its other activities, this way of enspiriting is natural. It is like breathing. One is born to it. Watch the child. She needs no instruction in placing herself within another's space. Her spirit is free enough to roam the universe of her classmate's predicament, the lion's roar, adventures on Alpha Centauri, a mouse in the wheat field. Growing up, as I have already pointed out, is a *social* exercise in learning the rules of the road handed down by previous generations. In modern learning, empathic competence gets lost in the maze designed for training the left brain.

So we need to exercise this capacity. If you have learned to give singular attention, as Ikkyu offers in the intensity of your being silence, then you are ready to rediscover the empathic disposition of your spirit.

The Path of the Imagination

By now have you guessed that being empathic is through the path of imagining? It is the bridge over which you cross to another's life. *Imagining is a way of your spirit.* Walk it to the other's space. Let it take you to the laughter and tears, the hunger and completion, the infinite variety of life's detail that sets this human being apart from the billions.

How do I take that path? As I deep listen, how do I give rebirth to my imagining?

The exercise that follows is one way. It invites you to loose your imaginative capacity from the corral. Let it breathe a bit, roam a bit, smell the roses and nibble the grass. As it begins to trust its newly found freedom, it will look across the distance to the other side and see that it is not so great a journey. "I can easily cross over to the other side of this exchange. My partner is telling me something. I have been silence. I have given focused attention to her telling. Now, let me enter *her* space. What lies beneath her words? Who is this person—what is this spirit—that invites my deep listening?"

Who is this Person?

In a workshop setting, this person is the partner with whom you've begun the enspiriting work. Perhaps it is a business colleague or a member of your congregation. In civic projects, it is a citizen who, with her fellow-citizens, has gathered in the *agora* to formulate a new policy, to address a civic problem, to build a new public-private partnership. It does not matter so long as you are prepared to inhabit the space she occupies.

Absent a living partner, let your empathic imagining roam where it will. I have seen enspiritors cross bridges to meet up with many persons, living, dead, not yet born, to future settings as well as past. One went to her father, long dead, and lived his unspoken dreams. Another gritted his teeth, tightened his tant'ien and became a Jew herded by Nazi guards into the boxcar that would take him to the ovens of Auschwitz. Still another, an older woman, visited a young Saudi bride on her way to her marriage ceremony, she imagining with joy and fear what lay before her and the old one *imagining her imagining.*

The infinite variety of human experience caught up in its biographies and roles is now open to you in this exercise *if you but seize the day* and let your spirit walk across the bridge of your imagining. This is a special kind of out-of-body experience, the one of which dreams are fashioned and strong tales are told. It is available to everybody if they will let go of body and mind constraints imposed by culturally narrow views of reality.

What is this Space?

Of course, the space is the context of that person or situation you invite yourself to imagine. It is both *outer*—the role, the situation, who else is there, the time (what century, what day, what hour?) and the place (is it dry, enclosed, jungle, furnished, etc.?)—and *inner.*

Inner is the key to the space you will occupy. Crossing over the bridge of empathy by imagining what it is like to be the other person must eventuate in entering into her inner space of feelings, thoughts, and experiencing until spirit is reached. For some, this may take a few seconds. Others may need minutes or hours to practice at it.

Can you fail? Is it possible to stifle the imagination so that it is no more? Not until and unless you stifle the spirit, a job which has been tried for hundreds of centuries without a great deal of lasting success.

Do you now understand that the human imagination about which so much is written and so little understood *is the voice of the spirit, nothing more and nothing less?* In this day and age when so many seek the new spirituality, a simple test will tell us that the quest for the spiritual is grounded in acts of enspiriting and not in platitudes and wish lists.

What is this test? It is the litmus of imagining. When folks are imagining, there spirit is. When they offer certitudes and platitudes, be clear that spirit is in hiding. Be sensitive, then, to this way that spirit calls and responds.

Do you see and hear and feel the imagination at work? Who is imagining? Who has cut loose from the colorless soup of things-as-they-are by imagining the alternatives, by letting her spirit—as well as her words and actions—live them in front of you?

One group of envisioners from middle management lived out their scenario of a new approach to problem-solving, one based on invitation, response and competence rather than role, hierarchical authority, and orders from above. As they lived their imagining, they invited the rest of us, one by one, into their problem-solving circle. What had we to offer? What had we to learn? Who was giving the orders? How were we to define the problem? Who was prepared to own what piece of this invented space? As we watched the team act in concert and as we joined them, an entirely new way of work opened for us, indeed an entirely new corporate culture to replace the existing one devoted to safety, fulfilling expectations, predictability, monopoly and untouchable dividends.

The negative side of culture is to constrain the imagination so that it pursues only safe tasks; that is, to control the spirit. At this moment in human history, we are called to break through those constraints so that we can participate proactively in the transformation of ourselves-in-the-world.

An Exercise in Being Empathic (No. 3)

As in all of the disciplines, preparation is essential: The inner quieting, the emptying, the deep breathing as body and mind relinquish control to spirit.

Review. You have become silence. You have given attention so that nothing else is present but your partner's words, spoken or unspoken.

Softly, now, easily, no abrupt movements of hands or face or spirit, you feel yourself move into the other. Do I mean this literally? Of course. All of the suggestions I make, all of the paths I seek to open for your own enspiriting are to be translated into concrete and specific actions. When I use metaphor, symbols, signs, I shall say so. Enspiriting is not metaphor. It is not ideology. It's not: "Wouldn't it be nice if..." It is direct and immediate *experiencing*. It is *concrete and specific*. Spirit is not metaphor. It *is*, simply, infinitely, and marvelously.

Again, who is this other? It could be an imagined other. It could be the palpable flesh, blood and bones of the other sitting next to you or across the circle. In either case, spirit lives. For its time is not chronological (from *chronos*, the giants, rulers of an ancient world where spirit dwelled not). Its time and space are infinitely everlasting in *kairos;* and there the other's spirit is present *if you will let it be present to you and if you will let yourself be present to it.*

Now live the other in any way and in all ways that come to you: Her feelings, her worries, her tasks, her happiness, her biography in any of its aspects. The key here is not to constrain yourself, not to self-control by saying: "I can't," or, "I won't."

This is deep listening at a foundational level.

When, in common parlance, one person says to another, "I know where you're coming from," he has entered into that person's space. We all do it. It is a human proclivity. In this mode of deep listening, we commence the practice of refining and honing this capacity until, finally, spirit breaks through, crosses the bridge, and enters the other.

When Is Being Empathic Called For?

All the modes of deep listening have their place. Learn to use one or another as the situation warrants. Beginners and those suspicious of the whole thing will find the competence of being silence and giving attention excellent starting points because they demand an inner discipline that can be readily learned if the will is there. Building on their foundation, the enspiritor then shifts to the third mode of being empathic (and eventually, to the Fourth Mode of Being Non-Judgmental and the Fifth Mode of Nurturing which are taken up in Chapter Six). Which mode depends on what is called for.

In the third mode of being empathic, the call from one spirit to another is about a merger which is a special kind of inner sharing. Each person in *dialogue* knows when to let this happen. The signals are not always given verbally. Remember the example I gave of the retired businessman and the woman bent on inventing her future? Trust that your spirit will learn when it's good for itself and for the other to cross the imagining bridge to enter the other's space. Time and again folks with whom I've worked report that they found themselves being empathic without premeditation. The call from their spirit or from the other's was too strong to avoid. Don't avoid it.

3
Deep Questioning in the Body and in the Spirit: Imbalance, Disharmony, Tension

Sensing the Pain

For most of us, enspiriting evolves from a confrontation between spirit and social biography. That dynamic interplay invariably translates into *deep questioning* about yourself and your world.

What sets off the confrontation? Often, dissatisfaction with job, mate, personal situations, sometimes grave concerns about the state of the world. Beneath dissatisfaction and concern may be pain. The alerting signal is a "sense" that all is not right. At the outset, this feeling often confuses. Your body speaks up, telling of imbalance, disharmony, tension. The mind has not yet caught up. There is an issue to be confronted but you can't say what or why.

Let me suggest that imbalance, disharmony, tension are the inner aspects of an out-of-kilter world on the path of transformation. And all bets are off as to whether or not we'll make it. It would be surprising if the external mess were not paralleled by an upsurge of feelings within each of us that portend crisis, change, opportunity and reconstruction within as well as without.

Over the last 25 years, I have worked with many whose outward calm hides an inner turmoil of dissatisfaction with themselves-in-the-world. The outward posture is called: "Keeping your cool." "Stay cool, baby," is the popular refrain as our worlds, inner and outer, heat up. But this is self-numbing. More, it is an imprisonment of the spirit. Here, then, is a piece of work to be done: Probing the inner space of feelings, thoughts and images to discover the ways in which each of us has closed off the doorways to the room where spirit resides. Deep questioning opens those doors. But first, you must deep listen to the pain—the world's and yours—both and not separate.

What pain is this? On the outside, it is a rending and tearing of the fabric of complacency in a Malthusian century now ending in a fit of anger, turmoil, strife, terrorism, environmental disasters, AIDS and too many mouths to feed. Tired of hearing that litany? Then go inside, to your own inner chambers where are lodged your fears of unemployment, cancer, meaningless jobs, unhappy marriages and, finally, death. Thus, to our addictions. How desperately so many of us try to consume, inhale, ingest our way into a surfeit of numbing oblivion. Do the addictions work? Scarcely. For as our spirit speaks its pain, it tells us through our body that what is not right in the outer world and what is not right in the inner world are part and parcel of the same condition.

How can you know this? If you will just get beyond your self-numbing, check out the feelings in your body, particularly your tant'ien. Remember from *deep listening*? It is the space of your spirit. It is also the space where social biography, feelings and energy reside. What feelings are these? Feelings of fear... the tant'ien tightens. Feelings of revulsion... the tant'ien heaves. Feelings of anger... the tant'ien boils. Feelings of despair... the tant'ien shrinks. Feelings of love... the tant'ien expands to take in the entire world, for then spirit cannot be contained. No matter the occasion, no matter whether you're adrift in your own private world of unmet aspirations and unfulfilled expectations or in the public world of political dishonesty and subterfuge, street gangs and carjackings, or planetary starvation, ethnic wars, and environmental devastation, spirit speaks out through your pain. It's a wake-up call.

What to Do?

What to do? Start with learning to listen to your body. Learn to listen to its language. *Deep listening* is a must, for it is a more likely path to your spirit than your intellect. As any T'ai Chi, Yoga, or Feldenkreis master will tell you, habits of the body are more easily discerned and more readily challenged than habits of the mind. Changing attitudes is difficult. Attitudes are habits of the mind: Toward the other gender, toward sex, race, work, study, brushing your teeth, toward everything. Especially toward yourself. Can attitudes be changed? *In enspiriting work, we bypass them.* We seek a much deeper source for intentioning and discerning: spirit. One way is *deep questioning.* One path is through your body.

Finding a Language for the Body

Words for the body, like words for love, are in short supply (except in medical science which has lots of words for the body parts and their chemistry and physics but nothing for its underlying spirit which pervades it all). "I love you" carries as many meanings as there are people who say it, billions of meanings that express spirit's quest for loving relationships.

So too with the body. Pain is pain. "Where does it hurt?" queries the loving parent or the caring doctor. Imbalance, disharmony, inner tension, a sense of loss, inadequacy, frustration, anger, despair: to where do you point? Your knee? Your elbow? Your gizzard? Indeed, maybe. Just wait.

Through the Body to the Spirit

The path is through the body. Body speaks the truth if we will learn to listen. Listen for what? Listen to what? *The language of feelings.* That is spirit's language when it chooses to speak through the body.

Let me get just a little "technical" here. Spirit speaks in many ways. As you move along the paths of your enspiriting, it will be helpful to be a bit knowledgeable about these ways.

First and most often, spirit speaks out through feelings in, through and of the body.

Second, spirit speaks out through images.

Third, and last, spirit speaks out through the mind, intellectually, so to speak. But be careful, here, and give attention. Initially, spirit's "words" come to us as intuitions. Don't reject them. Intuitions are the feelings of the mind. Only last comes the intellect, with its ideas, arguments and linear analysis. For spirit has learned—even if perhaps we have not—that the mind can deceive much more easily than the body.

What to do with feelings? Unlike the children, we grown-ups have learned to obscure, rationalize, hide from and, if we but could, dispense with feelings all together. Of course, that can't be done. Spirit will out, as Shakespeare might say. Stand on your head, stonewall, pay it cool, it doesn't matter. When your life is touched by events to which spirit must respond because of its life, it will. It speaks out in feelings. *Enspiritors do not deny their feelings. They do not deny the feelings of others. But they do not let their feelings tyrannize them.* They deep listen and, as we shall see, deep question. Unlike the rest of us, enspiritors do not call upon the center of command and control to shut down feelings. Sorry. Enspiriting is not a cool intellectual trip. *Feelings are a path back to spirit.* Enspiritors go to that path, search it out, listen to what spirit is trying to say.

Let me tell you a story about this.

Some years ago, a friend of mine who was a senior executive in a major transnational corporation and his spouse participated in a weekend seminar I conducted. The seminar focused on new approaches to leadership that emphasized the way of enspiriting. In that two days, we did a little deep imaging, *deep listening* and *deep questioning.*

Soon thereafter, she was diagnosed with a severe and inoperable cancer. What could save her? Chemical therapy was a must, according to her doctor, an eminent oncologist. The outlook was bleak.

Here's what happened, as best I can recall the events told to me.

The husband loved his wife dearly. He was an engineer. More, he was a "hands-on" guy who had worked his way up from the ranks to the vice-presidential level.

But as his wife's health deteriorated, increasingly he gave his attention, his energy, his spirit to her, not to his job. He relieved himself of senior executive responsibilities and demoted himself so that he could create with his wife a new world.

Most interesting, he was not an very good visual imager as most understand it. He had worked with his hands and his body senses all his life in sensual—there's no other word for it—interaction with extraordinarily complex machinery. He was a "machine healer" just as others are "body healers"; and in both, spirit is at work.

In short he was an enspiritor though it didn't show up in his *curriculum vitae*, his career record, or his job description. His wife was an enspiritor too, in the sense that now her spirit cried out for completion as she faced the very real likelihood of her death.

Some years earlier, they had purchased a piece of land on which to build their retirement home. But more than retirement was at stake. This home and land were to be her dream come true: a place designed to warm and nurture and protect her as she did her art. That was her spirit's longing. A certain kind of art constituted her inner life through which her spirit spoke, not to anybody else but to herself, directly and concretely.

As her condition rapidly worsened, my friend's tenacious spirit rose up in him: Let her spirit live, breathe, speak out, his spirit called to him. What is there to lose?

They began a remarkable nightly regimen of enspiriting together. Deliberately, they focused on her dream house and its special creation room. Nightly, sitting on the couch before the fire with a light supper, she did her *deep imaging* of that place. He deep listened, deep questioned and recorded. Nightly, that house, the land on which it sat, her creation room took shape, corner-by-corner, floor and ceiling by floor and ceiling, nails, wood, stone, wallpaper, furniture, windows: The entire shape and fabric of her future come to life, driven by her spirit through deep imaging, nurtured by his spirit through deep listening, clarified by the deep questioning in their dialogue together. Night after night for two, three hours, week after week into the months. Her body was imbued with her spirit's longing for completion and his spirit's caring energy.

She recovered from her cancer. She lived. They built her dream house. When he retired a few years later, they went to live there.

Learning Your Body's Language

The history of human development has produced marvels. One is the language of the mind emerging from grunts and groans (we still do some of that!) to a blossoming of the intellect that, at least on this planet, has no rival. With the advent of Guttenberg's printing press, that language has expanded enormously, particularly in those arenas of human endeavor that seek scientific knowledge and technological results. There are so many more words now than there were 350 years ago. With more words have come more specializations, more roles, an inordinate flowering of the educational institution, more professions, more organizations, more of almost everything that signifies the *thinking* activity as distinguished from the *feeling* activity.

But on this historic journey to the country of the mind, something happened. We lost our way. Many literati in different professions and academic pursuits have written about the "lag" of "culture" behind the spurt of science and technology. The internecine wars of ex-Yugoslavia are this century's Peloponnesian wars; and what have we learned in the 2500-year interval? That the nation-state in the killing matters is as useful as the hind tits on a boar. With this intellectual development launched by Renee Descartes', "I think, therefore I am," we have lost our ability to let spirit speak out through the body's feelings and discern what that is. We have neglected *its* language: To listen to it, to develop it, to endiscipline it so that spirit would speak out truthfully and forthrightly rather than continue in the game of hide and seek it has learned in order to survive. Even latter-day psychologists, starting with Freud and on to contemporary clinicians and researchers have developed a refined intellectual mode of explaining our behavior and feelings that denies the adventures of the spirit.

The trick is to listen to the body or, more correctly, to let it speak its own language. Carl Sandburg, the great biographer of Abraham Lincoln, reports that when Honest Abe first entertained the notion of becoming the presidential nominee for the Republican party, he voiced reluctance. But after a while, after getting caught up in the great and unique institution of presidential races and presidential politics, he admitted in a letter to Senator Lyman Trumbull: "The taste *is* in my mouth a little." (1954, p. 168). Just metaphor? I suspect not. I can taste a challenge. Why not Abe?

I've always taken these metaphors of the body literally. When someone says—more often *thinks* to himself, for to say it out loud is rather impolite—"That idea stinks!" I take that to mean that his body senses literally smell the idea and do not like the odor. Just consider the sayings when a person is confronted with a great challenge, even a fearsome thing: "My stomach dropped."—or—"I felt like I was kicked in the stomach"—or—"I have this sinking feeling." These are ways of stating the body's reaction to a situation. We brainy folks tend to rationalize. What we should be doing is *deep listening* and *deep questioning*.

Paining as a Path for Deep Questioning

What about this pain? Discomfort, imbalance, inner tension are often voiced first as dissatisfactions, concerns, problems, or issues. These constitute the *surface* of pain. Its depths have to be explored if we are to come to their source. *Deep questioning* does that. In this sense, pain is those feelings in the body that hurt *because your spirit is hurt*. Physically, the pain emanates from a change in the internal environment whose complex chemistry has reacted to a real-life situation of upset. Here, I am talking about upsets that involve and are to be addressed by enspiriting. Only you can discern what these are through the enspiriting discipline of discerning. But can you accept the pain, feel the pain, go to the pain in the first place?

In the Western culture of pain-denial, the pain part of the bodily sensing is difficult to accept in a creative, signaling, alerting way. It is a challenge to be avoided. Avoid it no longer.

In my early 60s, I developed a terrible case of what the doctors surmised was rheumatoid arthritis. For six months, I could sleep no more than 20-30 minutes before the pain awakened me in a sweat. Gradually, I learned not to fight it. Instead of taking sleeping pills, I talked to it. I went to it, deep, specific, being right there with it in my hips, my arms, my shoulders. Well, I didn't enjoy it. But I didn't hate it, either. I learned, literally, to embrace it. *My body was telling me something.* I had to go deep to find out what that was. With the discerning of some enspiriting friends, particularly Paul Burke of Edmonton, it came to me that I was turning away from a path my spirit had finally put me on, a quest that had caught me up and was giving new direction to my life and work...until I denied it.

A T'ai Chi master, Chiangling Al Huang, had taught me to go to the pain some years before. I had taken beginning T'ai Chi workshops with him. In one, he talked about back pain, a well-deserved symptom of the Western way of life. He would put his hand on my back. "Go to it," he would say. "Don't run from it. Embrace it. Warm it. It is trying to tell you something. What is it trying to say?"

At about the same time, in the 1970s, I read a book by Ivan Illich, *The Medical Nemesis.* He wrote about how we Americans avoid pain as if it were not only physically hurtful but also morally distasteful. The era of middle-class drugs is the consequence of not wanting to let the body speak out about the spirit's eclipse in our lives.

And finally, Yoga, more specifically Iyengar Yoga to which I was introduced by an American master, Andy Dufford who had studied with Iyengar in India. "Your body remembers," he would say while doing an Assana with us and correcting the outward posture while inviting us to look to the inward posture of the bones, muscle, sinew in proper alignment. I thought: Great athletes know this, intuitively or not. Why not all of us?

Learn the language of your body. Then, when it alerts you to imbalance within or without, you will begin your deep questioning with a "What's going on here?"

What is Deep Questioning?

It should be clear, then, that *deep questioning* is born of the spirit, not of the mind; that its occasion is a bodily sense of imbalance, tension, inner conflict. These, in turn, often hide a paining that is your body's way of alerting you to some enspiriting that demands expression and articulation; and that therefore the forms of deep questioning seek to penetrate through the numbing to that core where the truth about the matter-at-hand is to be discovered.

Whatever its forms and occasions, deep questioning means going to the heart of the matter. Where is that "heart"? Does it not beat robustly at the juncture of your spirit and yourself-in-the-world?

Sometimes the issue appears to be private. You would say: "This is my concern alone." Sometimes the concern rears its head in the outer world, is about you and others. However you first locate your issue and start to unpack it, you will discover, sooner or later, that neither the private nor the worldly, alone, can contain the issue. Deep questioning is a way of enspiriting that conjoins both the private with the worldly domains so that they interpenetrate each other.

That which pains you about yourself—your body image, your sex life, low self-esteem, your thwarted aspirations, your unwillingness to enter into dialogue with your God, your sense of shame, guilt, fear, anxiety about *anything*—is invariably bound up in what pains you about the world in which you live, i.e., yourself-in-the-world. The enspiriting disciplines reveal that continuity. Deep questioning might start with yourself-in-the-world or ourselves-in-the-world, the individual self or the collective self (i.e., the group, the organization or the community), the personal or the impersonal. It matters not. Once begun, deep questioning brings you to an interior space where *deep learning* changes everything.

Asking questions, generating images, or listening to others in conversation are universal activities. Everyone does them. After all, they are essential to social connection, to being human. Yet I use these very words, these very descriptors, to identify disciplines of the spirit. The difference, at the level of vocabulary, is to add to those generic activities the word *deep*, as in deep questioning, deep imaging, and deep listening.

In workshops, seminars, projects and other kinds of gatherings where people form themselves into a community of learners to learn, practice and apply these arts and crafts, they always ask: "But how do I know when I'm doing this? How do I know when I'm deep questioning?"

That question deserves a response sufficiently precise that, as you begin the deep questioning with the exercise in Chapter Five, you will know what you're about. The next chapter assigns four qualities to deep questioning that should provide you a framework for *your own response to how you know when you're deep questioning*.

4

How Do I Know When
I'm Deep Questioning?

Propriety, Politeness and the Culture of Self-Censorship

In going to the heart of the matter, *deep questioning* peels away the fabric of propriety and politeness that covers over so many destructive behaviors. The apple fell on Sir Isaac Newton's head unintentionally. But you have to shake that tree so that the apple falls, not of its own accord but of yours. Enspiriting is neither random nor accidental. Deep questioning, particularly of others, is often regarded as somewhat pushy. People may criticize you, even shame you, to try to keep you quiet. Deep questioning sometimes results in a conspiracy of silence, a stonewalling if the questioning gets too close to home. Sometimes, if the antagonist is in a position of command and control, he may try to neutralize your deep questioning, even by firing you. Senior management at the Pentagon did just that to the "whistleblowers" who were ferreting out waste and corruption in the defense industry until the U.S. Congress passed a bill prohibiting such malevolent behavior. More recently, the National Institutes of Health discharged two of its research monitors who had through deep questioning uncovered corruption and plagiarism in scientific research supported by government funds.

But don't we all react negatively to deep questions?

For example, parents often play the stonewall game when their youngsters begin to ask questions that are embarrassing, awkward, or inconvenient. Teachers, too. It takes a good teacher to allow a young learner to pursue her questions to their ends. The general preference is to play the lock-step curriculum game that adults have invented so that young people will grow up pretty much like them.

But the most insidious form of politeness and propriety is the kind applied to yourself. It's form is *self-censorship*. Self-censorship is the centerpiece of an internal culture by which your social biography seeks to control the adventures of your spirit, particularly those whose expression challenges the stories about yourself with which you grew up. Questions about your own conduct, your own habits, your own self aren't asked. You close off the paths to your awakening spirit. Your social biography wins out once again. The stories about yourself concocted, often lovingly, by others as representatives of the dominant culture smother the attempts of your spirit to find its expression and seek out its adventures.

No better example exists than among some members of marginalized groups. Such persons have come to accept as their due the put-down stories of the majority group. Such stories become part of an internal culture of beliefs, feelings, attitudes towards themselves. They are the internal referent of the external stories of prejudice that have survived for centuries despite the best efforts of many great enspiritors like Martin Luther King, Mahatma Ghandi, or Helen Keller to puncture by their great enspiriting the internal cultures that have such a hold on us.

But even members of the dominant culture and group suffer from the same disease. Politeness and propriety are surface protections against embarrassment, shame and guilt which, anthropologists tell us, are the socio-psychological measures of command and control that serve to maintain the way things are.

Getting on the enspiriting path to deep questioning is by no means a discipline that will suit everybody. As you work your way through the endisciplining experiences and practices, one or more will come much more easily to you than others. Not to worry. As I have said, they are all fingers on the same hand—your spirit. Competence in one breeds competence in another.

But how does one know she is in the deep questioning mode? Years of work with both would-be and accomplished enspiritors have given us a set of indicators that, when felt and observed, tell you that your deep questioning is not a chimera but rather a powerful way to engage with your spirit and to invite it to engage with yourself-in-the-world (your social biography) and ourselves-in-the-world (the rest of it). We have given some names to these indicators that I hope you will find helpful.

They are:

- Upsetting the person to whom the question is addressed—including yourself!
- Looking for alternatives;
- Questioning entrenched assumptions and strongly held values;
- Asking a compelling question.

I have found these very helpful myself, for they tell me I am on the right path of deep questioning; and they help me to get off that path when the other parties in dialogue are not yet ready.

An Indicator That You're on the Right Path: Upsetting People

One quality of *deep questioning*, then, is its upsettingness. You feel the upset. Your heart starts beating more rapidly. Inner discomfort and tension occupy your body. The delicate balance you have negotiated between your social biography and your spirit is thrown out of kilter. Sweat appears on your brow. Fingers tremble. You shift about uneasily. All these are manifestations that your body's homeostatic state—previously in balance, in harmony within itself—is coming unglued. Your body will use all of its internal physical-chemical dynamics to return your inner state to calm and tranquility. It will not succeed if your spirit is in disrepair.

Exactly the same quality of upset applies to deep questioning the outside world. And exactly the same reactions occur, this time in the body of the organization, in the body politic, in the sinews of habit that hold an unthinking community together. You can feel the trembling and shaking at the meeting, be it a school board, executive committee, city council, management retreat, professional/expert conference, or what-have-you. Denial is one reaction. Put down is another. Cold anger is a third. Violence, often subtle, follows. *When your deep questioning of others produces these, you are on the right track!* Be careful.

Upsetting the Powers that Be

In the early 1980s, long after "school reform" had been mandated by education officials, academicians, business leaders and politicians, colleagues and I began a leadership project with elementary and secondary school principals from a large public school district. In a series of day-long sessions held over a couple of months, we introduced to them some of the enspiriting ways described in this book. Soon, they began to distinguish between "managing" their schools and transforming them. Their self-espousal of transformational leadership—i.e., the enspiriting disciplines applied to leadership—and its application to their own issues, concerns and problems was swift, energetic, enthusiastic and difficult. For we offered no pat solutions to the central issue in American education that they brought forward, namely *learning empowerment,* i.e., how and why to put learners, youngsters as well as adults, in charge of their own learning. Soon, these school principals—20 in all—began the serious design work that comes with shifting educational governance and local-level problem-solving to the critical participatory mode, an essential pre-condition for learning empowerment.

Of course, word of their radical critique of their own educational culture got out to the state education department with its huge bureaucracy, to the college of education in the local university that "sponsored" the project, and to the school district's executive staff.

How well I remember our meeting with the school district superintendent and his assistants. We were ushered into his presence. No CEO of a business corporation, a national church (a bishop?), a university (a provost or chancellor?), or a federal agency (a Secretary/Minister?) could wear a mantle of executive authority any better than that superintendent. After a few niceties about how well the project seemed to be going, we began our *deep questioning,* framed of course in an aura of professional courtesy. "Did the superintendent understand the implications and consequences of our 'staff development' work with the school principals?" (You bet he did, but he didn't say so at first.) "Was he prepared to give them some backing with the (elected) board of his school district? Was he prepared to provide some backing to his principals when members of the local community, including certainly some parents, became upset over the re-design of learning that involved their kids not only as recipients but also as designers?" (Metaphorically, I could begin to see smoke coming out of his ears; but he wasn't being paid $100,000 a year for nothing, so his lips still held a slightly bemused smile.) "And was he prepared to go to bat for the project with the cognizant state education officer to acquire adequate funding?" (His eyes flashed and sparkled, for he knew, and we knew, that he had us there.)

Gradually, as the discussion continued and we framed and reframed our deep questions about education, learning, power, decision-making, empowerment, criteria and standards, curriculum design all within the context of our approach to transformational leadership that the participants were already beginning to execute, the superintendent and his point men could no longer hide their upset. When we pointed out that these questions were the participants', that our work with them consisted mainly in creating a supportive context within which they could raise *their* concerns and issues about the deficits in the district's culture of decision-making, the superintendent's eyes hooded over like a cobra's about to strike.

We knew that this leadership program for school principals was hitting the mark of *their* realities. We laid no ideology on them, no policy suggestions. We invited them to their enspiriting. Invariably, when that offer is genuinely made, people pick up on it with an alacrity and enthusiasm that runs exactly counter to the self-benumbing effects of a spiritless culture. Invariably, also, people get upset. Are you surprised to learn that the program died soon after, not a "natural" death of completion and application but an artificial death imposed by the school district and the cognizant state education officials in concert with the local college of education?

The indicator of upset applies equally to yourself. Enspiriting leads to transformation, not just easy social or personal change. The inner dialectic of transformation puts your social biography up against your spirit. The confrontation can be softened. It can be eased into. *It can't be avoided.* The chapters on *deep learning* take up this confrontation between your social biography and your spirit. That confrontation is the material out of which a new "self" is born. Having a community of learners to midwife this birth is, for most of us, essential. Without it, the travail—as well as the joy—becomes almost too much for a soul to bear.

Another Indicator that You're on the Right Path: Looking for Alternatives

Invariably, *deep questioning* generates alternatives. In ourselves-in-the-world, these alternatives eventually appear as new policies, new institutions, new programs, new actions. In the inner world, deep questioning eventually leads to new self-understanding, a fresh sense of who you are and what you're up to. If you have done the deep questioning, spirit speaks out in a voice not previously heard. The perspectives you gain are completely different from the old ones on which you have relied to see you through life.

The alternatives to which deep questioning leads can be dramatic. Consider the case of the abused wife. I have one in particular in mind, a Nancy S. who had hidden her spirit in that syrup-thick glue of co-dependency. All of that great and loving woman energy had gone into a caring concern and questioning (but not deep enough!) about *him*: "What can I do to help *him*? Why does *he* beat me? How can I get *him* to treat me as a human being? How can I get *him* some help?"

Of course, fair enough questions... for a time. A good way to start a dialogue if one is welcome. If not, take the abuse. "Finally," she said to me, "I came to another question: 'What is it in *me* that keeps *me* living with this fellow? What's going on inside *me*? Why don't I get myself and the kids out of here?"

She did. She had uncovered a fundamental alternative through deep questioning.

At the safe house to which she escaped, there were other abused women. She was introduced to a new community. Throughout their rehabilitation—she later told me—they deep questioned all of the values, sub-cultures, and institutionalized relationships of male hegemony, aggrandizement and violence. As a result of that liberating dialogue, she melded herself-in-the-world (her private agony) to the public agony of ourselves-in-the-world which so many of us (men *and* women) still deny.

If deep questioning does not ultimately bring you to alternatives, to new perspectives, to images, thoughts, feelings not previously entertained in your social biography, you have not pushed it deep enough.

Questioning Assumptions and Values: Another Set of Indicators

Of course, all of these aspects of *deep questioning* meet together at the vortex of the spirit. I separate them because persons with whom I've worked often ask: "How do I know when I'm deep questioning?"

Indicators are a way of answering that question. They are not infallible, which is why they are called "indicators" rather than "evidence." But they're pretty accurate *if in the first place you have accepted your self-invitation to commence that way of enspiriting.* But indicators can be misinterpreted. They can melt into suspicions. Sometimes, they harden into certainty.

These two, assumptions and values, are a bit tricky because their mode of the deep questioning is not of the body, of feelings, of images. Mainly, it is the mode of the intellect. The well-trained mind will always ask, "What am I assuming here?" The enspiritor is always ready to ask of his actions, his aspirations, his relationships, "What do these tell me about what I value?"

But checking out assumptions and values through deep questioning is so powerful an activity that most people never do it. A case in point. At one company with which I worked in an envisioning and leadership project with senior and middle management, the CEO and his reports group had decided to pioneer in the application of a new technology to an assumed marketing need. Implementation took place. For the first year or so, prospects for recouping the investment of a quarter of a billion dollars looked quite good. Profits were in the making, just around the corner. I myself used their technology in my own work. But...they didn't deep question into their assumptions.

One unexamined assumption was about the cost of putting this particular technology in place. The company assumed that the cost of marketing the technology within their own product line could not be brought down to a new and lower point intersecting with rising demand, a point at which the technology would be made available by other companies to hundreds of thousands of individual customers. But that's exactly what happened. So enamored was the company of *its* capacity to make the technology available that it didn't check out these assumptions.

Let me finish only by reporting that this company lost one quarter of a billion dollars in one year. It could not compete. It had to withdraw the technology from its offerings. The CEO and his reports group had not done their homework. He was furious.

This kind of deep questioning is crucial, and for more reasons than business profit and loss. Teasing out the assumptions lodged in your social biography, in your group and in your culture is every bit as important. Why? In the normal course of events, in the unassuming sweep of history over the exigencies of daily life, we can take for granted most everything. *But in a time of transformation, taking anything for granted is perilous. Among other things, transformation is just that: The old assumptions about anything and everything are tossed aside.*

Deep questioning our assumptions reveals to us that which we have carefully avoided all of our lives. Just take one assumption imbedded deeply in our culture and follow it through with deep questions: That "more is better." My colleague at Syracuse University years ago, Maureen Webster, could tease the "more is better" assumption out of just about everything: government policies, personal behavior, organizational theory, the variety of community life.

"More is better" lies at the heart of three centuries of "progress," industrial growth, rendering the entire planet a worldwide market place, eating up the limited reserves of our resources, etc. Of course, no one can demonstrate empirically that "more is better." But why try to do such a foolish thing? Everybody "knows" it, everybody behaves as if the assumption stood for a deep, underlying myth about how the world works, about how God works, and about what makes us human.

Challenging this article of faith—sometimes assumptions are located in the domain of faith and tacit belief—changes everything. If more is not better, then what is? Less? Less consumables? Fewer jacuzzis or VCRs or automobiles? A decrease in information overload? Clothes that don't have to be redesigned every season, that might even, God forbid, last for years with the same charm and durability that were put into their making in the first place? Fewer children to be birthed? A shift downward in the ever-rising curve of credentialing and what John Ohliger has called for years compulsory education? Less choice among breakfast cereals and fewer trees cut down to make cartons on which to advertise competing claims about wheat, oats, barley and corn?

Deep questioning doesn't have to be profound. Children's "Why, Mommy?" can uncover an unexamined assumption with the best of the philosophers. "Because, child, that's the way it is."

Digging into unexamined assumptions is an anathema to the status quo. Coming to a different operating assumption about the righteousness of plenitude would start the human race on a fundamentally different path. In a world culture of never-ceasing rising expectations among rich and poor alike, the culture of production and consumption would cease substituting mammon for enspiriting . . . and might even save the planet!

I will tell you now that the discipline of the spirit I call deep questioning will lead you to unpack and examine a host of assumptions, like that one, that lie at the heart of our modern culture.

"What am I assuming about myself?" That is the crucial question. As an enspiritor, ask it. If you want help, seek to tease out these assumptions with the help of a fellow-enspiritor. Her *deep listening* and *deep questioning* are the best safeguards against the mindgames that we can play in this intellectual mode of deep questioning.

Enspiritors also explore the *facts* of their values in much the same way. The idea here is not to enter into that endless debate over "values," as if they were some disembodied entity floating around in the air and bumping into someone else's values. Your values are to be discovered by deep questioning who you are and what you do in the most concrete and specific instances. When feelings of anger arise over incidents, relationships, words and gestures, often that which you value is revealed if you will deep listen and if then you will deep question. Don't say that you value freedom, justice, love if you don't find that in your actions.

A great question is to call out your behavior—or that of your colleagues, your associates, perhaps the entire nation—and ask: "What does this tell me about myself—about ourselves?"

Deep questioning assumptions and values is a difficult but necessary piece of the road into your inner reaches, to that unmapped territory of your spirit where new assumptions and new values may be aborning. In the chapter on deep imaging, we shall explore exactly how that is done.

The Compelling Question

But of all the characteristics of *deep questioning* by which you know you are traveling its endisciplined path, the quality of compellingness is the most salient. You can feel the compelling question in your bones. It is the quality that cements this discipline to the domain of spirit and frees it from a sole reliance on mind. Though voiced in words, a compelling question erupts from deep inside. *It is the question that you have to ask.* You cannot not ask it. You can't help yourself. The roadblocks of propriety and politeness which your spirit seeks to avoid like the plague are swept aside. The thick, sweet syrup of self-censorship no longer drowns the act of deep questioning.

A consequence of asking the compelling question is that it is not raised lightly. Unprepared for it, the recipient can be thrown back on his heels by its force. That force comes not only from its intellectual vitality. It is also the force of spirit-energy. Like a volcano erupting days or weeks *after* the underlying mechanisms of pressure, heat and fissuring have done their work, the compelling question is forced out into the open by the enormous strength of spirit engaged at last in piercing to the heart of the matter.

A compelling question is about essence: What is the essential argument being made, what is the founding assumption, what is the very ground on which you stand, and does it crumble under the weight of the question or does it remain solid and steadfast? Ask that compelling question of yourself. Ask it of another. In either case, prepare the recipient.

Despite their strength, compelling questions are not acts of hostility. They emerge with great force but not in anger. Exactly the opposite is true. Compelling questions are asked with affection for the recipient, be it your partner in dialogue or your social biography receiving your spirit's deep questions. Nevertheless, be prepared for an emotional reaction. A compelling question usually challenges habits of the heart and mind, yours or others'. In the chapters on deep learning, it is the compelling question that unfreezes those habits so that you can return to the space of *intentioning* by which your spirit lays its claims on the world.

Once again, as in *deep listening,* you will learn to yield, this time to your compelling question. Don't fight it. Prepare its recipient, yourself or others, by some gesture of affection or friendship that indicates your underlying community. And ... *don't demand an immediate response.* Let the question sink into deeper and deeper levels of consciousness until, if all goes well, spirit is reached, including your own from whence sprung the compelling question in the first place. How is that possible? In the discipline of *discerning* (Chapters Nineteen through Twenty-One), I share with you the remarkable capacity of the spirit to interrogate itself so that it discerns good intentions from bad, true images from false, and right actions from wrong. The ancient quest for the philosopher's stone is found where it has always resided: In the capacity of your spirit to cut through the effluvia of a false reality to that which we are invited to be and do on this planet. The gold is in us, in our spirit. Learning how to open up the mine is what deep questioning is all about.

The compelling question is a great shovel.

5

A Way of Deep Questioning:
An Exercise

How to Start the Deep Questioning: An Exercise (No. 4)

In this exercise, it helps to work with a group of would-be enspiritors who are prepared for both *deep listening* to you and *deep questioning* the initial responses you provide. This exercise invites you to an inner work that starts you on a quest into the recesses where your spirit lies in readiness *if you will not censor your responses and if you will let yourself be surprised.*

The exercise consists of a series of questions. They lead you to an ever-deepening inquiry into the sources and consequences of your concerns.

A First Question: What Am I Concerned About?

Prepare as usual: Sit quietly by the stream of your spirit. Find the quiet space, leave the busy space. Shutout the outside noises, distractions, tasks. Getting on the path to enspiriting most often means doing the inner work first by yourself.

So the start-up question is asked by yourself of yourself. Sharing the concerns with another, perhaps even within a community of learners, happens later. Look inward rather than outward.

As you ruminate, perhaps you might make some notes. An initial list of concerns can be quite long. What are your concerns?

A Second Question: Concerns about What?

This is the first piece of *discerning*.

Does it go without saying that these concerns should be yours, not someone else's? Watch out for what has come to be called "political correctness." Go deep inside to avoid listing concerns that were laid on you by your organization, your memberships, or your ethnic, religious, or cultural heritage.

Seek here the concerns of your spirit. We live in a world where an individual's deepest reflections count little if they do not match up with a popular version of issues and problems. Such intolerance goes far beyond the phenomenon of peer pressure. It is the consequence of a culture in which differences are appreciated only when they do not challenge but serve as a multi-colored frosting on an otherwise bland cake.

In one multi-billion-dollar corporation, mid-level managers identified their concerns by a *deep questioning* that began this way. Are you surprised to learn that their concerns, responding to questions just like these, resulted in a strong *cultural critique* of their organization, one that from the outside was popularly known as a great place to work? Almost unanimous, their concerns had nothing to do with the official organizational mission and goals. Senior management was upset. The corporation had sponsored the project to help address corporate futures, but the participants were unimpressed when invited to their own enspiriting. Rather, they brought out into the open a jungle of fear, avoidance of risk, lack of team work, mistrust of subordinates and envy of superiors.

This second question generates two issues: Self-trust and ownership.

The First Issue: Self-Trust

In this corporate project, we invited the participants—remember, now, mostly middle-management with a few more senior people sprinkled in—to create an atmosphere of self-trust. In that atmosphere, the *deep questioning* implies not, "What am I prepared to bring to the public surface" but, prior to that, "What am I prepared to ask about myself-in-the-world?" In that atmosphere, encouraged by our invitation and example, the participants took it from there.

Some posed concerns about social, planetary, environmental matters that were not within the direct purview of their corporation but hovered on its horizons.

Others went immediately to their private lives, their intimate settings of family, self-esteem, self-empowerment, fear of old age, disease, death, all leading one way or another to the malaise and absence of spirit in their lives, an absence that schools, churches, businesses, unions, universities were not designed to give attention to and usually didn't.

The Second Issue: Who Owns these Concerns?

Ask yourself, "Do I? Do I own these concerns?" " How do I know that?" "How do I find out?" "Might other people own them?" "Should they?" "Why?" Again, "How do I find out?"

In the politically correct language of the contemporary environmental movement, I call this "the spotted-owl" question.

The spotted owl, living life in the old forests of America's Pacific Northwest, is in danger of extinction as its ancient habitat is timbered. The controversy over timbering, jobs, capital investment, private and public ownership of the lands, wood for houses for exploding human populations, not interfering with nature has raged for years among lumberman and families at risk, corporations wanting to timber on public lands, environmentalists wanting to save the spotted owl for its own sake and environmentalists using the spotted owl as a strategy for saving the total human nest we call planet Earth.

What happens in substantial disagreements of this kind is that the people-in-conflict are rarely invited to sit by the stream of their spirit—my metaphor for the inner work—before they launch onto the raging waters of public conflict.

Public conflict is the very stuff on which a strong democracy, as Benjamin Barber calls it (1984), thrives. In modern times, however, the possibility of strong democracy's *participatory* requirements has been hoisted on the petards of single-issue advocacy, "I'm right and you're wrong," of the kind that keeps pro-lifers and pro-choicers at inescapable odds rather than in dialogue founded on the enspiriting disciplines of *deep questioning* and *deep listening.*

I have learned over 25 years in this work that *concerns, if they are owned, have roots in the person's spirit.* That as the deep questioning continues, politically correct, organizationally correct and culturally correct concerns dissipate as the froth on a wave when it comes ashore and begins its undercurrent journey back to its source.

Likewise with the deep questioner's social biography. As you dig deeper, you arrive at a space where social biography and spirit have come face-to-face and merged to produce your persona, i.e., who you are in this world (which I have named "yourself-in-the-world" or "myself-in-the-world"). That space is the focal point or interface between *other* people's stories about who you are that you have come to accept and the adventures of your spirit. *All of the enspiriting disciplines arrive at this pivotal point, one way or another.* It is the space of *deep learning.* It is in this space that the question about the *ownership* of your concerns is addressed.

Is there a way of steering a straight path through the tangled web of ownership? How do I find the self-honesty to which deep questioning invariably leads, the self-trust in which I am prepared to learn from my spirit and not censor it. Of course there is. How? By addressing the *consequence* issue.

A Third Question: What Are the Consequences If My Concern Is Not Well Addressed?

This question reveals much about the concern. It reveals much about you. To my mind, consequence analysis is what we humans do most poorly at a time on our planet when our survival as a species rests squarely on our learning to do it better.

Consequences are about happenings, about events neither random nor accidental. Consequences are the result of taking action, including the decision *not* to take action. In this third question, the consequences for which you search result from *not* addressing your concern but rather from letting it lie there like a cold potato floating on the surface of an unappetizing soup. Simply put, if the consequences don't bother you, the concern is not very important to you. Perhaps you'd better drop it from your initial list.

The willingness to acknowledge and live the consequences of one's actions is the essence of human responsibility. Not addressing your concern means that you take no responsibility for it. Find that out. *Deep questioning,* after all, is not fun and games. It is a discipline of the spirit *which tells you what is important.* The inner work in deep questioning is to open up the agenda for enspiriting. It is to free up and bring into ourselves-in-the-world the claims of your spirit. *Deep imaging,* as you will soon discover, puts substance to those claims. Deep questioning reveals what they are. This fourth consequence question leads you to gather the inner space of your spirit to the outer space of your action in the world. At their juncture lies the very source of your responsibility to yourself and to others.

The consequence question, then, enables you to discover the *weight* of your concern. What are your feelings about it? What spirit-energy does it call forth? Do you really give a damn? How to find out? The weight of your concern is directly proportional to its resulting consequences. Consider, then, that some consequences for yourself may amount to very little. Their negative or harmful qualities are not strong enough to put you into that inner state of tension which, properly queried, leads you to your spirit.

Suppose, for example, my concern is about winning the state's lotto. Over a cup of breakfast coffee, with just a bit of bemused anticipation, I read the lotto numbers in the morning newspaper. No luck. My numbers weren't picked. I shrug my shoulders and move on.

What is the nature of this concern about winning the lotto? In fact, it doesn't amount to a hill of beans. Indeed, why call it a concern? Rather, it's a game whose losing amounts to so little—for *me*—that it doesn't deserve the accolade of words like concern, issue, problem, dissatisfaction, tension, disharmony. These words, all, point to a condition of conflict of which I am a part and of which I claim ownership if *when I do the consequence analysis of "my concern not addressed," I discover that I can't live with that neglect.* Perhaps I have in the past tolerated doing nothing. But now that I bring this concern into conscious awareness, it grabs me and *won't let go.* That is a mark of your spirit.

The point is that searching out the consequences of a concern you have named helps to show how important that concern is to you. This exercise is not about un-important concerns.

Note, however, that what is of little consequence to you may carry more weight with another person. Substitute $200 sneakers for a lotto ticket and walk around in the urban ghetto. Some young people will kill other young people to get a pair. In my home town, a youngster of about 14 was pulled to the ground and shot to death so that his equally young murderer could possess his victim's L.A. Raiders football jacket. The concern, here, is about wishlists, a syndrome that has invaded our culture of consumption via the open gate of lack of self-esteem. Consuming helps us to buy the self-esteem that otherwise escapes us. Perhaps killing does too.

Lack of self-esteem invades many people's lists of concerns when they dig deep enough. That lack affects even affluent people well positioned in life. A culture of put-down of others and of self-doubt about our own worth has emerged as a substantial agenda in this deep questioning work. Unpacking a concern like this is not easy. What do you name it? What are its consequences if not addressed? Its negative consequences obtain both in your own life and in the larger social milieu where putting down others is built into the institutional fabric of society. Poverty, racism, anti-this-group or anti-that-group, feeling that you're better than a specified group of people is endemic in our society. It is also not accidental. In a society where opportunities for the full expression of our spirit through the gifts and talents God granted us are in short supply, valuing ourselves often comes at someone else's expense, i.e., undervaluing them, believing them to be less than fully human. For example, in Whiteman's culture, if and when banks make business loans less frequently to or fund fewer mortgages for Blacks, Hispanics, Native Americans, or women, these practices of discrimination based on prejudice are part of a total package of differential human worth inside of which is found a low sense of self-esteem among some of those wrapped up in that box.

So the consequences of an unaddressed concern, unlike my participation in the lotto game, may amount to a very great deal. In this third question, that is what you want to find out. How?

Consequence Analysis

Consequence analysis is a fancy name for the ordinary "if... then" question. Ask it about your concern. *If* you don't give attention to this concern, *if* you don't address it, *then* what consequence does that have for you... for others, those whom, in an earlier question, you thought ought also to be concerned about the same matter?

The practices of *deep imaging* provide lots of inner space for this conjecture. Discovering the consequences of an image of the future, consequences both positive and negative, is a key competence in the envisioning activity. At this stage of *deep questioning*, the competence is less sophisticated. Nevertheless, you are invited to put yourself—conjecture, imagine—into a space where your concern is *not* addressed. Who cares? Why do they care? Do you? Move inside, now, to the space of feelings, even into your tant'ien and deep listen, smell it out, feel it out, picture yourself or the world in a state where the conflict and tension underlying the concern still existed. So what? Now feel it. Feel the tension. Is it there? Feel the pain. Is it there? Many politically correct concerns are of this nature. They are not yours. You don't own them. You're not going to do anything about them. They're somebody else's concerns that were laid on you and which you also name, when asked, until you begin the deep questioning.

I'm convinced, for example, that poverty exists in the United States because most Americans don't give a damn. We can live with it. Why? Most folks don't care enough. They are concerned much more about getting cancer as individuals than they are about addressing this social cancer. For to do so would entail consequences in our cherished way of life so deep and powerful, so *transformative* that we don't want to mess with it.

Better to find out now than to pretend a concern, a dissatisfaction because you think other people want to hear that. Search, therefore, for the pain. Listen for the rumblings in your tant'ien. Become sensitive to inner tension, to the bodily manifestations of inner conflict. When you find it, you've got something to enspirit about and work with. Deep questioning has led you to the space where spirit speaks out.

6
Deep Listening: Part Two: Nurturing, Non-judgment, the Empty Vessel

Why More Deep Listening?

D*eep questioning* is greatly aided in probing to the heart of the issue by colleagues who are adept at deep listening. After all, many folks tend to understand deep questioning solely as an intellectual project. All of us can use questions to obscure truth and hide from our spirit. One can engage in that kind of strong self-talk wherein the two competence work closely together. But that takes considerable practice. When deep questioning is initially self-applied, social biography intervenes to save itself and to protect the cultural situation from which it sprang. A deep listener, bonded to you in that special way of a community of learners, helps purge the dialogue of those barriers to an inquiry that spirit must overcome if it is to arrive at its transformative moment.

Put another way, you can learn to ask yourself a deep question if you can stand the discomfort, the pain, the challenge to your most cherished beliefs and feelings about yourself. In the next chapters on Deep Learning, that course of inner action is exactly what I shall invite you to. But it helps so much when joined to yours in collegiality is a loving spirit who, by virtue of her competence as a deep listener who has untangled her spirit from her social biography, will ask you the hard question that perhaps you have avoided.

How will that question be asked? This is the mode of non-judgment.

The Fourth Mode: Being Non-judgmental

The competence of *deep listening* called for in this mode are quite different from the third, empathic mode described in Chapter Two. At the beginning, qualities of non-judgmental listening include a form of communication in which spirit is not involved at all. Among these qualities are participation in discourse where the listener possesses so little information or understanding about the subject-matter that little response is warranted. This is the expert-neophyte relationship embedded in a culture that worships specialties, experts, credentials and the certification of anything and everything that walks and breathes; we are familiar with it in the academic lecture style, the traditional doctor-patient relationship, or the plumber's $45 per hour charge to fix the leaking faucet.

When a spouse, a child, a friend, or a colleague says, in effect: "Be quiet. I need a listener, not an advice-giver. Just be still and listen," that plea is usually for non-judgment.

Lots is at stake in that plea. The speaker wants something that she finds difficult to articulate because it is so foreign to ordinary conversation. When, however, a person's spirit is endisciplined in the way of deep listening, that stake becomes clearer. "What I really want," the speaker means, "is to be able to hear my own words coming back to me through the open gate of your spirit so that I can discern what my spirit is trying to tell me."

When Is the Non-judgmental Mode Called For?

Non-judgment is called for when the other person is enspiriting about something important to her which is also potentially contentious.

The universe of contention is enormous. It includes spirit's call to all of the alternative ways of being and doing that are the very stuff of transformation. The "spotted owl" conflict is a case in point: so contentious that it demanded—but did not get— non-judgmental *deep listening* by all of the parties who owned part of the stake.

The public conflict, however, finds a parallel in private and in intimate settings. When self-empowerment, a new self-perspective, a new mediation between spirit and social biography are in the making, these also are occasions for non-judgmental listening. The enspiritor doesn't need an argument. She needs a deep listener whose aim is to create a climate suitable for clarification of ideas, of images and of feelings. How is that climate established? When the speaker feels and knows in her bones that the other is judging neither her nor her offering.

A great deal of human conversation involves judgment. A raised eyebrow, a slight grimace, a nigh imperceptible shrug, even the smells we give off carry judgment. One of my friends, trained in the tradition of academic scholarship, can't stand it when I speak of enspiriting. He won't say that. I know it from his body and the slightly disgusted and at the same time amused grimace on his face.

That's one good reason why in deep listening, the listener looks away rather than at the speaker. We want the speaker to listen to herself. We want neither to put her on the defensive nor to give her soporific support when we don't yet know what we're supporting.

This is a delicate issue that will arise again when we unpack the deep listening mode of nurturing. Children whose spirits leap out and blossom right in front of you need all the welcome, support and deep listening they can get. Immediately. Never mind their craziness. Delight in their imagining. Let them try anything, words, ideas, images, feelings, roles, behaviors so long as they do no violence to themselves or others. This support is nurturing, just as a warm rain gently helps the branches bud unless thwarted by an ice storm. The great thing about grandparents is that they have the patience to deep listen...being silence, giving attention, nurturing.

My experience tells me that adults are a different kettle of fish. When the suggestion, the alternative, the strong talk, the new image emerges into the exchange with spouse, lover, friend, colleague, boss, employee, the idea is to let it come out with neither the put-down nor the praise of judgment. If you have prepared the speaker for deep listening, she will understand that your task is not to give her or her ideas support before you have heard them and before she has deep listened to herself. One of my dearest colleagues in this work, Donna Cardinal of Edmonton, bows her head so that no one in the circle, including the speaker, has the faintest idea of what or how she thinks, feels, reacts. But we know she is deep listening because this has become her way.

This mode of non-judgmental listening is difficult to undertake exactly when it is most needed. When is that? Just when the enspiritor is trying for a new self-definition, a new policy, an invention that is counter-cultural, an alternative that challenges what we hold most dear. You see now why being silence and giving attention are initiated as outward, visible actions but must, soon on, become the inner posture of your spirit. Without that inner work, non-judgment is impossible. For if you do not trust your spirit to be what it is, to maintain its integrity and its ethos in the face of another's challenge, who will?

This is strong stuff. Don't use it lightly.

Judging...Judging...and Judging...

Deep listening goes hand-in-hand with *deep questioning*. Together, they walk beside the stream of your spirit and rest in its cool waters. How is that possible? Because there's more than one kind of judging. Understanding the differences lets you deep listen and deep question in the same dialogue.

Deep questioning involves the deep listener in raising clarifying questions. These are questions of an analytic kind. Analysis is a form of judgment, no doubt about it. It seeks to generate understanding by a method that in philosophy goes under the quaint name of *unpacking*. Take it literally. Everybody does this. Just unpack a suitcase. It's closed. What's in it? Open it up. Start to pull out its contents. What's this, a shirt? Clean? Dirty? Mine? My son's? Does it need a button? Is it for fancy wear or loafing around at home? Next a hair brush? Whose? Not mine. I don't have enough hair to cover a boiled egg much less a boiled pate. They're both kind of shiny. Ah, my wife's. How can I tell? The hair's long. A bit of gray in it. Can't hide that gray from a hairbrush. How did that get in my suitcase? I thought everything in there was mine!

Now, unpack the image, the idea, the issue or concern. What's extraneous to it? Did George Bush need his wife's hairbrush to make his case for a *new world order?* Maybe that's why he didn't make the case. It couldn't be unpacked, at least in public. He didn't show us the concreteness and specificity of what lay within his image. And his fellow politicians knew neither how nor why to deep listen or to deep question.

An analytic judgment seeks understanding and clarification by pulling apart or unpacking an image, a concern, an issue, a proposition so as to reveal its inner structure, its inner meanings, its consequences. A deep listener is perfectly at home in the enspiriting dimension when she raises questions like: "I'm sorry but I don't understand. What are you getting at? Is this what you mean? Can you explain? Will you give me an example? What are you assuming? What are the consequences? Where are you coming from? How do you feel about what you're saying?" etc.

My mother did this to me when I was growing up. She had a built-in crap detector. She was the first high priestess in my enspiriting journey through the cosmos. Seeing right into my soul, she'd say: "Warren, you can do that. You can do anything you set your mind to. Just be clear about what that is."

The analytic judgment may hurt. Deep questions do that. But they are value-free in this sense. Analytic judgments are not constituted by the questioner's values. The deep listener is raising questions to generate clarification by and for the speaker.

Though strong, the analytic judgment is offered on behalf of the other so that the latter may come to a more powerful *discerning* of who and what she is and is becoming.

Not so with the other two kinds of judgment, the *plausibility* and the *preference* judgment. These two kinds make up a great deal of human conversation. They can be devastating.

Suppose your mate makes this announcement after dinner over coffee: "I'm going to quit my job and search for another. My work is at a dead end. I'm not getting anyplace and besides, the owner is a turkey who hasn't the faintest notion that his employees are human beings."

A deep listener might respond: "Do you want me to deep listen?" Literally: "Do you want me to be silence and give you absolute attention? Or are you letting off steam after a bad day at black rock and want a little sympathy?"

In the ordinary play of intimate human relationships, the listener will more likely respond with a plausibility judgment or a preference judgment or both. They are antithetical to deep listening. They are also difficult to avoid.

Plausibility judgments are about believing. They arrange themselves in conversation in many different ways. Their bottom line is: "I don't believe what you're saying. I don't believe you can do it. I don't believe you. I don't believe in you."

The number of ways we convey non-belief are myriad. Body language offers a rich repertoire of signals. The speaker catches them right away. The plausibility judgment signifies lack of belief in the efficacy of your mate's will and ability. But she will push that judgment to its root, understanding by your words or gestures that you don't believe in her.

Equally abrasive to the human spirit is the preference judgment in which you convey disagreement, sometimes without words, sometimes in words: "I don't like what you're saying, or doing, or proposing." However rendered, the preference judgment puts your mate on the defensive. What is worse, this attack often comes before the speaker has even completed her thoughts. A great deal of human conversation consists of rendering explicit preference judgments: "I don't like what you're saying ...I disagree with you...How stupid can you get?...Stop that!" (particularly to your children)..."That's not the way we do things around here," etc.

What is the source of these judgments? The speaker has challenged the values, attitudes, habits, tacit beliefs, or articles of faith of the listener. I call these the KBVAF (knowledge, beliefs, values, attitudes and faith). But what are they? They are constitutive of one's social biography. They represent one's life history. We are creatures of our habits. When challenged, we fight back. The response is automatic. Like the electric charges that spark the muscles of the heart to contract rhythmically, preference judgments are not within our deliberate control *until and unless we gain competence in the enspiriting discipline of deep listening.*

A Moment for Patience

A moment arrives in one's personal history as well as in public life when deep listening is called for, when withholding these kinds of judgments may be tantamount to survival. When is that?

Not in light conversation, certainly. Not in the ordinary exchanges of daily living, within families, at work, in schools, in nursing homes, at the ball park. Here, politeness, propriety and the humdrum are the rule, covering over the plausibility and preference judgments that jump back and forth like a pingpong ball, hidden though they are. That's O.K. Indeed, they add spice to what might otherwise be a boring life.

Then when?

Exactly when the stakes are high or when discovery and invention are involved. Mediators must be non-judgmental. As most of us don't mediate disputes but are party to them, we will want to deep listen when one or another party signifies that the issue at hand, the concern, the image, the idea is important.

Often, that importance is measured by the emotional charge invested in the exchange. Listen for the upset, the anger, the amazement, the disbelief, the contention in the situation, in yourself, in the other. Do you feel your bile rising? That's exactly the signal for *deep listening.*

I came to the non-judgmental phase of deep listening as a consequence of our envisioning work in discovery and invention. People were trying out ideas, playing with new situations, feeling their ways through relationships, imaging possibilities (alternative futures) that went against the grain. In envisioning the future, this is the usual situation. True envisioning is always counter-cultural and involves *deep learning* in which we unfreeze our habitual ways of being and doing to uncover our *intentioning* spirit.

In hundreds of projects and workshops with people of all kinds, in civic and community settings, with the business corporation, in churches and schools, in organizations, people work together to generate alternative approaches to problems, concerns, situations of frustration, dissatisfaction, conflict, pain. Sometimes the inventions are superficial; sometimes they are deep-seated. In either case, when the ideas and images begin to emerge, it has proven essential for the listeners in the group to withhold judgment until the baby is born, until the discovery has been made, until the invention has been fleshed out enough that both the envisioner and the listener know and understand its concrete and specific details.

Personal discovery and social invention are fragile. They are easy to kill. In transformation, they may offer the only passage through perilous waters.

In sum, preference and plausibility judgments are anathema to deep listening. Contentious argument and creating alternatives tend to produce a dynamic field of feelings, reactions, questions that represent negative judgment, concealed or explicit. The deep listener leaves that field. She will not play on it. Where does she go?

Of course, to that space where ego dwells not, where superior knowledge and expert credentials are left behind, where self-aggrandizement is not welcome, where habits of mind and ingrained culture are absent. It is the inner tableau empty of all but spirit. Spirit waits and listens.

The Fifth Mode: Nurturing

As I have already suggested, the nurturing mode is a direct extension of the empathic mode discussed in Chapter Two. To nurture through *deep listening*, you first must have moved into the other's space, lived it as she does and noted that it will benefit from further exploration.

In being empathic, the deep listener has warmed the other's spirit and thus brought trust to the relationship. In being non-judgmental, she has shown that the images, the idea, the concerns generated out of the other's spirit are accepted, perhaps to be clarified but not to be denied. Now come the nurturing and growing of the other's spirit to new dimensions.

In common discourse, nurturing is found in phrases like: "Have you thought of this? What about this? Would you consider this add-on, this extension, this modification?"

In the enspiriting world, the nurturing mode includes but goes far deeper than intellectual support. It is a loving, warming, caring action of one spirit with another. Nurturing provides an inner context for the other's spirit to grow, to take on added life and energy, to try out new ways of thinking, feeling, imaging, taking risks and confronting challenges that might otherwise be denied.

Good parents do this with their children. Bad parents don't. Good lovers do this with their mates. Bad lovers don't. Good friends do this with their colleagues. Bad friends don't.

A case in point: A woman deep listener who has accepted the vulnerability of her own spirit now nurtures another to his or her vulnerability. How often have I watched men fight the tears, stiffen the upper lip, deny the pain, battle to maintain a stoic posture in the face of people and situations that affect them to the core. A woman might more likely accept the nurturing not as a challenge to her self-worth but as a loving act of enspiriting between the two of them.

But what is this nurturing by the deep listener? It is a two-fold activity.

First, her spirit holds his, literally, in the warm, refreshing glow of her energy so that his is replenished, is rested, is calmed.

Second, her spirit gives energy to his so that his spirit can expand the horizons of its journeys, can try out new ways of expressing itself.

The enspiriting process itself goes like this. Initially, nurturing is inner action, where the spirit can confront itself within the protective embrace of another's spirit that has no motive other than *deep listening*. At some point, the action moves to that space where spirit and social biography conjoin. That dynamic is nurtured so that the space shifts towards the adventures of the spirit and the restraints of social biography diminish. Eventually, the action becomes outer. The person whose spirit was nurtured by a deep listener goes public. What then happens? Things like this:

The leader who demands obedience over truth is challenged.

The leader who demands blind followership or expects subservience is confronted.

The mate who is accustomed to a relationship of put-down is denied his power.

The co-dependency relationship so frequent in intimate and organizational settings is replaced by the free and empowering relationships among spirits who are bent on inventing their community to replace the aggrandizement of those who seek to imprison the spirit.

The Sixth Mode: Deep Listening the Empty Vessel Way

The enspiriting discipline of *deep listening* comes to completion as the empty vessel mode is realized. Persons who learn this competence enter into the space of spirit and know their spirit because they are that which that is and nothing else. That knowing is a beingness and unity, not a subject knowing an object as we understand knowledge in the Western way. It is a satori; it is a Biblical knowing; it is coming to the essence as Almaas describes. But keep in mind that the empty vessel way is originally fashioned out of *dialogue* with another—or others, though that is a bit more difficult—in which deep listening is, more than anything else, a sharing even though it initiates in the sole person.

Thus, the gate to deep listening the empty vessel way is entered by yielding, emptying and waiting.

What are yielding, emptying and waiting? You already have clues. Being silence and giving attention both introduce you to these activities of enspiriting competence. But understand, now, that deep listening, in any of its modes, *is not a task. No one can force spirit. No one can mold it.* One can do those things with social biography, personality, upbringing, socialization...but not spirit. Rich or poor, old or young, black, white, or other, Christian, Muslim, Jew, Hindu, Animist, Agnostic, ghetto-reared or suburb-reared, Ph.D. or illiterate: None of these shells can force, mold or contain spirit once it is liberated and endisciplined.

The Centrality of Invitation

Yielding, emptying and waiting are paths to the empty vessel way of *deep listening.* They can be learned, can be practiced, can become part of the enspiriting competence. But they are not tasks.

They are invitations. All of the disciplines of the spirit start with invitation from you, in your own person, to you and to other persons in the enspiriting dimension. Some dissonance in you, some crack in the shell of your biography, some tearing in the fabric of your reality gives an opening for spirit to emerge in response to the invitation. *If it doesn't believe you, if it feels that your invitation is false, forcing, constituted by agendas you're hiding, it won't accept the invitation.*

There are no tasks in this work, so there is neither success nor failure. There is only invitation and response expressed in the endisciplining practices (sometimes introduced and learned through exercises). These lead to the enspiriting competence of which deep listening the empty vessel way is surely a grand, wondrous and satisfying example.

Because these are neither task-oriented nor outcome-driven activities, yielding, emptying and waiting have few parallels in the outer—what we like to call the "real"—world. Indeed, all of the enspiriting disciplines are domiciled in a universe of interiority that is as broad, expansive, infinite, complex, multi-layered, dense and rich in seeming contradictions as any other universe that eye can sweep, Hubble telescope can reach, light rays can span or imagination can create.

How to enter this universe? Deep listening is a way. But there are no secrets here and no sophisticated or over-specialized entry points. *You have to want to do it.* But that *intentioning* is not grounded in guarantees of success, in a goal-orientation, nor in achieving expected outcomes. All of those drive tasks. They are neither intentioning nor deep listening.

Yielding

Wanting to enter this interior universe is the first step in yielding. Of course, wanting to let go is no guarantee that you will the first minute, hour, or day. But spirit, *your spirit,* is listening...and will help you, will come out to meet you. The Yoga way of relaxing your mind through giving attention to your body, joint-by-joint, muscle-by-muscle, sinew-by-sinew, or the T'ai Chi way of moving your spirit energy through your body in flowing postures of circular movement are, among others, great ways of letting go into a yieldingness. Your mind cannot anticipate if your spirit will respond in your foot or ankle, your shoulder, this posture or motion: but it will respond to the "wanting-to-do-it" invitation if generously proffered.

Being silence is a powerful form of yielding. This outer posture of "no-words" is constituted by an inner posture of "no-thoughts." They are *assanas* of the spirit. Being silence, the first mode of *deep listening,* turns out to be the first mode of all the disciplines. For in that silence, spirit will prick up her ears, sensing that finally, after all of these years of mutual imprisonment, a gate is being opened for you, in all of your biography, to *enter* and spirit, in all of its innocence, sprightliness, verve and spontaneity, to *exit.*

If yielding is initiated by being silence, what then of emptying? What is that? Pouring water out of a glass? Of course. Then the glass is empty, to remain empty or to be filled. What do we "pour" out of ourselves? What is left when we have emptied? What have we removed?

Inner Data

Earlier, I referred to the tant'ien, the center of your vital life force at the pit of your stomach just above and behind your pubic bone. Here, spirit rests. But the tant'ien is also a storage place for three sets of inner data. Acting together, these three sets play the key role in defining who we are. They are the source for our greatest energy outlays. They also leave little room for the play of spirit.

One set is our social biography. *It is that which other persons claim is true of us which we have come to accept.* The formational stories are those which our parents and significant others have told about us to us (including having overheard them when not intended for our ears) in our formative years. Such stories are often grounded in overt action among our growing selves and the others. The immediacy of our experiencing that action, that relationship, gives substance to these stories and vice-versa. We have come to believe them.

Another set of inner data stored in the tant'ien are the emotional states. These are active responses of our bodies, our minds, our feelings to the interaction or exchange between our social biography and its outer world contexts—people, events, situations. These emotional states include anxieties, fears, conflicts, angers, hates and despairs, as well as loving states.

A third set of inner data stored in the tant'ien is the energy source of our hopes, our ideas, our aspirations, our commitments and our intentions. What is this energy source? It is that which the social biography borrows or takes from your spirit in return for spirit's quiescence in the deeper issues of yourself-in-the-world...who you are and what you're up to.

You see now why the Chinese named this the center of your vital life force. For if you could empty the tant'ien of all these things, you would become an empty vessel, a chalice bereft of everything but spirit and feeling.

An Exercise in Emptying (No. 5)

Its movement is inside. *Emptying is physical movement in a literal way.* It starts with the centering, the yielding, the relaxing, the meditative state in which by giving attention to the body you loosen the mind's grip. So this is not the headtrip of modern Western psychology. It is not a cognitive, analytic activity.

Emptying is moving into your tant'ien; feeling yourself turning inward until the entire focus of your attention is in your tant'ien. Feel your body turn inward. Feel yourself swallowing yourself. Feel yourself moving downward in an elevator from the top of your skull to your tant'ien. Step off into the caverns of your spirit.

Search, now, for your social biography, your emotional states and your energy sources. Embrace them, warm them, love them *for are they not the you you know and have lived with all your life?*

Now ask them to leave. Ask them to let you push them aside, to take them out of the tant'ien and place them in another part of your body or even outside the body where they will be safe, undisturbed, reposing until you bring them back into the tant'ien.

Take these suggestions as literally as you can. *Don't think of deep listening the empty vessel way as a mindgame.* It isn't. Let your imagining move you inward to that reality obscured in a spiritless culture that celebrates outward manifestations yet staunchly denies an inner spirit. Launch yourself on the stream of your spirit. It will take you to its source. Swallow yourself as you swallow your pride. Feel the tant'ien welcome you to your old home that you left as a child but now return to as you listen to the call of your spirit.

I call this an "exercise"; but there are many ways to do it, practices that you have learned or will shortly that move you to this deepest level of your interiority. In one envisioning workshop I did with a group of school teachers, one of them was incensed that I used phrases like enspiriting and deep listening. She was adamant in her refusal to use the language of deep listening. Then she said that she and her partner, in the practice of their Christianity, had meditated and prayed prior to their sharing their deepest images of the future of teaching and learning. Then, a bit non-plussed, she turned to the larger group and said that she had heard and received feelings and picture images from her partner—and vice-versa—that they simply had not shared verbally, in so many words. I maintained my silence except to offer my congratulations.

For some, the social biography, the emotional states and the energy sources are so deeply entrenched that we think no amount of prodding, pleading, digging, dynamiting will loosen their grip. But that grip can be loosened. For many, quite easily. Many with whom I've worked in deep listening learn to empty the tant'ien the first time around.

The Healing Part

One participant with whom I recently worked queried me quite critically during my introduction to *deep listening* in a workshop where he and 30 others had accepted the invitation to invent their futures the envisioning way. His critique was not hostile, but very strong and quite disbelieving. This was a person—found more often among men than among women—who by role, status and social biography was a "show me" skeptic, loyal to the rules of practicality and caution. He fought it on the several occasions he was invited to deep listen with another person. We, meaning also many in this community of learners, kept nurturing him and extending the invitation lovingly.

Then he exploded. On the second day, we met—literally—in the washroom where I had gone to relieve myself. As I was washing my hands, he, leaning against the wall, out of sight and sound of all the other participants, said to me: "Warren, is this deep listening really true?"

Silence.

"Warren, do you expect me to get rid of my biography?"

Silence.

Then with a sob, plaintively, desperately: "Warren, what if it won't come back? Where am I? I have so much to lose."

He walked into a stall to hide from the world...and began to sob.

After a few moments, I said, "The social biography always comes back. It is yours. You can't give it away. Now, when it comes back, there is the possibility of transformation. Deep listening is about re-discovering the space where your spirit will listen unencumbered. It's not about personal trauma or psychological counseling. But...if your emptying has been frightening, if the temporary moving aside of your social biography has been too traumatic, this is probably the beginning of the healing that your spirit has waited for so long and wanted so much."

I left the washroom. It had become his external space for the inner work. Some healing occurred. Some spirit emerged. Within an hour, he became the gentlest, most nurturing, most participative of the deep listeners in the workshop. He had reached the space where his own spirit could listen to others. They thanked him for it.

A Tale from the Source

Deep listening the empty vessel way is removing everything from your center, from your tant'ien, so that all that remains is spirit. My words to describe the emptying —as well as the yielding and waiting—do no justice to the experiencing of it. Chuang-Tzu's description might. In the early 1980s, I discovered this passage in the Chuang-Tzu (1968) translated by the eminent Chinese scholar, Burton Watson. It shone as a brilliant light piercing the densest obscurity of my non-understanding. I had read this passage many times without giving attention. Then one day, in re-reading it, it caught me up short, shook me like a water-rat, droplets flying in all directions along with all of my neat theories about communication, and pierced me to my soul. "Attention!" the passage said. Master Ikkyu was right there, beating me about the shoulders with his stick. "This is how spirit listens."

This is how the story begins.

Centuries ago, a disciple of Confucius named Yen Hui came to Chuang-Tzu for advice. Yen Hui had accepted a position of court-counselor to the ruler of Wei. The ruler was an impetuous young man as likely to chop off Yen Hui's head as to take his advice. Surely Yen Hui wanted to preserve his head. But more, he wanted to offer sage advice for he took his professional calling seriously. Chuang Tzu and Yen Hui discussed the options. But they found each option wanting in one respect or the other, and all departing from the selfless conduct of the Way (i.e., bereft of social biography).

At first, the dialogue focused on how to give advice. As the story progresses, that focus shifts from giving to receiving, and that of a quite special kind. Each advice-giving option has negated the way of counseling *that rests on non-speaking rather than on speaking.*

Finally, somewhat desperate, Yen Hui tried to go deep inside himself to find some answers. "I will," he said to Chuang Tzu, "become grave and empty-hearted, diligent and of one-mind....(I will be) inwardly direct, outwardly compliant and (do my) work through the examples of antiquity....If I go about it this way," he asked Chuang-Tzu, "will it do?"

Chuang-Tzu replied, "Goodness, how could that do? You have too many policies and plans and you haven't seen what is needed. You will probably get off without incurring any blame, yes. But that will be as far as it goes. How do you think you can actually convert him? You are still making the mind your teacher!"

Yen Hui said, "I have nothing to offer. May I ask the proper way?"

"You must fast!" says Chuang-Tzu. "I will tell you what that means. Do you think it is easy to do anything else while you have a mind? If you do, Bright Heaven will not sanction you."

Yen Hui now offers: "My family is poor. I haven't drunk wine or eaten any strong foods for several months. So can I be considered as having fasted?"

"That is the fasting one does before a sacrifice, not the fasting of the mind."

"May I ask what the fasting of the mind is?"

Chuang Tzu answers: "Make your will one! Don't listen with your ears, listen with your mind. No, don't listen with your mind, but listen with your spirit. Listening stops with the ears, the mind stops with recognition, but spirit is empty and waits on all things. The Way gathers in emptiness alone. Emptiness is the fasting of the mind."

Later in the discussion, Chuang-Tzu added: "It is easy to keep from walking, the hard thing is to walk without touching the ground. It is easy to cheat when you work for men, but hard to cheat when you work for Heaven. You have heard of flying with wings, but you have never heard of flying without wings. You have heard of knowledge that knows, but you have never heard of the knowledge that does not know. Look into that closed room, the empty chamber where brightness is born! Fortune and blessing gather where there is stillness. But if you do not keep still—this is what is called racing around. Let your ears and your eyes communicate what is inside, and put your mind and knowledge on the outside. Then, even gods and spirits will come to dwell, not to speak of men!" (1968)

What to take from this tale? Deep listening is that emptiness of the spirit which waits on all things, waits to receive that which the other offers, without comment, without expectation, without judgment. What have we to empty? Our emotional states, our social biography, and our energy sources. Then a great and attentive quietness settles in. As a consequence of deep listening, we may speak to you that which is true of us, without fear, without false pride, without cover-ups that we have used to protect ourselves from the adventures of our spirit.

7

Ways of Deep Learning: An Overview

What is Deep Learning?

Deep learning is the soul-food of the spirit. It is the discipline that puts spirit in charge. In deep learning, spirit learns itself. It is the learner. It is the learning. It is that which is learned.

This is a very awkward way of talking about learning. It departs from standard behavioral, information-management and neurological definitions. But so too does spirit. Deep learning is spirit experiencing itself in all of its immediacy and presence that is so absolutely powerful, it sweeps all away. The "I" part of your social biography disappears under its onslaught, to be replaced by a new "I" that is your spirit in direct relationship with the outside world.

Does any of this make sense? After you have entered into this discipline and experienced it directly, you might respond affirmatively. For now, just mind that deep learning is so different from what we conventionally call learning in schools that you must shift completely the focus of your thinking about it.

Let me tell you a story about my own deep learning to give you a taste of it. I have to do it this way because in the stories and examples given in the earlier chapters, I have been unable to enter into my colleagues' deep learning, only observe its effects. For example, my colleague who took the occasion of her husband's abrupt announcement of divorce clearly entered immediately into this way of enspiriting;

but her account of it to me is on the outside. For example, the reluctant deep listener who finally pushed aside his social biography so he could enter into the yielding, waiting, emptying of *deep listening* clearly also experienced a deep learning episode; but my account of it is on the outside.

To get on the *inside* of it, you have to be and do deep learning. No one can do it for you and, as you shall soon read, it's very difficult to talk about except in generalities that may not apply to your enspiriting journey. Even in the story of my own deep learning, it has proven easier to surround it than to get to its core. For deep learning is spirit experiencing *its own learning*, nothing more, nothing less. Deep learning is a state of beingness like the mode of being silence in deep listening. You don't "do" silence. You *are* silence. So too with deep learning. Doing the learning and being the learning, from the viewpoint of spirit, are one and the same.

What could all of this possibly mean?

Let me give you a hint as to what to anticipate based on my own experience and on that of friends, colleagues, students who have entered into it. When you live in the space of deep learning which is also the space of your spirit, you won't recognize yourself. Your "I" will have disappeared. When you come out the other side, you still won't recognize yourself. Oh, your clothes will still fit (unless part of your deep learning has to do with the very structure of your body itself). But your "personality" won't. I don't mean that you will have cast aside all or even very many of your "traits" and behaviors. In the ordinary course of events where nothing much important transpires, most will note no difference. But you will have cast aside those portions of your social biography that now, after deep learning, don't fit your spirit. Your actions in and towards the world will be different. You will have started growing a new "I" as the essence of your spirit emerges into "real" life.

My Own Unlearning

For many years, long before my entry into the professional ranks of adult education, I knew intuitively, strongly, compellingly, that a great deal of fully human learning was *not learning new stuff but getting rid of old stuff, of unlearning it*. I mean taking out of yourself, literally removing from your persona, your gestalt, your biography an important piece of it. But I didn't know how to do it myself, and so I didn't understand what was happening when other people working with me claimed they were unlearning.

Until I experienced it. Each person's unlearning is unique because her spirit is. Experiencing it is pretty powerful stuff.

As we enter into unlearning, an inexpressible experiencing of ourselves takes place at one point or another. We come face-to-face with our spirit. We cease being in object-relation to our body, our feelings, our mind. Once again, we become as we were when spirit entered our flesh. When does that happen? Most frequently, in moments of great pain and great joy. Exactly in such moments, as we live them in their immediacy, the habits and biography of a lifetime shake loose. Like withering leaves in a strong autumn wind, they drop away, leaving bare a stark core of inner biography which is the spirit itself.

Forgive, now, a little rendition of part of my social biography. There is simply no other true way to get into this story. As I am myself a private person, this story is pulled out with some effort that now, as I understand it, goes by the name of *yielding*.

From the time that I was a youngster, I sensed that the games I played with schoolmates, the rules we made up, the moral and emotional order we created that fit into the larger culture did not match my own internal dispositions, i.e., my spirit. To a large extent, the social biography I was trying on like a new suit of clothes did not match my needs, my proclivities, my energy levels, all that I now understand as expressions of my spirit (though I did not then). What I did "know" was the empathic quality of my spirit. Carefully, and without much success, I tried to hide that quality from my family and classmates. I knew not what to call it; but that empathic spirit placed me unwittingly into other persons' beingness. I broke through the skin and flesh and, later on, the "personality" and role barriers that protect and sustain our culture of privacy and super-individuation. I suspect this is true of many youngsters born with an empathic quality to their spirit. But in my youth I thought I was alone in this, all except for one young friend, a girl whose naive and powerful imagination —she later became a marvelous actress—led her across the bridge between our spirits in a joyous rather than a secretive way. For the most part, I worked very hard at growing up in a masculine culture in which hard body blows—in youth—and hard spirit blows—in adulthood—dominate the ways things are. No doubt, that's why from early on I had such empathy for homosexuals. The way their spirit expressed its lovingness through their sexual behavior had to be hidden too. The masculine culture could no more permit that expression than it could most of the enspiriting ways talked about in this book, of which being empathic was an early one of mine.

In short, I felt myself to be an "other" among my friends. I learned to protect my vulnerability through the mechanism of an easy smile and jovial laugh mixed with the weapons of an aggressive posture and the armor of an intellectual hauteur, the latter emerging particularly in my university days when I finally learned to use my mind as a weapon.

Thus, for example, could I create conflict with and among others—which also became an important early mode of my teaching style—because I had learned to render myself impervious to its consequences...or so I thought and so I told myself in the self-stories that constitute the outcome of continuous negotiations between spirit and social self. Thus had I become accustomed to wearing the mantle of intellectuality on those many occasions when the expression of feelings and the presence of sheer body were invited. Only with the closest of intimates, and then not very often, would my spirit break through. One revolutionary church leader—a dear colleague with whom I did enspiriting work for many years—more often than once had to bear the brunt of my spirit's anger which broke through the propriety of "playing it cool" when her social biography smothered her own great adventures into the byways and laby-rinths of the princes and principalities. But she gave it back in kind—though in a much different and loving way—when my spirit faltered in the face of my own bio-graphical habits that denied the invitation to join those who were building of a covenant community of spirit.

In recent years, the occasions for my enspiriting have rapidly multiplied. More often do I now raise the shades that hide a lifetime of spiritual insularity and private journeys so that others can look in through the window of my soul; and now, sometimes, I hold out my own or grasp another's welcoming hand.

In short, I learned something that pierced through these barriers of invulnerability: The ready smile, the hearty laugh and the machinations of creating conflict and intellec-tual dispute no longer suffice. I have learned to deep listen; and so my spirit is revealed. How did that happen?

Through a trauma existential beyond reckoning, so immediate that time and place took flight, so armor-piercing that my social biography and the twentieth century evaporated...and so I was left naked with my pain, my despair, my utter helplessness...and my spirit.

From Death to Healing

It was when my third born, a son in age not much beyond three, a spirit from Alpha Centauri, birthed by my second wife, was dying. Though he lived and flourished, that time of dying, as we understand that in a scientific/technological/medical culture of making a body better, was upon him like a great black cloth laid over a fragile body and shrouding its effervescent spirit. And though I have loved all my children, the imminence of Zachariah's death drove me to where we all stand naked and bereft.

Zachy lay in intensive care for three weeks, I with him every night for 12 hours, his mother with him every day for 12 hours. As he wasted away, his heart three times its normal size with a wall as thin as tissue paper, the medical staff couldn't handle their foreseen failure to keep him alive. They retreated to the central place of counter, desks, computers, coffee. Except for two who helped save him in the wondrous mating of their medical art, their science and their spirit. The others disappeared.

For three weeks, my nights were spent on a floor bed, up every hour or two to be with my dying son. Often, when I went home during the day, I would awaken in the middle of a lost moment and find myself furiously bashing my head against the wall of our bedroom in a self-denuding onslaught of such pain that, as I came into conscious awareness, a flicker would catch my left brain: My God, Warren, what are you doing? Who is this that is bashing his head against the wall?

Other times, driving to my night watch at the hospital where Zachy lay, a small figure flat and motionless, wired to all the machines ever invented by humankind, I would suddenly see my knuckles whiten on the steering wheel as screams for help, loud enough to blow away a kingdom of habit and self-protection, tore forth from my tant'ien.

Before my son began his slow healing, I did not know who I was and cared less. This was not sorrow or depletion. It was, simply put, the unnumbing of spirit, no longer to stay in hiding after 50 years, being rebirthed as my son lay dying. Can you imagine taking a piece of sheet steel in your bare hands and tearing it like you would an old cloth? Can you imagine the shriek of the molecules as they are rendered asunder, forgetting the story that they feel no pain. That was my shriek.

Until finally, the last day of this journey, I entered the back door of my house at 7 AM to seek respite, with such despair wracking my body, my brain, my very soul that I was ready to die myself. At that moment, my mother, dead for 20 years, appeared luminescent in white, feathery, shimmering, not three feet away. From the last step into the house I had just entered, she said: "Don't worry, Warren. Zachariah will live"… and disappeared.

Zach's healing and mine began that day, he with his body, I with my spirit. It had finally broken through because nothing was left except my utter vulnerability, my haplessness, my yielding, not out of an intention to yield, but because there was nothing else. That's all there was.

This was my *deep learning*, not the only one but the one I share with you so, by story, to give you a glimpse of one way of its experiencing.

There are many stories like this. My good friend and colleague, Paul Delker, told me of a spontaneous deep learning that occurred when his wife died...of her spirit and its living presence with and to him even though modern science, as most of us and he too have been led to understand, denies the domain of spirit as a reality which we can enter and which enters...indeed lives in...us.

Not all moments of great joy or pain constitute occasions for deep learning. Are there other occasions, or must it always be a trauma, a death or dying, that brings on the deep learning? Can we create and live the enspiriting of deep learning deliberately? Is there any *intentioning* here? Or must we await the cymbals, gongs and clashes of men-at-war and women weeping before spirit enters the fray as deep learner and we cease our violent ways? And if we can, how?

These chapters are about that: Offering you some experiencing tools that help you to open the door to the deep learning of your spirit.

The Space of Deep Learning

The space of *deep learning* is vast. It contains all of the holographic images of the universe lying in the implicate order waiting to be born, all of the realities that were, are, and ever will be. (In the chapters on Deep Imaging, some of these images will be teased out as spirit learns to express itself.) How does this enormous space enter into us? Consider. Spirit enters flesh about eight weeks after human conception when zygote becomes foetus. At that point, this vast reach of spirit consciousness focuses in on a specific time, place and culture. The carrier of spirit is the body. In its infinite neurological/chemical/physical system, a collage of so many billions of cells, their molecules, their atoms, their quantum stuff formed into particles and waves, each person replicates within the infinity of the universe outside. But the carrier is not that space. That space which spirit brings to us is filled with all possibilities and no realities.

Then that space's filling-in begins. Possibilities become realities. The ingredients of social biography form. Empty at first, the space is soon filled with stories of ourselves-in-the-world. Social biography begins to emerge. The stories, interlocking with genetic predispositions and the accidents of historic time and place, begin to shape what we have named as *personality, character, body-shape, feeling modes*—different for each person on the planet—and what I call *yourself-in-the-world (myself-in-the-world)*.

What of spirit? It has entered untarnished, untamed, undisciplined, raw spirit-energy that we do not understand because our culture offers us so inadequate a language for understanding spirit and so few practices that ground spirit in the everyday world. In the formation of our personhood, spirit makes a pact with the storytellers and their stories. *If the stories are not about spirit and how and why to discipline and bring it into the world, spirit retreats.* It lays back, mostly unresponsive, in the tant'ien, the center of our vital life force *which is our spirit.*

Does spirit ever emerge? Of course. Usually, in one or another of your facets, well-contained, well-hidden or well-disguised. Shortly, you will be invited to an exercise in which you can test out the qualities of that pact in you *(My spirit speaks out—No. 10).* Occasionally, then, it is allowed to emerge, but only in ways that your social biography has programmed for it. Most of us do get a glimpse. Were this not the case, we would be neither willing nor able to enter into any of these disciplines, enact their competence, and enspirit.

But we do.

This deep learning space is at the end-point of a journey to the origins of your social biography. Here, spirit joins to body through its original enfleshment, seeking its focus, its purposes, its projects in the world and body into which it was born. Much of the inner work in deep learning is designed to bring you to those origins, to that space, by *bypassing your social biography.*

It's a bit more complicated. Stay with it before we come to the actual practices of deep learning to which half-a-dozen exercises will introduce you.

The Continuum of Learning Space

Consider the space of *deep learning* as a multi-dimensional continuum. One part of that continuum eventually fills with stories that I call *ourselves-in-the-world*. The other end fills with stories from the storyteller's own pact between her social biography and her spirit... what amounts to *herself-in-the-world*. These stories tend to be more private, and shared with few persons. The first kind are more social and are usually widely-shared in your group. It is because my mother acted out (witnessed in my presence) some of her "private" stories about spirit in her life that I came, eventually, to my own enspiritings.

For most of us, the space of deep learning is filled with these social stories learned from parents, peers, teachers, or other belief-authority figures. Whence came these stories? *From the storytellers' own reservoir of habitual knowledge, belief, values, attitudes and faith, what I call their KBVAF.* (More on that later. The KBVAF is the dynamic glue of your social biography, and holds its stories together in an iron grip.)

By far, these stories fill up most of your learning space.

The other—private—kind of learning space, also originally empty, is filled with the ways these same persons (parents, etc.) *had integrated spirit into their* own social biographies, usually to the detriment of spirit unless you were blessed with unusual enspiriting storytellers.

In our era, Mahatma Ghandi, Martin Luther King and Anwar Sadat were such enspiriting storytellers. Such persons, at least on the world scene, have been rare. Because ours has been an age of dispiriting rather than enspiriting, the reconfiguration of this other kind of learning space (the *private* part of the continuum) has become the source of the psychiatric project in the 20th century and also accounts for the appeal of the New Age movements from the Eastern cosmologies. Many of the founders and practitioners of dynamic and depth psychology—and almost all of clinical—have eschewed the vocabulary of spirit in the name of proclaiming their work and profession "scientific," befitting the 19th century's model and glorification of science, progress, industrial management and human perfectibility. Whatever its successes and failures with individual persons, the psychiatric project has sought to deal with the spiritual deficits in one's social biography by *bypassing spirit in the name of ego-reconstruction.* In short, the psychiatric project has neglected spirit. When and if befouled social biography inhibits enspiriting to the extent that its barriers can not be overcome by learning and practicing the disciplines of the spirit, then the psychiatric project comes into play. But it is not a substitute for enspiriting. Hope only that whosoever plays with your psyche understands that beneath it lies spirit and is able to recognize the signs that it wants out!

The premise here, may I remind you, is that our social biographies are made up of stories told to us when our learning space was empty, stories told us by persons who meant us no harm, may indeed have loved us and respected our emerging personhood, whose stories were the internalization of their life experience mediated, interpreted and legitimized by the stories they learned in the same way. Such is the process of socialization and education. All well and good *so long as these stories are well and good.* But what if they're not? What if they are no longer? Too much damage to our spirits, too much damage to our planet, too much damage to each other, all in the name of the habitual KBVAF that we must now get rid of.

Deep learning, then, is a matter of getting rid of rather than accumulating? Right.

Is Deep Learning Like Learning?

At first encounter, spirit presents a fathomless face. Much of the work in the enspiriting disciplines is designed to put you in touch with your spirit. Have you already discovered that when spirit smiles, it is unlike any other? Its suffusing light radiates outward to warm the furthest reaches of the ice-country. In *deep learning*, the rigid habits of social biography melt away in the radiance of spirit's welcome. When spirit angers, as it sometimes does when *deep questioning* leads to the *discerning* of malfeasance, of error, of self-denial as social biography protects its domain, of hidden violence towards yourself or others, your very self trembles as your familiar stories crumble like cement with too much sand in it.

What is it like when spirit learns?

It is not the learning of schools, colleges, or other training establishments. Curricula, texts, test scores, classrooms fly out the window and run away. Planning, design, outcomes, goals and objectives, resources—the very vocabulary of educational systems—obsolete under the hammer blows of deep learning's onslaught on the self-deceit of these self-perpetuating mechanisms of cultural hegemony. Unlike all conventional notions, deep learning is uncertified (and uncertifiable!), undesigned, spontaneous, surprising and shaking all to our very foundations.

What kind of learning is that? Can I get it at the campus bookstore, in a 5th-grade civics class, through a management training center? Can I buy it, sell it, store it, use it to get a better job, document it (a term paper, an E-mail, a report)? Don't count on any of that.

Well, can I at least talk about it, share it, live it with another (like together going on a hike, preparing a meal, making love)? Can I at least convey what it is like? Maybe yes, maybe no.

Yes, if you are both enspiriting at the same time. Your partner might be *deep listening* while you are deep learning, and both present to each other in *dialogue*. (Then how come this book? It will not "teach" you deep learning. Reading it is not deep learning. I offer you *starting points*. We have learned quite a lot about those in 25 years. *But your deep learning is your own, not mine; and if it is mine, it is not yours.*)

No, if you or your partner are not on enspiriting paths. These are never the same paths, of course. Quite often, it is only a few steps. But you're both on it. If you're not enspiriting and she is not enspiriting, don't look for deep learning between you.

How to get to that path? Where to look?

Starting Points

In each chapter so far, I have talked about finding the right starting points. This I learned from my teacher Aristotle in the ancient days of a past life when I was a Hebrew slave in his household. He always talked about it when his friends (he didn't have many) and students queried him about where the inquiry was leading. "Get to the right starting point," he would say as he turned to confront the questioner, "and all else will follow as a bird returns to her nest to feed her fledglings. The question is the parent," he admonished, "and the answer is the child."

In the modern parlance, we are wont to say: "The answer lies in the question." Discover the right question and all else follows. I believe that. Much of *deep questioning* can be understood as coming to the right questions about ourselves-in-the-world, the inner and the outer in combination.

But note: I have pluralized. In *deep learning,* as in all of the disciplines of the spirit, there is no one, single starting point. *There are many.* Out of my own work, I have teased six modes of deep learning. You may discover another. Feel free.

The first three modes I call start-up points of departure. They are set forth in the next three chapters. The second three modes of deep learning are practices in *unlearning.* In these, spirit invites the social biography—it can't force it—to relinquish its ways; not all, to be sure, but those that inhibit spirit's expression. The last three modes go very deep. For some folks, their enspiriting craft invites a more sophisticated "technique"; unlike the first three start-up modes, these last three move a bit beyond the common-sense approach to a more difficult path. They are set forth in Chapters Eleven, Twelve and Thirteen.

These six modes of deep learning are summarized below. As you read the summary, keep a few things in mind.

First, you might want to scan these chapters, dipping in and swooping out until one of these start-up modes entices you. Try that one first. If it leaves you high and dry on the shore of your social biography, try another. One will get you started; and I don't think it matters which one.

Second, do remember that the first three modes are starting points. Don't expect or seek instant revelation. Of course, that is true of all the ways of deep learning. Some modes may take you further along the path into deep learning than others. None will get you there. For while spirit is permitted, even cajoled and invited to learn itself, we humans are not permitted to crack open that door and watch what is happening as spirit learns itself, much less write about it. Why? Is this a copout?

Deep Learning Is Not Mystical; But It Is Mysterious

Deep learning is sacred, but not like the face and name of God at the burning bush or the Tao that is unknown and unknowable. It is sacred in the sense that all enspiriting is: Special, protected, powerful in worldly matters, not just of this earth but of the universe (though unbelievably present in us and with ourselves-in-the-world).

Now here's a twist. The sacred and the secular, the "other worldly" and the "this worldly" unite in the enspiriting disciplines. The inner work—self-confrontation until spirit is liberated—and the outer work—confrontation with others in dialogue about the justice issues go hand-in-hand. The idea of the "sacred" is removed from our discourse about how the world works. So too is the idea of the "secular." They merge into a unity that I have named the disciplines of the spirit. Neither private "salvation" nor public "making the world a better place to live" is, by itself, sufficient unto the day of transformation. It may be that by itself, each is an abomination; spirit must join both paths or we have lost God's grace.

But in the final analysis, deep learning shapes the whole universe much as the hand shapes the whole body. Watch the hand and you see and understand what the body is up to. If we describe the actual experiencing of deep learning by spirit learning itself, if we "explain" it, if we give it a cause-and-effect kind of analysis, if we seek to predict outcomes and set goals for it, we are on the road to command and control of spirit.

Religion may seek command and control; but I won't. And in the institution of education, that is exactly what it does with learning. To set learning free of educational systems by placing the learner in charge of her own learning (this, by the way, is one of the modes of deep learning) is a most radical and transformative act in modern society. The outstanding work of Paolo Freire, John Ohliger and Allen Tough in rediscovering the *learning* of adults as distinguished from their education and training amply demonstrates that certification of the learning experience reduces it to those skills, knowledge and attitudes that the prevailing culture deems appropriate to maintain itself.

We are not after survival in enspiriting. We are after discovery and invention of how we might all live together on this planet so that spirit is free rather than devastated by our religious, language, ethnic, cultural and biographical differences.

As I invite you to deep learning, I am constrained to share starting points, not ending points. My aim is not to issue edicts of command and control. Indeed, the first mode of deep learning, self-empowering learning, is characterized by its spontaneity. We must seek to conceptualize without controlling, to name without commanding. Remember Chuang Tzu? *"... the mind stops with recognition, but spirit is empty and waits on all things."* That we can only experience in its mystery.

Your spirit will come to its deep learning when it is ready. You will know that. How? Because you will have got beyond your social biography. The modes of deep learning help you to do that.

The Six Modes of Deep Learning; A Summary

These are the six that I have discovered, learned, been taught. Let me summarize them.

The first three—start-up points of departure:

1. *Self-empowering learning:* In which you seek out the learning that empowered you.

2. *Imbalance:* In which you discern and acknowledge your inner disquietude and imbalance.

3. *Dissonance:* In which you come to realize the conflict between what you have been taught about the way the world works (and the way you work) and the immediacy of your own experiencing of it.

The second three—the unlearning modes:

4. *Unpeeling:* In which you enter an unlearning that is an unpeeling, and so discard aspects of your social biography.

5. *Unfreezing:* In which you enter an unlearning that is an unfreezing of habit and a re-discovery of your original *intentioning* before habit is formed.

6. *Moving from past to future:* In which you tease out the learning involved in imaging a future of that which is expressive of your spirit.

All the modes work; but they work selectively for one or for another enspiritor. The start-up modes may open gates to a new path for your enspiriting. If you have already gone through these gates, move on to the unlearning modes. There is no necessary sequence among any of these six. Read among them, skip about them, mix them as you will. I describe each mode. Its occasions are set forth. An exercise accompanies. At the end, we'll once again take up the question: "How do I know when I'm *deep learning*?" Perhaps we might even unravel the mystery of *spirit's learning itself!*

8

A Start-up Point of Departure: The Mode of Self-empowering Learning

Here Comes the Parade!

It is true that I have said you should scan each of the six modes of *deep learning* before you decide which one to initiate. It is true that enspiritors come to this pivotal discipline with a history of their own spirit, a history perhaps untapped but nevertheless present. That history, which is the story of the negotiated relationship between spirit and social biography, may well incline you to one or another of these modes; and you intuit that. Also, some like to start with the most difficult: unpeeling and unfreezing. *A strong spirit, one that trusts your invitation to its own learning, one whose venturesome disposition takes it to spaces previously unexplored may select one of these more difficult modes of deep learning even at the beginning.*

How do you know a strong spirit?

When my first son, David, was nine, he took a sail with Bill and Kathy Saltonstall, two intrepid and experienced sailors, on Buzzard's Bay, on a cold, windy but beautifully clear late October day. Bill gave David the benefit of his vast experience: how to steer, how to watch the wind meet with the sails, why to watch the whitecaps, and much more. David soaked it up and, within a half an hour, was given the helm. He sat in the stern, steering a straight course set for him by his mentor. Half a dozen of us sat back on the sides of the boat, enjoying the stiff breeze. But David wanted to experiment. His was a questing spirit that has guided—and *pushed*—him into bold adventures ever since he could ride a tricycle. He would try *anything* just for the experiencing and learning of it! Over went the helm, hard aport, as far as he could push. The boat heeled. We were about thrown off. The boom came swinging through, just about beheading us... but we ducked. Bill must have cursed under his breath (I never heard him do that in public!) and yelled at the young boy: "WHAT ARE YOU UP TO, YOUNG MAN?" as he jumped to the helm and righted us.

You, too, may swing the helm hard aport and try one or another of these modes as your spirit disposes you. But try the self-empowering exercise first. Discover what it uncovers for you. Then go to the start-up modes, *imbalance* or *dissonance*. Take it easy on yourself—your social biography—as you begin. After a while, this discipline takes hold and won't let go, no matter how much it hurts. Oh, you'll recover, have no fear. But in their experiencing, the "advanced" modes of deep learning give no quarter and demand a depth of interior action, of inner work, that may leave you a bit discombobulated.

Experiencing deep learning is a bit like going to a parade. You stand at the curb, heart beating a little faster, milling about to find a good spot in the crowd. The street is empty. Then, in the distance, you hear the first faint call of the bugle... perhaps it's a cymbal clashing in the mist or a drum beat or two, making that far away but imperious call to your spirit. You look out over the curb. There, rounding the corner half a dozen blocks away, comes the drum major—you can barely see him—followed by the first echelon wheeling into a flank right. Then it begins, that parade, creeping up on you, getting a bit louder. Can you hear the Sousa march now? Your heart picks up its beat, your whole body careens forward in anticipation, now you can make out the color of the uniforms, individual bodies take shape, the movement of the parade, its rhythms, its sounds, its bands, its floats, become increasingly present. And as the first group marches right up to and past you, you are caught up in that unbelievable excitement of full beingness with the parade, and you lose your identity, your social biography, your hopes and fears, for you and the parade are present, fully, to one another.

So if you like parades, begin the deep learning with *self-empowering learning* ... and it will take you from there.

The Mode of Self-empowering Learning

I have framed self-empowering learning into an exercise that follows because in giving you a clue about *where* to look for this entrance gate to *deep learning*, it will also provide a clue as to *how* to look.[3]

---

[3] I have used versions of this for many years, particularly with my colleague Bob Luton whose selfless dedication to putting people in charge of their own learning and pastoring them through its travails will give him a seat close to the throne of the Mother of Wisdom.

You begin the search by looking for self-learning that is empowering. Self-learning is that which you do under your own direction, and thus is a clue as to what your spirit does in *its* learning. You are in charge; not a teacher, not a parent, not a boss, not even your dearest friend. *Empowering* goes hand-in-hand with self-learning. Because you're in charge, responsible for your own learning, once undertaken, the experience becomes a source of inner strength. Inner strength means that you have learned to tap into your spirit-energy; more precisely, that your spirit has learned to trust you enough to share some of its energy.

What is self-empowering learning about? It is about yourself in this sense: You are in the learning both as initiator and as recipient. Self-empowering learning often gives an insight into your social biography: its limits and its possibilities. Many people have recounted to me stories of early learning about their own physical prowess or social competence: The first difficult rock climb when they discovered they could do it, the first social dance when they discovered that boys found them attractive. Often, that discovery clashed with an earlier self-perception. The Outward Bound movement was founded for urban ghetto youngsters whose self-perceptions (i.e., their emerging *social biographies)* denied them a powerful sense of themselves by virtue of their lower social class and their impoverished living conditions.

Later, the focus of self-empowering learning shifts directly to your spirit. But don't rush that shift of focus. It will happen naturally as a part of the deep learning discipline further along its path.

Is it a big thing, this self-empowering learning? It might be. A revelation about yourself or a substantial breakthrough that brought you to a new place of knowledge or skill.

But it might be a small thing: The first fish you caught all by yourself when you were nine years old as you brought it into the boat or onto shore. Do you remember its flapping about frantically? Do you remember grabbing it close to the head, feeling that very special quality of cold, wet, frantic fishskin trembling in your hand (or were you the one that trembled?), and trying to get the hook out of its mouth without tearing more of the flesh? What was it like to throw it back into its watery home? What was it like to feel that sense of accomplishment, of responsibility, of risk-taking with no one around to hold your hand, to show you, to judge you? That is what it means to be in charge of your own learning. Deprived of an experiencing of learning that is self-empowering, your social biography has little to fall back on when your spirit invites you to its adventures.

But most of us have this experience, though often not in our formal schooling. The next exercise invites you to this search. Don't worry about learning of earth-shaking proportions. Who is to say what is a "big" learning and what is a "small" learning, so long as it belonged to you?

The Exercise Itself: Self-empowering Learning (No. 6)

As you begin this inner work, do remember that "exercises" are to give you practice at the competence as well as insight into your progress along the path of a discipline. By themselves, exercises are as worthless as a hen scratching in the dust for a kernel of corn that wasn't there in the first place. But as guides to experience and to reflection on that experience (praxis), they may help you to those early steps that put you at the right starting points and hold out hope that your crawl will soon turn into a walk, a run, into spirit flying. Be sure to have a piece of paper handy, for you will want to capture some of your inner work for later reflection.

The "headlines" at the start of each paragraph are my starting points for this mode which is itself a starting point for *deep learning*. Starting points and starting points! Is there no end in sight? Not in sight; but there. Use them freely...but with an inner discipline of *yielding* to your responses until you find your own starting points.

Preparation. Will you mind it? Still essential. Don't neglect it. Warm up the muscles of your spirit! Be quiet. Listen to the sound of your own breathing. A self-note that, though not the whole thing, it is a good start. Give attention to it. Perhaps, even, a little emptying.

Searching. Search the body of your experience for that revelation or break through, literally and figuratively. Your experience always leaves its mark in your body. I have already talked about that in *deep questioning*. Your whole body remembers what happened, not only the memory cells in your brain. It too will speak to you if you will but listen.

As in deep questioning, have no expectations about what you will find. Let your mind roam through your life, through out-of-the-way times and places as well as the ordinary.

The first time. Isn't this a good place to look? It is full of surprises, for you know not what to expect. Unexpected, the self-empowering learning was not planned; but it happened and you can describe its detail.

Spontaneity. Another word for the unplanned and the undesigned. Why this quality? Like others, it is a clue, not a directive. Along the path to deep learning will be found spontaneous experiences that may well constitute your spirit speaking, more likely, taking in. It is giving attention even while your conscious awareness is not.

Ownership. This is the self-knowledge that you are or were in charge of your own learning. "I own this learning," you say. "It is mine, not some one else's."

What could this possibly mean? Like a house, a car, a suit of clothes, you "own" it? Not at all. This is not proprietary. Then what is it?

The body sense, which you already know. You can feel this learning in your "bones," in your tant'ien, in your body. It is palpable.

The impact sense. Something changed. Whether in the mind, in the body, or in the feelings, there has been a perceptible *shift* as Eugene Gendlin talks about it in *Focusing.* The shift involves a reduction, a peeling away, or an addition, a growingness. It is a change that you can begin to name, though not necessarily explain. What you seek in all of this is description, concreteness, specificity of the learning, not a psychological or sociological account. Those tend to lead you into a discourse about educational or psychological behavior rather than self-empowering learning. Bring this impact sense to conscious awareness if you can so that you may enter into an internal dialogue through *deep questioning* and *deep listening.*

The consequence sense. If all that goes before holds up under your reflection and discovery, you can then name some consequences of this empowering learning. What are/were its consequences for you, for others, for the situation or learning setting? We shall do much consequence analysis in the disciplines of *deep imaging* and *discerning,* for that is one of their chief competence. It's not too soon to get started.

The situation. See now if you can remember and describe this. These are the familiar *what, when, where, who, why, how* questions. Here, seek to place the learning in its total context, inner and outer. Describing this learning setting may give you clues about how you got on that pathway to learning empowerment in the first place, and so may open the gate to deep learning a bit wider.

Some start the entire line of inquiry with this headline or category, sort of surrounding the experience until the memories rush back and you focus in on exactly what was happening.

The empowering. What could that mean? Certainly not having or acquiring power over another person. Perhaps taking away their power over you! Well, you could move away. Folks do, to a halfway house, another apartment, city, even country. Self-empowering learning is an inner experience. That's where the move takes place. The "in charge of" phrase, as in "being in charge of my own learning" (or my own clothes, my own work, my own sex life) gets close to it. Another notion is *competence*. I can do this (ability, skill) and I *want to* do this (intention, will). Joining them together into competence is generated by self-empowering learning.

Strength. You became strong, at that moment, in that arena of self. Big learning or small, it doesn't matter. Quantity is not an issue. Impressing people is not an issue. Feeling, knowing, living, experiencing that inner strength and competence is the thing. When that happened, didn't you afterwards let out a "whoosh," or something like that? Your spirit acknowledging through your body: "It's about time."

Can This Be Shared?

Now you've got the most of this mode. If you are working with a partner, give yourself time to do this inner work by yourself, and give her time too. Fifteen minutes, half-an-hour? You decide. Then start the *deep listening* and *deep questioning*. Begin by preparing yourselves for that dialogue. Each gets a turn, though if you have become adept at these competence, turn-taking can move into a faster-paced exchange. However that sharing happens, give yourself plenty of time. An hour would not be too much. For the whole of *deep learning*, would a lifetime be too much?

Clues to Deep Learning

While there is a mystery to *deep learning*, as to any of the enspiriting disciplines, we have discovered gateways, pathways, starting points. Even in this first mode, some of those might lead you to the inner spaces where deep learning occurs. One trail leads to *hidden learning or the hiding space*. We have learned that some people hide from their self-empowering learning because it is/was counter-cultural or anti-biographical. Not proper. Too dangerous. Perhaps just not permitted to be talked about, sometimes even thought about, much less lived.

In many cultures that are mainly anti-body and pro-mind, that search for learning empowerment might well lead to hidden memories of the early sexual exploration of your own body or with another person. I am not inviting you here to revisit violence or abuse. Rather, the search might be for the glorious sense of your own awakening sexual self where spirit and body joined, a learning that was yours and not someone else's; that might have been spontaneous, surprising and impactful, that was your own sexual power and prowess.

How Is Self-empowering Learning a Starting Point?

If this mode of *deep learning* works for you, you have entered an inner space that is difficult to colonize from the outside. By virtue of your ownership, you have enfranchised your general learning capacity. Now continue the exploration. Retrieve into conscious awareness more episodes of self-empowering learning. Dig deeper to ascertain the conditions under which they occurred with such questions as:

Who else was involved? How? Why?

What did you feel in the actual learning experience? Can you describe those feelings?

What impact did this have on your social biography? Any? Did you begin to feel differently about yourself? How? Why?

When well undertaken, the mode of self-empowering learning produces two results.

First, it returns your learning to yourself. The culture of learning that emerged in the industrialized world took away a great deal of learning's grand empowerment very much like modern medicine has taken away much competence in self-healing. In the Information Age, it is essential that we retrieve control over our own learning. Otherwise, we relinquish to enticing and manipulative systems and institutions that "manage" information the solution of to what to give attention. In the world of spirit, that self-abrogation is, quite simply, devastating.

Secondly, when considered in its interior dimension, self-empowering learning reaches to the juncture where spirit interacts with social biography. You have already begun to explore that junction through *deep questioning*. It is a space—often placed in the tant'ien rather than the brain—where deep learning begins. Why? The accouterments of social biography like career, marriage, family, intimacy, self-concept, how you feel about yourself, your habits of accommodating to your life circumstances: All of these begin to loosen their grip in deep learning. Once again, you have re-entered an interior space where agreements between spirit and social biography can be renegotiated.

That space is characterized by imbalance and disquietude, the very same that often starts up the deep questioning. That imbalance is the second mode of deep learning, one of its chief starting points.

9

Another Start-up Point:
The Mode of Imbalance

The Mode of Imbalance

In earlier chapters on The Ways of Deep Questioning, I speak more fully of the inner sense of imbalance, disharmony and tension, signaled by the language of feelings, the voice of spirit speaking through the body.

In this start-up mode, *we seek to describe that interior space where social biography and spirit are in conflict.*

It is easy to think of this as self-analysis, the poor person's approach to psychotherapy, self-counseling, or a short course in clinical psychology. But the mode of imbalance is none of the above. I consider imbalance, disquietude and inner tension to be conditions, endemic qualities of great conflict between ourselves-in-the-world (our collective social biography, so to speak) and our spirit.

What is the tension that *deep learning* searches out? It is a conflict between spirit as *it* tries to express itself and social biography as *it* tries to confine spirit to culturally acceptable expressions. Celebrate this tension. Go to the inner conflict and embrace it. Do not avoid it. We are in transformation. The tension within is a sign. Disquietude is the hallmark of our times. Begin the deep learning.

Spirit Will Out: My Mother's Story

It has been more with women than with men that I have seen this conflict between spirit and social biography at work. In the masculine era of the last several centuries, at least in the West, women have sought to free themselves from aspects of their social biography in favor of what their spirit calls them to. Waves of political, social, economic liberation of women have swept through the Western world every 50 years or so; but like the ocean beating on the shore, each bit of erosion is accompanied by a returning undertow. The movement of seachange against shoreline is inexorable. Its effects are not always visible unless you watch for a long time.

Yet each mass movement in the world, every shift in collective consciousness comes into being by virtue of an inner struggle among its initiators and early proponents. They create the outer fray—themselves-in-the-world undergoing transformation—as they seek their own, new inner balance. That was the case with my mother.

My father died as I turned 14. Among the many consequences, one stands out. My mother re-entered her inner conflict of spirit with biography, a conflict never completely submerged but one that had moved to the back burner in 20 years of marriage. Friends offered her jobs so that she could support herself and her two sons. She refused them all; and some of these friends, after admonishing her to play it safe and sensible, thought she might have gone a bit off the deep end. She refused these job offers because she intended to be independent, a trait that had caused her husband a bit of upset when he was alive, a trait that was constituted by her spirit that she did not intend to give up even when the protection of a middle-class, fairly affluent lifestyle suddenly disappeared that summer of 1941.

In retrospect, I realize that her indomitable spirit had sparked and risen from time to time in her marriage to a rising young surgeon of great promise. But our cultural institutions still conveyed a singular and intractable homemaking role to the wife and mother. So the occasions of her enspiriting were probably fewer than they came to be after her husband's early death at age 48.

As she began to journey the economic survival trail, it didn't take long for spirit to awaken. The inner conflict she rarely showed me, but the tension was obvious as she threw off the outer apparel of style, affluence, accommodation to reach for a new self of independence, survival, integrity, all the while keeping the semblance of a home for her two sons.

For example, after refusing the job offers, she began baking and selling fruit cakes. Folks thought this was laughable. Her gas oven could bake about 11 pounds at a batch, in one or two pound tins. Her recipe was antique and unique in the history of fruitcake-making; and soon she was selling them throughout the United States and, within a year, abroad. Her fruitcake sojourn and recipe were written up in

Gourmet Magazine. What is the point? Between October 1 and December 15, 1941, she mixed, baked, sold and mailed from her apartment hundreds of pounds of fruitcake. Not much money... but lots of independence!

One winter afternoon, just after Pearl Harbor, during Christmas vacation when I was home from prep school to which I had been granted a partial scholarship after Dad died, my grand uncle—the millionaire in the family—visited us. My father had been his favorite nephew and the executor of his will. On Dad's deathbed, his uncle, tears streaming down his face, had promised to take care of his family and ensure that the two boys would receive whatever financial assistance was necessary to continue their education at the best "private" schools and colleges.

With the visit from the Granduncle came an interview: What had I been doing? What was I learning? Was I minding my P's and Q's? Since I had been back on vacation, had I visited my father's father—my Grandfather? Questions came fast and furious to verify my conduct.

When it became obvious that my responses were not suitable, my Granduncle's tack shifted. He beat against my breezy and no doubt wise-acre responses. You had better do this and you had better do that, he said. My mother, of course, was present during this interview. I was not watching her. I could feel the heat rise. Then she spoke.

"No one dictates to my son."

Flatout, unambiguous, not yet passionate but hard and straight as a dagger.

"If he doesn't do what I say," my father's uncle retorted, "I will not pay for his schooling."

Her voice rose in firmness. "We neither want nor need your help." Note the "we." I did. Again, repeating: "No one dictates to my son."

Now I was watching. How her chin set. How her eyes flashed. Spirit had just exploded. Whatever had been working within her in the five months since her husband's death, no doubt an inner cauldron of loss, pain, grief, fear, determination, a new sense of herself was emerging. She was confronting the exigencies of rent, clothes, food, health care, tuition for her sons, one at college, one at prep school. Perhaps her spirit was in constant and still ambiguous struggle with her social biography. This moment was an invitation her spirit could not refuse.

"Please, leave now," she said. He did, furiously bashing his hat on his head and swinging his gold-tipped cane. Out the door he flew and with him all the promises this very wealthy man had made to his favorite nephew.

For the next 20 years, as she continued to earn her living, my mother was in a continuous state of liberating her spirit and negotiating her social biography. I don't mean her "personality" changed. What happened over the next 20 years was just this: Her indomitable spirit came to the fore. All of her character traits, her idiosyncrasies, her behavior patterns were subsumed within her enspiriting life.

Sometimes we are privileged to catch a bit of the outward manifestation of imbalance, renegotiation, inward turmoil.

The "real" story of your own inward struggle only you can know. It need not be shared until and unless a partner is invited to the *deep listening*. That invitation must be extended *and* accepted with great care. Spirit sharing with spirit is no light and easy small talk over a cup of coffee or a glass of wine.

The mode of imbalance invites you to cast the struggle within upon your shore of what Harry Stack Sullivan called your *conscious awareness*.

Struggle, turmoil, disquietude are sometimes taken as illness. They are not. They are the main healing going on in this world right now, for the outward healing is still beyond most of us.

Imbalance Signifies Health

Should my mother have visited a psychiatrist or a career counselor when she refused the job offers? Nowadays, if you had the money, that would be a reasonable road. This is the era of mental health. How does this popular perspective equate with the disciplines of enspiriting? Why is it healthy to celebrate imbalance, inner turmoil, tension, and disquietude?

Simply put, enspiriting work is not about your achieving "mental health" in a world in turmoil. It is about freeing up your spirit to speak to you and through you to ourselves-in-the-world about our transformation, about the ways we live within ourselves—the interiority—and the ways we live with others—the exteriority. *Deep learning* is not a product of the upsurge in mental health practices. The mode of imbalance does not posit mental health problems among any of its practitioners.

Exteriority has to do with justice issues: how we might best live together on this small planet. Interiority resides where spirit is in conflict and negotiating with social biography. In my view, the two domains, though named differently according to a perspective of inner action or outer action, pinpoint the basic tension of our world. But this start-up mode calls you to your inner action, to your rich inner life always in creative conflict.

Imbalance, disquietude, tension are not bad, evil, sick, or "to be cured." In deep learning, you travel far beyond simplistic moral and medical models to the great on-going event in your life: The entrance of spirit into flesh and spirit's quest to speak out to you about who you are and what you're up to. For years, I have named that your compelling image, that which you can not not be and that which you can not not do. Later on, in the chapters on *intentioning*, we shall explore in detail the practices of discovering *your compelling image*. For now, concentrate on the nature of this imbalance, this disquietude, this inner tension. It is a grand starting point for deep learning. But it is also a difficult starting point. As you will soon discover, social biography seeks to protect its kingdom from the inroads of spirit. Where they meet is where you will now travel.

The Exercise Itself: What Is the Imbalancing? (No. 7)

Can you invite your social biography into this dialogue with spirit? More precisely, will your social biography permit you to travel to the juncture to listen, to watch as spirit and social biography interface in an extraordinarily dynamic interplay? You'll need the imaginative and persevering skills of a topnotch journalist who, eschewing the daily briefings by the center of command and control, goes to the battlefield and lives with the troops. But you must *force* nothing. Spirit may respond and social biography may yield just a bit if you frame your invitation openly and lovingly. Yield to the responses. You know that at this stage of the negotiations both sides have a case to make and both would like to complain just a bit. Let them.

To the Biographical Side

See if you can identify and name the characteristics of your social biography that are most upset or most at risk. What are they? Don't be afraid of mis-naming. This is not a test. Deep listen to your feelings. On the social biography side, is it a conflict about money (and what that signifies: riches, affluence, security, prestige, consumerism)? Is it about sex? Is it about self-esteem? Is it about a useless, unsatisfying, frustrating, uncreative job or relationship? Is it about stories of yourself that you never liked, know are false and wanting in some respect, that fall short of the mark? So far as I can tell, these categories comprise a large portion of social biography that impedes the spirit.

Begin making your own list. Recall the events in your life that stand out as significant, i.e., they mattered, their effects were lasting, you can still relive them with all of the feelings involved, as if they were happening once again. If they hurt, hold them, embrace them, ask of them: "What are you trying to tell me? What does this happening mean?"

Does this produce tears, pain, sorrow, a sense of loss, anger, frustration? So be it. Who told you—beyond a false culture—that "life" was invariably and continuously a steady bombardment of pleasurable sensations that would woo you into the soporific sleep of avoidance?

Of course, the counter is also true. Moments of great joy, even ecstasy, as well as the enduring and endearing relationships with other humans, with animals, with all living creatures including our Mother Earth, await those of us who learn—who re-discover —the ways of enspiriting.

Embrace the Tiger

Go to the inner tension, the sense of imbalance, the conflict that wells up through your body senses. Don't fight it. Don't push it aside. Embrace it even though this is not a "happy" feeling.

Some years ago, my dear colleague Mary Link and I were facilitating a workshop on envisioning a world without weapons. *Deep imaging* was the main enspiriting metier; but we invited participants to their *deep listening* too. After a while, we formed ourselves into a tentative community of learners and began our praxis. For 20 or so minutes, the participants, mainly good, solid middle-class Americans held discourse on what it was like to do the envisioning. Then one person, a woman who kept herself neat and tidy, a matron of solid repute, good intentions and pleasant manners suddenly lost it. She erupted in passionate tears of deep pain just as we thought we had all maintained our cool in the face of a holocaust imaged away by our spirit. She could not. The world destroyed was with her, in her, of her. Her spirit cried out in desperation; ours turned towards her, though many fought hard to maintain the semblance of a cool exterior demanded by their social biographies.

Each person who spoke tried to calm her, solace her, hold her. When my turn came, I remembered the words of my Tai Chi Master years before. "Embrace the tiger. Pull your pain to your bosom. Hold out your arms and welcome it. Love it. Count your tears a blessing. Feel the pain. Feel the feelings. Run not from them. Your spirit speaks out through them. Thank God for that. We need no words of comfort. Live through the holocaust and all that does to you in the life of the imaginal. Retreat not. Embrace. At some point, you will come out the other side. There is always another side, for spirit's journey is never over."

To the Spirit Side

Through the disciplines you have already learned in practice, let your spirit speak. Yours. How will you know it? You'll know it. Let your invitation ring true. Feel the welling-up from your tant'ien of the white light of your spirit through your body.

What is it saying? Don't try to make sense of it yet. The mode of imbalance is a starting point, not an ending point. Jot down notes if words come to you. Some of us keep journals. In my own life, I have found that arising early in the morning to write in my journal before the "day" begins is a helpful way to invite spirit to speak out before social biography intervenes to silence it. But words are not necessary. Pictures may come to you or movement. Dance your spirit's feelings in your body as its energy moves.

What if, despite your yielding invitation, spirit does not "speak"? Not to worry. It can't be forced. It can only be invited. Perhaps this is the first time you've made the invitation. Your spirit can't believe it, not yet.

One person I knew was a spirit's poet. When her spirit spoke, it was in her poetry. This she offered to a reluctant world of family, peers and colleagues. "Listen to it yourself," I offered, "What does it say to you about you?"

Rapidly, then, her poetry brought her to the juncture, to the interface.

Another person I knew chopped wood, literally, cursing and mouthing, sweating out the poisons in his biography, fighting its stubborn resistance until, exhausted, he slipped to the ground, his back against a tree, into a dream-like state. Eyes staring inward, not seeing the outside world, he listened to his spirit as it came, once again, to the juncture of imbalance.

To the Juncture, Then

For those who invite spirit's *deep learning* through the mode of imbalance, the space to visit is that where spirit and biography meet. Just listen. That is all.

This is not an exercise in personal problem-solving. Don't give yourself advice. At this stage, such advice will be social biography and inbred cultural constraints falsely stating the issues.

This is start-up. What is the question? What disquiets you? Coming just to that is an event of deep insight into the interface where spirit and social biography are now in movement, in re-negotiation, where the two grind against each other like two tectonic plates of your soul slipping and shearing against each other for new position.

To Silent Dialogue

Of course, this dialogue is inner. First your biography speaks, then your spirit speaks...or vice versa. Let them. Do not intervene. You are the deep listener, the deep questioner, standing unnoticed at this interface.

What kind of a jargon is this? Who, for heaven's sake, is the "you"? There is a technical point here, to be unpacked in a later chapter on *discerning*.

But for the moment, say to yourself, "I am the dialogue itself. I am the energy that lets this happen, that invites the conflict or tension to emerge. I am neither biography nor spirit, neither body nor feelings, not even mind. I am only energy in motion, kinetic energy."

For the moment—half an hour, a nanosecond, the whole day?—allow yourself to be in *kairos*, neither fish, fowl, nor good red herring, as the saying goes. Be the interface of spirit and social biography. Let each speak its tears, yells, growls, gnashing of teeth, grinding of jaws, false enticements. This is true inner work, not psychologizing. Specific. Concrete. Descriptive. What is going on here? What is the conflict? Wherein lies the imbalance? Learn it. Learn to let it happen. When you learn to do this, you are halfway to spirit's core, its essence.

Your spirit is learning to trust you.

10

A Third Start-up Point:
The Mode of Dissonance

Reality's Continuum

Much of what I have introduced invites a looking inward, to your social biography, to your soul, to your spirit. In these times of confusion and disharmony, many look inward to find new keels that might provide them a semblance of balance. For many, that is the path of least resistance because to seek redress, renewal and reconstruction in the exterior domain which no one controls feels impossible.

Transformation, of course, bonds the inner and the outer. I believe that. I believe the traditional distinctions between *inner* and *outer*, between *this-worldly* and *other-worldly*, between the *sacred* and the *secular*, between *action* and *contemplation*, between *subject* and *object*, between the *personal* and the *impersonal*, are, simply put, false. Enspiriting creates a seamless web, a new wholeness, a new integrity between spirit and ourselves-in-the-world that is at the heart of our transformation, inner and outer. *But you have to experience this yourself.*

In fact, each of these "sets" is a continuum. Most land on the inner side of the continuum first, in learning the discipline of *deep learning*. This next exercise is crucial to opening up for you some of the *external* or *outer work*. It is still inner work, to be sure. But its focus encompasses much that lies outside your skin and, conventionally, outside of your influence, much less control. It puts you on a continuum on which you will learn to move back and forth, from one edge to the other side, quite rapidly.

The Mode of Dissonance

What is *dissonance*? How does it serve as a starting point for *deep learning*? How is it different from the mode of imbalance? Imbalance, as we are using it, comprises a conflict between spirit and social biography. The aim of that approach is to come to the juncture or interface where that conflict can be described.

Dissonance focuses on a distinction between *knowing* and *experiencing*. The two modes of imbalance and dissonance certainly interact. But, as you will soon discover, the deep learning mode of dissonance involves more use of the intellect while the imbalance mode relies more heavily on a *discerning* of feelings. Thus, the dissonance mode is designed to appeal to folks who have found the feeling and intuiting aspects of the first two modes difficult to enter.

In the conflict that breeds dissonance, there are two sides, sometimes more.

On the one side is a central part of the social biography, defined by *knowledge, beliefs, values, attitudes,* even *faith.* Taken together, these constitute your "official" posture about anything and everything. I call this your *KBVAF* "core." These you are prepared to enunciate and declare, as in "This I know. This I believe." Some portions of this core are tacitly held. Rarely do they enter conscious awareness unless provoked by an ordeal or stress of significant proportions. But when they emerge into daily discourse and action, the tacit KBVAF positions you vis-a-vis the rest of the world. Your KBVAF core is vital to your maintenance, even survival as your social biography defines you.

Knowledge, beliefs, values, attitudes and faith each attract a very large literature in philosophy, sociology and psychology. Have I lumped together into one mode that which must be kept separate? Not in the enspiriting discipline of deep learning. For this point of departure is about a striking dissonance between that core of your social biography, your KBVAF, as one element, and *experience* as the other.

Your KBVAF core has been constituted by what you have been told is true by all of the authority figures in your life. The KBVAF may have been molded by your parents, your teachers, a minister or doctor, even a political leader. Your KBVAF has been filled by what you have read in authoritative texts, by what you have been taught in school, by what you have imbibed as true from TV, radio, the movies; and from what is held to be true in the popular culture.

Consider the KBVAF core from an information-management perspective. From that fix, your social biography is formatted into a huge neurological program. This is a dense, multi-phased program packed with such an infinity of data that its behavior is best understood by a quantum mechanics approach in which the data alternate between particle behavior and wave behavior depending on what you are looking for and what questions you ask of it.[4] I bring this up to alert you to a problem with this mode of deep learning. That problem is to insist that distinctions among knowledge, beliefs, values, attitudes and faith are crucial. In this work, they are not. What is crucial is the quality of their *social truth* that lies at the core of your social biography.

What is on the other side of this dissonance? It is *the immediacy of your experiencing life in any of its myriad dimensions.* Dissonance arises when that experiencing reveals the lie, the incompleteness, the tarnish, or the capacity to manipulate this social truth. In times of transformation, it is not only the "outsider," the one we name "strange," "peculiar," "a little touched" who lives this dissonance in everyday life. It is all of us, though many of us are afraid of acknowledging this dissonance and so look for authority figures to keep us in a state of true belief. Eric Hoffer called these "true believers"; in today's currency, they are the upholders of political correctness.

The key phrase is "the immediacy of your experiencing." To make that phraseology even more awkward, let me call it the "is-ness" of being. What you experience in this immediacy or is-ness is like experiencing a lightning strike on a 14,000-foot peak. As you jump out of your skin, what has happened is unmediated by anything or any one. It just is.

Do you see what I am coming to here? The immediacy of experiencing breeds a genuineness whose authenticity is diffused when we seek to certify that experience as *true* by an appeal to our KBVAF. Needless to say, this immediacy or is-ness quality of *experiencing* has troubled philosophers for centuries: How to render experience intelligible without changing it.

This is no longer an esoteric issue best left to philosophers. It has become a peculiarly twentieth century question that cannot be avoided without grave risk to our sanity and the health of our spirit. Look what Chairman Mao had to say about this, an idea that affected hundreds of millions of folks in its application.

---

[4] In the chapters on deep imaging, I rely on holographic theory and quantum mechanics, both at the forefront of modern-day physics, to help us understand how it is possible for spirit *enfleshed in each of us* to generate an infinite number of images of the future, so many of which are not fastened to present-day realities or histories of the past.

"If you want to gain knowledge you must participate in the practice of changing reality. If you want to know the taste of a pear you must change the pear by eating it... All genuine knowledge originates in direct experience."[5]

You inhabit a world where dissonance is rife, where the eternal verities, the "truths" of your culture, your sub-group, your upbringing come under direct challenge not only by events and people with whom you are not in direct contact, but by your own experiencing. This dissonance is not only a gateway into the path of deep learning; it is also the very ocean on which you will sail as your spirit seeks to steer a true course in its discerning discipline.

The Aim of the Dissonance Mode

The aim of the dissonance mode is to invite you to discover and acknowledge the incongruities between what you have been led to believe is true and the immediacy of your own experiencing. Shortly, I will invite you to make two lists that reveal those incongruities. By acknowledging them, you render public your inner knowledge of how things are through the rawness of experiencing them. That carries with it its own validation separate from that of the popular culture. You will blow Joshua's ramshorn. The walls will come tumbling down. If the outward vestiges of culture crumble under the trumpet of your own experiencing, then you may hope that dis-assembling a social biography and creating another closer to your spirit is a worthy project.

Who Owns My Spirit?

Here's how one person came to the point of acknowledging her dissonance. Because her story is about spirit itself, the question of ownership may be universal.

She was a community development consultant, a professional in her early forties, who had participated with 30 of her colleagues in an introductory workshop on the enspiriting approach to leadership.

It might appear that not much can be done in an introductory six hours. But if people are ready, starting points framed as invitations spark serious conflagrations very quickly. The disciplines require extensive work to bring them into the realm of competence, but inner action can begin at once.

In this workshop, the community builders focused on *deep listening* and *deep questioning* about their professional concerns. Some sought refuge in discussing

---

[5] This quote from *On Practice* was shared with me by my old friend and a great sociologist, Bill Westley, then of McGill University in Montreal, as he watched and participated in the incipient practices of envisioning as I developed these in the 1970s.

theories of community or celebrating the "real-politik" practices of leadership. Others wanted to deal with the intransigent issues generated in a society bereft of community that seeks to formulate policies to deal with the symptoms of that loss: teen-age pregnancy, children-at-risk, the homeless, racial and ethnic tensions, maldistribution of opportunities, resources and rewards, etc. But some understood from the outset that deep questioning their work, their profession, their official lives was a thread in the rich fabric of both their inner lives and the world at large. They began experiencing the immediacy of the enspiriting to which they had been invited.

Late that afternoon, we gathered for a final reflection together. Tired, flushed, pale and distraught, satisfied and completed, awed or confused, they began their praxis about what they had themselves discovered. Many reflected out loud about what it had been like to do this work; what they had learned; unresolved problems and new questions.

I now shift this story into the present tense. Perhaps that will help it to become more present to you.

When she speaks up, the tremble in her voice brings us all to that startled recognition that she is in travail and about to share it. The issue we all feel is not, Can she handle it? It is not, Can she handle it in front of us? It is, Can we handle it? Deep listening helps some of us; others have not yet come that far.

"When I was young," she begins, "I grew up in a very religious family. We went to church regularly and participated fully. That's where I first experienced my own community. We said grace at every meal. The Bible was our bulwark, and we read together in the evenings rather than watching TV."

A lengthy pause.

"My spirit side, that which we have opened up here, today, was taken care of. I was told about God, about how that works, about the practice of liturgy and prayer proper to my church."

She pauses again. She breathes deeply. She turns to me.

"Warren. You have helped us create a community of learners this day. It will evaporate by 5 PM as we go our ways. But this is a trusting space for me right now, so"...she takes another breath, "I must say this to you all, otherwise I can't say it to myself."

Tears well up. Cheeks thin and the bony structure of her face shows through. Another breath, this one very deep indeed, a sigh rather than a gasp as her spirit gathers its courage.

"I have learned today...in this work...that my church does not own my spirit." Pause. "Perhaps I always knew that. Now," more strongly, "I say it. My church, no church, no religion has a monopoly on the spiritual." Her words become more powerful with each statement. Tears pour. "I was told, and I grew up believing, that my church was the only house in which I could—to use your word—enspirit. Not just the house of God. But the house of my spirit. In this work today," she turned to two colleagues with whom she had been deep questioning and deep listening for most of the day, "I learned, I discovered, I now say what my experience has always told me. My spirit belongs to no one but to me and," she gives a half-laugh, half-cry, " I'm not even sure that it belongs to me. Maybe it belongs to God. But it certainly doesn't belong to any one else."

She had come to her dissonance. She had penetrated one version of an outward reality by admitting to an inward reality of her own experiencing. Some of that experiencing took place within the ambience of enspiriting I had introduced and we had all sought to share. Some prior experiencing—she did not share that in the larger group—had broken through to a level of consciousness that proclaimed the authenticity of her own inner life and at the same time defied someone else's version of how the world of the spiritual works.

This mode of *deep learning* invites you, now, to search out the dissonances in your own life between what you have been told is true, beautiful and good, and what you have experienced as true, beautiful and good.

An Exercise in Dissonance (No. 8)

This one is short. Again, a piece of paper may be helpful.

Part One

Start by making a list of social truths, claims about what is true, beautiful and good that you have learned and that, in this first listing, you believe are true. These social truths could be about child-rearing, working, family life, government, politics, intimacy, earning a living, love, specific ethnic, language or geographical/regional groups, religion, art, leisure, mountain climbing, "foreigners," dishwashing and drying, how to cure warts, anything and everything.

As you get into this, extend the list from a handful to lots of truth-claims. It is incredible how long your list might get. The human being is, after all, a walking pattern of programmed behavior...until that human being says: "No." By saying "no" to some portion of an inherited social reality, that human being begins her search for the truths to which the disciplines of the spirit might lead her.

Part Two

For the second part, search through your life (much like you did in the exercise on self-empowering learning, page 84) for "experiencings" that share the following qualities. Make a second list of them.

Presence. Seek an experiencing of which you were a vital part. The immediacy of experiencing, the "is-ness," does not happen if you are merely an observer. You must be *present.*

Spontaneity. Again. Neither programmed nor planned by your expectations. Perhaps surprising. "I didn't expect it was going to be like this."

Genuineness. Some core in the experiencing vibrates with its truth. You can't unpack it. You can't explain it. But try to describe what that experiencing was like: Feelings, body states, thoughts or images that flashed (if they did).

The Setting. Describe it. The who, what, when, where, how, why of it. Specificity and concreteness are always invited. You might discover that the situation was bereft of authoritative components; that as you searched for meaning, explanation, expectation fulfilled, none showed up and you were left alone with the *is-ness* of it.

Part Three

This is the meat of the exercise: Comparison.

Finding the Dissonance. Compare the two lists. As you do, search for categories for items from each list. (Hint: Experiencing is quite specific. Social truths often—not always—are offered up in abstract and general terms. Level of generality is not important in this comparison, i.e., a specific experiencing might well fit into a category in which the truth-claim is very general. That's OK.) Don't get too fancy about naming the categories. Search for what a category is about: The content and focus of your experiencing, the content and the focus of the social truth.

The dissonance mode of *deep learning* relies heavily on reflection. Take your time. Dig a little. Don't give up if no instant categories of incongruity show up. This is not comparing apples and pears, for both sides of the equation possess the same focus. The level and character of the material is quite different, however. It is easy to miss a dissonance. Sometimes you have to feel it first; then, do the analysis and reflection.

Partnering with a colleague who has *deep listening* and *deep questioning* compe-tence is helpful. She may enter empathically into your KBVAF core and into the acts of experiencing you recall. She may even nurture your reflection by helping to search out items on both sides of the dissonance equation that you may have missed.

What to Do with This Dissonance?

As yet, nothing. At this stage in deep learning, as Heidegger might have put it, *apprehending* the dissonance is much more important than *comprehending* it. Your realities approach the bottoming-out condition. You are beneath the surface... or heading that way.

Just let the dissonance be there. Does it shake you a little? OK. It shakes me. My first marriage was indissoluble. As I grew up, I had learned from *everybody* about marriage's sanctity. It lay at the core of my own KBVAF. What happened? The *experiencing* of it, its multiple issues in dissonance, challenged that mental core. For years, for the sake of the children, I lived with that conflict. Some do all their lives. So... you can live with your dissonance for an hour, a day, a week.

No Solutions, But a Great Opening Up

Dissonance within your inner life or between your interiority and the exteriority is real and serious. It is difficult to acknowledge to others as well as yourself. But it can't be avoided. For it is exactly at these juncture points and interfaces of dissonance, of imbalance, or of self-empowering learning that we might begin to feel the exciting, surprising, awesome vibrations of our spirit at work in its *deep learning*.

No "solutions" to anything have been offered yet. Deep learning is still mysterious and opaque. But as you have now searched your life through one or another of these start-up modes, can you not feel your spirit at work? As you—not your social biography but the *you* of the interface, *you* of the inner *dialogue*—have begun to invite, cajole, probe and listen, gates have been opening up for your spirit.

"What's going on here?" spirit is asking. "Can I trust this person? Boy, this inner work isn't in the script! Who's the author now? Am I? Could I be? Is there something here for me to learn... about myself?"

Spirit also asks: "Can I trust *myself*? After all of these years, can I trust myself to learn what I am about and up to in this not-so-friendly world? Can I learn *myself?*"

Go now to the *unlearning* modes. Discover how your spirit responds as it enters its deep learning.

11

Unlearning:
An Overview

A way to *deep learning* is through the difficult mode of unlearning. When I first began to talk about unlearning with my education colleagues 25 years ago, I was rewarded with a fugitive smile that quickly turned into a runaway response: That's a no-brainer, or something like that. Still, even then I knew in my bone-of-bones—deep knowing, which is a way of *discerning*—that what was in short supply on this planet was not new knowledge but unlearning a great deal of what we took for granted.

Why Unlearning?

Why unlearning? Because to arrive at the point where spirit learns itself, confronts itself, enters into its own *dialogue* with itself is to stand naked before your God and discover that which spirit invites you to and demands of you. That is what *deep learning* is all about. Unlearning is its path, a path of unclothing, of throwing off the effluvia of the generations that has been woven into the fabric of your social biography.

How far can each of us go on this journey to the core of spirit? That you will discover. What I have learned is that each of us embarks on our own journey at our own pace, and goes our own distance. There is neither rule nor requirement in deep learning, only invitation. This book extends that invitation, primarily through the exercises; but by now, you understand that *only your self-invitation counts.*

Invite yourself, then, to your unlearning. Go as far as your social biography will allow. Eventually, you will reach a stage in the journey where social biography, that whom you believe you are, stops.

"I can go no further with you," it says. "Here's where I get off. Come back to me after your deep learning, return to me with the freshness and beauty of your spirit. We'll tell new tales about who I am. We'll re-invent ourselves-in-the-world. But for now, I must leave you to your spirit."

Unlearning is an endisciplining that leaves you at that halfway house where biography stops to rest and spirit continues on alone.

In this halfway house, there are three rooms. Enter each of them and explore.

The Unpeeling Room

Unpeeling is a mode of unlearning wherein the impediments to deep learning in which social biography is clothed are removed. In this room, you may disrobe with impunity. Of course, you need not shed all of your social biography. Take off only those stories that get in your way of enspiriting. For some, there are many; for others, few.

At a certain point, you will have unpeeled enough to open the door and enter the next room.

The Unfreezing Room

Here you unfreeze habits of your life, of your culture, of the generations of humankind. These we don't just shed. We shred them to bits and pieces. We disassemble them into their original molecules of *intentioning*. (More on this in Chapter Thirteen.)

Educators talk about freezing what is learned at one stage to set the foundation for the next stage. But the learning that fits enspiriting is heuristic, always exploratory, always testing out. Now, in the unfreezing room, we begin to move backwards in time to regain the open and fluid space of spirit prior to its freezing. We aim to arrive at a point of original intentioning before the learning to which it refers became frozen. Unprogramming the neurological connections? Yes, you'll do that. Don't be surprised if this mode of unlearning generates heat to melt the ice of habits and disassemble the molecules. The kinetic-molecular theory applied to *deep learning*? Why not?

The Futures Room

A door opens to the next room in the halfway house of unlearning.

This is the futures room, the inner setting for your *deep imaging* (Chapter Fourteen). The room is empty of habit, biography, culture, even history for those who have truly unfrozen and unpeeled. *History will return in a new and challenging way, and culture will be invented along with new myth.* That is transformation. The futures room is a tabula rasa. Here we shall discover that which is in us about the future. In unpeeling and unfreezing, we have shed the accouterments of the past. Here, we shed its tyranny.

These rooms share one thing in common. It hovers like a ghost from the past, though it is not frightening. Indeed, it is a familiar ghost, one that we always welcome. It is the ghost of time, chronological time, the time that comes and goes, counting the rows.

To do deep learning, this ghost of chronological time, the time that comes and goes, must be exorcised.

Let me tell you its tale.

Chronus, the Giant

Spirit confronting biography and seeking to enter into human history is an ancient story. In one such tale, giants roamed the earth, eating their young (not unlike what we do now in the decimation of our children), dominating that reality which was birthed from the implicate order where all things are possible. But an alternative hologram entered the universe of consciousness and became real. It had various names: The Gods on Mount Olympus, Istarte, Buddha, Yahweh, it matters not except that the thunder of the Giants loping the earth looking for their victims disappeared from human consciousness.

Myths and legends die hard. Chronus left a legacy. Time, chronological time, that inexorable tyranny that holds us in its iron grip.

Don't we measure our realities through the story the Giants taught us about counting the minutes, hours, days, months, years, centuries? The story is just this: We think about time as something to spend, give away, lose, waste, do something "worthwhile" with, as if time were a commodity in short supply. Can Chronus's legacy be challenged?

Other Rhythms

We are rediscovering that there are body times, body rhythms, some of the day and some of the night, some of a lifespan. And we are re-discovering that there are spirit times, spirit rhythms, infinite, flowing, endless, some focused in a lifespan *but not captured by it.*

It is spirit's enduring quest for freedom that we seek. We want to give it a chance. Yet spirit is channeled into lifespan and through social biography. Through unlearning, we may yet depose the internal culture of constraint that parallels the external devastations we create for each other and for our Mother Earth. *Spirit cries out for release and for enspiriting action.*

How to find this out for yourself?

Deep listen to your spirit and to the spirit of others in a community of learners where *dialogue* is practiced.

As spirit speaks most truthfully first through body, and thus through body's rhythms, listen to those rhythms as they interpolate into the conventions of chronological time. Some of us are learning to enter into the rhythms of career changes, mate changes, learning changes when our spirit implores and our body demands. That rhythm has peaks and troughs different for each person. Social institutions smooth out those unique peaks and troughs in the name of social predictability, social consistency, social expectations; and so breaking through the barriers of social biography through *deep learning* is to disrupt not only *your stories—yourself-in-the-world—but all of our stories—thus, ourselves-in-the-world.* Such is the transformation that is upon us once again.

In the three rooms of unlearning, we shall practice at entering into Kairos, the space of the Gods where spirit dwells and time stands still. That is what it means to unencumber the spirit by unpeeling and unfreezing and so, through unlearning, inviting spirit to its deep learning.

Breaking the Tyranny of Time: Some Stories

Do you remember your moments when time stood still? When the clock stopped ticking? When the day-night sequence of earth rotating on its axis no longer mattered? When punching in on the timeclock or rushing for an appointment with hair-dresser, dentist, or lover no longer mattered?

Was it when you rocked your baby in your arms, inhaled his body's sweet smell, were lost in the infinity of that bonding?

Was it the spinning kaleidoscope of branches and leaves, sun, blue sky, brown earth, up and down and around as you fell off your cantering horse and waiting—a moment, a year, a lifetime—for the ground to come up and hit you?

Was it when you were making love... lying on the hospital bed as it moved down the corridor to the operating room, looking downside up at all of the faces upside down rushing past—lost in that joyful space when your colleagues and friends celebrated your presence on the planet... scaling a rockface whose distance above the ground was the distance to the moon... feeling the sweat run off your face and back as you flung the dirt off your shovel from the ditch without end you were digging?

Once, I envisioned with 50 or so folks about the future of health care. Sponsored by the Sisters of Mercy, the project was about healing and wellness, not hospitals and genetic-molecular engineering. Among those present—the sisters, administrators, technicians, professionals, etc.—were some old nuns, perhaps in their 70s.

As we took our mindleap into the future 25 years away, one of the older sisters, her skin so clear and fresh you could see right through to her spirit, said to me: "Warren, I won't be alive in 2000. How can I image a future in which I won't be alive?" She was just a bit agitated that she thought herself unable to respond to the imaging invitation.

"But you know the answer to that," I responded. "That which is worthwhile in this world transcends time. Certainly your faith does."

She looked inward, her agitation ceased and she gave me a slight but loving smile. She nodded and turned to her colleague, perhaps even older than she and listening avidly. "Mother MacCauley (the founder of their Order in the 1840s) is with us this day." She and her sister, colleagues who had lived 50 to 60 years in the rigors of vows invented for them centuries before, *mindlept* into the space of healing and wellness in a future-present moment long after their deaths. Their images were fresh, innovative and healing, and not of chronological time. Then what were they of? What else but spirit?

Shall we explore: A brief exercise so that you too can break the tyranny of time?

When Time Stood Still: An Exercise (No. 9)

After some inner quieting, invite your memories into conscious awareness. Find your state of suspended animation, when body and mind stand still. Listen to the sound of your own breathing; concentrate on your exhaling, feeling and listening to it and nothing else.

Now invite the memory. Only, it isn't quite a memory. It isn't rolling the film of your life back to some point and starting up the inner camera. The invitation is to locate the space when time stood still. That space is a whole sense of mind, body, feeling and spirit melded into their original oneness. It's not a memory marked off by chronological time. It's a feeling of absolute wholeness, a knowingness of space rather than time or place. There may be a dream-like quality to it, not the content of a dream so much as the feeling of it, so that you don't think about it or analyze it, you live it and are in it.

Let this time-stood-stillness come back to you. Live it. Feel it. Let it embrace you as you embrace it. Let yourself re-enter this space. Savor it. Smell it. Taste it. What color is it? How does it feel on your skin? You are there. It is with you, in you, of you, and you are with it, in it, of it. You are no longer object. You are no longer subject. This is the wholeness we seek. You are beingness itself.

Have you got it? Have you let it invest in you again? Great.

You may want to create an outward "space" wherein the inner space comes to life once again. Have you learned yet—perhaps you always knew—how to create that outward gentleness that nurtures the rebirth of that which is within us. If not, look again. Create again. It is there.

In Preparation for Unpeeling

Like other enspiriting practices, unpeeling is a series of deep questions whose indicators you now know and whose qualities you have by now experienced. As in deep listening, the idea is to *unencumber spirit so that its learning is not smothered in the need of social biography*—others call that ego—*to confirm itself. Unpeeling is about the stories of ourselves we have learned and internalized that get in the way of deep learning.* Rarely do our parents, friends, teachers, priests, and leaders ask us about our spirit or tell us a true story about that. Who has queried your spirit? Have you? Has anyone? If they didn't, be prepared. For that is where deep learning brings you, a querying of your spirit, aided by the foraging of *deep questioning*, softened by the nurturing discipline of *deep listening*.

In the inner work that follows in the next chapters on unpeeling and unfreezing, you are invited to relive those stories in which your spirit was queried, your spirit was tested and invited out. In the end, these are good stories, though not always in their beginning.

But that is not all.

You are also invited to grasp to your bosom those stories about yourself your spirit *doesn't like,* and to love them a little, and *then* to kick them out of the barn because for too long have they fouled your inner atmosphere.

Be clear, though, that unpeeling does not deny all of you. *It seeks to relieve you only of that in your biography that gets in the way of enspiriting, of deep learning.*

What part is that? Which aspects of your biography? Abuse, violence, putdown, neglect, unlovingness, hatred of you or by you of others, no chances, little space to grow, blossom and flourish as a human being? *Only you can sort out which of these— or impacts like these—have denied your spirit and which haven't.*

For deep learning is *about,* is *for,* is *of,* and is *by* your spirit. In unlearning we shall bypass your history, your biography, and the stories of you that someone else created. Later, we shall return to your social biography. Later, spirit and biography dance together again to a different tune and with new steps. By then, spirit has come into its own. It can partner with your social biography in new ways, as a pro-active partner in the transformation of yourself-in-the-world and ourselves-in-the-world.

How to bypass your social biography? That is the strategy for the unlearning I call *unpeeling.* By finding the entrance into the space of kairos wherein time stands still, have you not already entered the unpeeling mode?

For this next exercise, live in that space. That will enable you to locate in your own history, detach from and then deal with those stories that block your journey to spirit, that have told you: "No," when your spirit has called out for release and affirmation.

Shall you begin?

12

Modes of Unlearning: Unpeeling

This piece of inner work involves many probes and self-questions. I have put the unpeeling practices in a certain sequence to facilitate your unlearning. Do read through the entire story of unpeeling so that you can get a good sense of this enspiriting path to *deep learning* before you begin.

The Method of the Unconscious

Unpeeling involves many probes and self-questions. Give yourself plenty of time. As you begin to *live* this mode of unlearning, it will occupy much of your *un*conscious awareness, i.e., levels of consciousness that are not part of your conscious thinking and conscious memory but are always in operation... the *whole* iceberg of which the cognitive capacities are the top 10 percent. From time to time, your conscious awareness will kick in. An insight will materialize out of "thin air"; but in fact your spirit, your body, your inner feelings, your multiple levels of consciousness have been at work in the unpeeling *if you have read the unpeeling story, gone through and accepted its questions, and extended the invitation to spirit and to social biography to begin this work. When these inner levels are ready, they will make an offering to your conscious mind. Each offering is an insight into what aspect of your social biography has gotten in the way of your spirit's speaking out and so has curtailed its involvement in your life, and in the process kept your spirit from its own learning.*

Removing these barriers to *deep learning* is what unpeeling is all about.

The path to unpeeling looks like this.

Roadsigns and Practices: The Path to Unpeeling

• The first step along the unpeeling path is to reacquaint yourself with what it's like when your spirit speaks out (*The First Probe: My Spirit Speaks Out—No. 10*). This gives you a palpable sense of what it's like when you have arrived at your destination after removing barriers and constraints to spirit's expression.

• The next step along the unpeeling path is to identify barriers and constraints in your social biography (*A Second Probe: Self-Stories My Spirit Doesn't Like—No. 11*). By locating such stories about and within your total life experience *that got in the way*, you have opened up the possibility of removing them.

• A third and parallel step is now offered: To identify stories in your social biography *your spirit does like*—and there may be many! (*A Third Probe: Self-Stories My Spirit Likes—No. 12*). But how do you know which stories about yourself your spirit does and doesn't like, i.e., which stories enhance and which inhibit the entrance and expression of spirit into yourself-in-the-world? The answer lies in the discipline of *discerning* to which you are introduced in another practice (*A Fourth Probe: To What Do I Hold?—No. 13*).

• As you move along the path of unpeeling, you begin to unpeel these stories. Like shedding your clothes, you shed these stories. Initially, a good part of this work takes place out-of-awareness until the unpeeling "kicks in" to your conscious awareness. Still, a number of practices are suggested for the shedding or unpeeling as a preparation for the actual inner dynamic. Getting you ready, so to speak.

• But we have to deal with the "peels." As you discard them, you don't want them to trash your nest—your social biography—anymore. So you remove them from your nest in a piece of work I call *shelving* or *clouding* (*The Shelf and the Cloud Exercise—No. 14*).

Unpeeling is only one path to the space of spirit's *deep learning* through the mode of unlearning. While not the only path, it is a straight one. It takes you right to the barriers and constraints *within you*, your self-stories you have learned, you have believed that have kept spirit—*your* spirit—from becoming present to you.

We begin with the first probe.

The First Probe: My Spirit Speaks Out (No. 10)

What is it like when your spirit speaks out? Has it happened? How can you tell? When did it happen? Will you describe it to yourself, in detail: Its conditions and occasions, the setting and situation, what happened and, most importantly, *how do you know your spirit speaks out?*

This last question is a doozy. In all of the enspiriting work this book describes, e.g., the exercises and coming to understand the disciplines and practicing their competence, that question looms. How do you know you're enspiriting? How do you know your spirit is speaking out? How do you know your spirit calls for transformation of yourself-in-the-world and ourselves-in-the-world? With what certainty? What evidence? How to distinguish truth from falsehood in these matters? What of kidding yourself, of self-fulfilling prophecy about your spirit because you like this spirit story, enspiriting sounds good, everybody's doing the new spirituality, etc.?

No finality is offered in this book. My method is discovery, inquiry, testing out within a community of learners (enspiritors like yourself), experiencing and learning to live with that heuristic and *seeing what happens to you.* The chapters on *discerning* explicitly address the questions of *knowing* spirit and of spirit *knowing;* but even that may not satisfy you if prior to your experiencing the endisciplining of your spirit, you seek a final proof. There is none, to my knowledge.[6]

The lack of an intellectual certainty and finality—conceptual, theoretical, analytic, etc.—has not deterred thousands with whom I and my colleagues have worked, particularly in the envisioning mode which relies so heavily on deep imaging.

Do now begin again. Be of courage. Without you, the world is lost.

So we begin the search for the unpeeling with this quest for your spirit speaking out. Don't force it. Give yourself as many examples as come to you. If uncertain about when this happened and what it was like, don't dismiss its experiencing out-of-hand. For those of us whose social biography swamps the spirit, its speaking out may be shrouded in ambiguity, less than pristine, less than a clarion call. OK. *There is nothing to prove here, only to discover.*

What Are the Indicators that Spirit Speaks Out?

As recounted to me by fellow-enspiritors and out of my own enspiriting experience, here are five. You may uncover others.

• An upsurge of spirit-feeling and spirit-energy, when you are carried away and move outside the conventional forms of interpersonal behavior that constrain people

---

[6] But see Ken Wilbur's *Eye to Eye: The Quest for the New Paradigm,* 1990, particularly the chapter on "the Problem of Proof." I think he and I agree that, ultimately, it is in its *experiencing,* in its *immediately apprehended, grasped, experienced, intuited* state that we *know* spirit. What Wilbur calls "intelligibilia" will take you just so far and then, as I invite in this book, you shall want to enter into the domain of spirit itself.

to play it safe, not to announce the conflicts, dissatisfactions, dismays and disquietudes that may stand for their spirit's response to an intolerable situation. Frequently, prevailing customs and entrenched behaviors lodged in the culture of propriety, power and politeness cordon off the upsurge of spirit-feeling and seek to play it cool in the erupting cauldron of spirit-energy.

• Losing your self identity, that identity defined by your social biography. Your old "you" is gone. Your sense of yourself proclaims a new "you," unfamiliar, perhaps even strikingly strange at first, but clear that its source lies at your very core.

• When time stands still and place disappears: Entering kairos.

• A deep quieting, so deep, so emptying of your tant'ien that the "you" in your *deep listening* can only be of your spirit, and the voices you hear—that speak to you, that take you in and lodge in your tant'ien—can only be those of spirit, whomever that is.

• When your competence, your performance, your *doing* of something takes over your entire being and you are supremely focused in that act, you *are* that act. Doing and being merge.

Two reminders: First, these indicators interact. They are synergistic. Each, indeed, marks a facet of the same experience; a different piece of it; a different way of identifying and signifying the enspiriting. So look for all or some of them, and perhaps be not satisfied with just one.

Second, enspiriting indicators are just that: Clues, possibilities, suggestive occurrences that are specific and concrete but never final because always subject to interpretation as to *what they indicate.*

Still, this is a start. For if you can locate occasions in your life when your spirit has "spoken"—I put this in quotes because not always does spirit speak through words or verbal utterances—then you have obtained a more precise and experience-based insight into *what is absent, what is missing, what is denied when your social biography has constrained, limited, swept aside, said "No" to your spirit.*

A Second Probe: Self-Stories My Spirit Doesn't Like (No. 11)

Two kinds of inner action are invited in the unpeeling exercises: One is about self-stories to get rid of, the other, stories to keep.

The first set of self-questions goes like this: "What are the stories about myself my spirit doesn't like?"

Put another way: "What are the stories about myself I choose to get rid of because they present a barrier to my spirit?"

Start with the first rendition. It's a bit different from the second, for the second implies a piece of inner action that goes beyond describing the stories, *and that straightforward, specific and concrete description is what is immediately needed to undertake this probe.*

There is a third question. It follows in sequence and is the focus of the next chapter on *unfreezing*. It is: "What are the stories about myself I no longer believe?"

These three questions interrelate, as do the unlearning modes of *unpeeling* and *unfreezing*. But for starters, don't fret about their complexity. Begin with stories about yourself your spirit doesn't like.

"But which stories?" you ask. "I'm a complex of a million stories." Try for some like these:

1. Stories that are excuses.

2. Stories that explain something in yourself, but you still don't like them despite their habitual and even convincing explanations.

3. Stories that explain something in the world—an event, an institution, a piece of history—that you still don't like despite the habitual and even convincing explanation.

Quite often, these stories are about justice: Justice to and in yourself; justice within your relevant action-setting of family, work and job, school, church, neighborhood, etc.; justice in the world. For justice, substitute your *feelings of fairness.* If you say, "I'm not being fair to myself," or "Others are not being fair to me," or "I'm not being fair to others," you have begun your story. Now finish it. In detail: The who, what, when, where, how, why of it. Write it down or speak it to a colleague in your community of learners who is prepared to deep listen and deep question. Don't escape into generalizations—e.g., "The world is unfair to me." We do that too much, to hide from the immediacy of the pain that we feel or that we inflict on others. For pain, like joy, is specific and concrete, here and now.

Can I give you examples? You bet. But I will offer very few. Why? Because our experience shows quite plainly that this quest—into your biography and its confrontation with spirit—is highly susceptible to pollution by the examples drawn from others' experience. That is the history of the pollution of our social biographies through false stories about the ephemeral, "touchy-feely," unreal, non-operational, unpragmatic, "theoretical," devil-inspired nature of spirit. It is a significant part of the cultural history of several centuries in the West. *You must move yourself beyond and beneath—or on top of—culture and social biography to spirit and to your spirit.* Can you do it? Start by looking for your examples. Get the feel of this work. Look back through previous exercises. Take your time. Enter kairos. Renew your experience with your own enspiriting, when your spirit spoke out, (Exercise No. 10) and juxtapose it with these stories. Believe me, you'll feel in your tant'ien, in your bone-of-bones, what that conflict is like.

A Third Probe: Self-Stories My Spirit Likes (No.12)

The same questions, the same inner work as in No. 11, the same process, except the query is different.

"What stories does my spirit like?"

They may be many. They may be few. No matter. Perhaps it's a small thing, something in childhood or adulthood, a little incident, a microcosm that enclosed the universe of your spirit.

Once, when I was 10 or so, my mother and I were walking down Lexington Avenue in New York City, an afternoon stroll, perhaps going shopping at Bloomingdale's or to the fruit market on Third Avenue. It was before the time of supermarkets and malls, can you imagine... or remember?

On a crowded corner, as we were about to cross the street, a man standing alongside collapsed. Hit the pavement. Out of it. People looked, stared, backed off, stepped off the curb, continued on their way. My mother, decked out in her Saturday clothes—she was a great dresser—stooped by his head, then knelt down. She asked some questions. No response. Then she crouched over, lifted and cradled his head a bit, talked again, he groaned and whispered, and she stayed and held and nurtured until an ambulance arrived. For 15 minutes, as people walked by or stopped and stared and then walked on, she was with him.

That was her.

What about me?

I was embarrassed... afraid... what was she doing?... inappropriate things like bending over, her face a few inches from his, people staring, in broad daylight... I grabbed for her arm. "Mom. Let's go." She shook me off. I pulled. "Mommmmm." Then, for a split second, she turned and pierced me with her eyes. No words. Just got into my spirit, right through my 10-year old "developmental" biography.

I unpeeled. Wow. Right then and there. Hers was not behavioral training. She witnessed her spirit expressed through her biography—who she was—and that witness called out my spirit. No longer, ever again, was I able to appeal to the protections of propriety, politeness, shame, embarrassment, fear, following the crowd when my spirit spoke to me.

That story started out not so good. It has ended OK. My spirit and biography have made a great pact here, though it took a continuing self-confrontation for another seven or eight years through my adolescence before I felt comfortable when my spirit spoke out. This is just one little story that my spirit likes. So do I.

Which Stories, Which Questions?

There is more than one story. There are many questions. Does it matter with which set you begin? No. One side—the "My spirit likes" variety—flows into the other side—the "My spirit doesn't like" response. There's not a lot you can do about interrupting that flow except when you take notes. Though the self-questions are presented on these pages line after line, the inner work is not linear. Most inner work isn't. Spirit, body, feelings, images are not linear.

Let the flow happen. Don't fight it. Go back and forth between the "likes" and "doesn't like" if the stories emerge that way. Keep plenty of paper handy—or a tape recorder.

Great. But *which* stories?

It doesn't matter. A big story or a small one, who cares? *No one is listening.* Not your friend, your counselor, your husband or wife, your psychiatrist, or George Orwell's Big Brother. Only your spirit is listening; and *it probably can't believe its ears!*

When To Do This?

Essential to this inner work is to locate within yourself some space for unpeeling. Can you find or create an outward time and an outward place that lets you discover your inner space of kairos? Taking a walk in the woods? Sitting by yourself in your living room filled with the music of Pachelbel's *Canon* or the singing of the whales? Driving along a country road and stopping by a roadside table or glade for a cup of coffee or tea hot from your thermos? Lying in bed in the early morning and letting your spirit leave your body, to hover overhead and speak for the first time the constraining tales of your social biography it has been listening to all these years but has never told you?

All these ways work, and many more besides. They offer this in common: You will have entered the inner space of kairos. Here, time stands still and place disappears. In this space, spirit dwells and social biography—which is *always* a creature of time and place—slips its hold on you.

Is This a Time for Deep Listening?

In the chapters on *dialogue,* this question receives its proper due. Still, you may have formed and/or be a member of a community of learners who practice together *deep listening* and *deep questioning.* Be careful, here; for less than that can stop your self-probe cold in its tracks.

A case in point: One of my dearest friends was going through her unpeeling. She had found her inner space for that. For six months or so, she was at it, distancing herself from much of the daily effluvia that usually attends a person at rest on the planet, as most of us are most of the time. Her biography was in upheaval; and I could sense that she was distraught much of the time even while showing an out-wardly calm, if somewhat fragile, demeanor. I wanted to help out and to participate in that complex confrontation between her spirit, now re-awakening, and the rich portfolio of self-stories that stood for her life, the life that most of the rest of us knew.

But I couldn't enter her space. I was unable to empty my tant'ien. That essential *yielding* action which lies at the heart of the empty vessel approach has always been difficult for me with persons whom I love. Endisciplining is a continuing practice. Rarely is it over, finished, once-and-for-all. My own *deep learning* which I described at the beginning of Chapter Seven was at the depths of my spirit, to be sure; but many habits were still frozen, habits that in this instance got in the way of my deep listening.

Thus was I reminded, once again, to "practice what I preach"; to prepare myself through and for deep listening so that the other's space, precious, fragile, open, vul-nerable to spirit's awakening and social biography's unpeeling is not violated.

For each of us, there is a spirit-brother or a spirit-sister, perhaps more than one, with whom unpeeling, unfreezing, deep learning can be shared. Such begins the community of learners in which dialogue itself becomes a reality. Forcing does no good; yielding does.

From Imbalance to Unpeeling

One strong starting point for these exercises is the earlier inner work I have called the mode of imbalance (Chapter Nine). Do you remember it? Did you not seek to acknowledge and identify a sense of imbalance between spirit and social biography? Did you not seek to describe that conflict as best you could? *How far did you get?*

As the focus of unpeeling is to pull out the stories about yourself your spirit doesn't like and to get rid of them, where better to look than at that conflict? It is an imbalance, a sense of deep disquietude and inner tension where spirit and social biography no longer meet easily, where spirit can no longer contain itself and begins that kind of "speaking out" that your body acknowledges through your feelings even as your mind keeps fighting in the service of your social biography.

The conflict between spirit and social biography becomes clearer, more precise and more actionable when you bring into conscious awareness those stories about yourself your spirit doesn't like. That's the long and the short of it.

It's not every story. It may be many stories or few. It's not all behaviors and certainly not all of your KBVAF.

Two more questions: Why doesn't spirit like a particular story? How do you know that?

A Fourth Probe: To What Do I Hold? (No. 13)

Body sense, feelings, intuitions become important paths to respond to this probe. Coming to know what my spirit does and doesn't like is not a theoretical activity. It is practical, proximate (not absolute), judgmental in the sense of *discerning*, actually grounded in your *experiencing* this inner conflict.

"This is how I feel," you say. "This story about myself hurts. It puts me down. It takes me to a place I don't want to be. It's disquieting. It stresses aspects of myself *I have never held to when I have gone deep enough and asked myself just that: "To what do I hold?"*

That question: "To what do I hold?" is a *deep questioning* of your spirit *by* your spirit.

A deep learner once came to me in tears. We met in a hallway outside the seminar room in which a group of 15 of us had been learning, practicing and applying the enspiriting disciplines for several days. She was distraught. That intense shedding of tears was, no more and no less, getting rid of part of her biography.

Her words:

"Warren." Silence. "Warren, I can't go on with this."

"With what?" I asked.

"I can't take enspiriting back to and into my place of work, live it and apply it."

"Why?" I asked.

"I can't go back to work. I can't hold to that job anymore. It goes against everything I hold to." Sobs. A hug.

Spirit is out. As Luddy Ledbetter used to sing: "Get back, get back, get back, get back." As we speak to the temptation: "Get thee behind me." As spirit cries out: "Give me some space."

So the unpeeling goes.

It's not easy. Have we yet to learn…it's always a new learning…that there is a pain that is healing, there is a rending and a tearing that is healing.

To what do I hold? reveals why your spirit doesn't like that particular story. With each person, every case is different *in the particulars*. Don't compare. Don't try to generalize from your case. The story is always different. Listen to *your* story. Let spirit cry out: "Stop. No more. To this I hold." Yield to that. I don't know how it will fit into your new social biography. Too early for that reconstruction. In *deep imaging*, we shall begin that. For now, learn to deep listen to your spirit in these matters.

The "Physics" of Unpeeling

Is there an actual unpeeling? Does the snake shed its skin? Have you ever peeled an orange or banana and tossed aside the peel? Have you ever watched in stop-action photography a seed burst forth and burst out as its cover disintegrates, peels away, slips off?

In unpeeling, you do exactly that, though the precise body feelings, the internal kinesthetic movements and the external settings will vary for each person. The entire exercise of unpeeling, after all, puts you on the inside, doing the inner work described in these pages; and that is always unique.

Let me share what I have seen and heard from colleagues or experienced myself.

• Feel your biography shed its stories. Breathe deeply, down, down, down as deep as you can go, to your tant'ien, and exhale the negatives that have constrained your spirit.

• Visit a sweat lodge. It may take several sweat lodges. Respect the Native experience, listen to the songs, the poetry, the incantations. As the aromatic steam from herbs and water swirls around your head and body and the mist of spirit becomes present, feel those inhibiting, spirit-repressing stories literally pour out of your sweat glands and dissipate into another world, back to the implicate order.

• Exhaust yourself physically—swimming, jogging, a day's hike, etc.—so that your body moves to an inner state of complete relaxation as if you were lying on a bed of soft, warm mud, just completely letting go. Your body can no longer fight the release of these self-stories. A Yoga relaxing is good, too, with the slight tensing and then the absolute letting go, muscle group by muscle group. Bring the self stories to the surface of your skin. Peel them off your body. Your social biography can no longer use a tight shoulder, an aching leg, a strained back, a nervous stomach, a crick in the neck, a headache or *whatever* to protect itself.

• Dance movement or massage, facilitated by a serious healer, may become an avenue for unpeeling as the body acts out whatever story has constrained the expression of your spirit.

Children let their bodies act for their spirit all the time. Then we adults stop them or push them into narrowly conceived avenues of physical expression. We adults can re-discover the functions of our bodies within the larger integration that binds spirit, body senses and feelings, musculature, organs and skeleton into the whole it has always been throughout history until we invented the idea that body, mind, and spirit were not only separate but, indeed, antithetical.

You will want to relearn—re-discover—that integration. For some, the "physics" of unpeeling can happen in an instant. For others, there may be a longer focus on coming to love and nurture your body so that it will once again become a full participant in *deep learning*. Then find your way, that which suits, that which fits your spirit.

The unpeeling will happen in its time, when you are fully ready and competent.

What Do I Do with the Peel?

This may not be an obvious question. It is practical and important. Do you throw the peel away? Where? Let's be careful here.

Fouling the inner nest with our throwaways is not different from fouling the outer nest of our environment. The location is different. The act is much the same. So are the consequences... choking off the sources that give us life.

In the enspiriting practices, *always* search for and leave yourself open to discover the concrete and specific. So, what to do with the peel, with those parts of the social biography that you peel off to free-up spirit? Is this unpeeling a metaphor... or must we truly deal with the peelings? What nest is fouled with our peels, our throwaways, our discarded self-stories? Do you believe that these stories have no weight, no mass, no density, and so can evaporate into an entropic mass of hydrogen atoms that float throughout the universe? I myself consider this to be a most serious question. Stories that we tell about ourselves-in-the-world carry with them an energy that propels us into action, into creating beautiful relationships but also into generating the most despicable acts. Stories, some new, some very old, about ethnic, language, religious, group, clan animosities and social characteristics lead to "cleansing," to the transformation of energy (i.e., the stories from your KBVAF) to mass (i.e., bullets).

The Shelving and Clouding Exercise (No.14)[7]

When I came to the final mode of *emptying* (hence, if you remember, naming this the empty vessel way), I asked myself: What do we do with the material in the tant'ien that gets in the way of *deep listening*? That material consists of images, hopes, feeling, much of our social biography. It fills up the tant'ien and in so doing smothers our spirit, leaving little room for another's to enter.

Go back, now, to your unpeeling room. Do you remember noticing that it has lots of storage places: shelves, chests of drawers, closets, bookcases? Take your self-story, give it a loving kiss or a pat on the shoulder. Say: "Thanks. You've been with me a long time. I don't hate you. I'm not angry. But I've decided to grow my spirit. It grows anew in me. You won't fit here any more. You'll be frustrated, unhappy, out of joint, misplaced. Here, let me put you on this shelf. Or perhaps you'll be more comfy in this drawer. You'll be happy there. You can listen to yourself. I won't be back, for I'm leaving this unpeeling room for the unfreezing room on the other side of that door. Then I'll go on to the futures room. Perhaps spirit, once freed-up, will invite you back. For now, stay warm on this shelf. You'll have your memories to keep you company."

Does this work? Yes. Try it. Test it. Use your own words. Don't push it beyond its limits. Some stories won't be put aside like this. Hence, unfreezing. But we have discovered additional ways to deal with the peels: put them on a cloud!

Clouding, as I call it, came to me when Bob Luton and I were doing a self-empowering renewal workshop for a group of New York school teachers one summer's week on a suburban campus of Long Island University. My, they were a frustrated, unhappy bunch with a great deal of spirit within, swallowed and frozen by a school system that understood only too well that learning and spirit are inextricably combined and, if allowed their head, would transform just about everything that school system stood for and practiced.

We were sitting on the grass next to what Luton called "a learning tree," a great embracing oak that held within its loving grasp all of the hopes and fears of anyone sitting within its protecting outreach. What to do with their anxieties, their worries, their inner stuff of social biography that held such a grip on them as to imprison their spirit that wanted so much to help out in their own empowerment and renewal and in the learning of their youngsters? For there were no shelves about, only grass and that great oak ... or so we surmised.

---

[7] The practices of *shelving* I take from the research of Eugene Gendlin and his colleagues at the University of Chicago as it is described in *Focusing.* I discovered its applicability 15 years ago in my research on the practices of deep listening.

What to do with the peels, with the stories to be discarded, with the contents of the tant'ien to be placed aside so these teachers could prepare themselves for deep listening by emptying?

The sky was so blue that summer day, the sun so brilliant; but we sat cool under the learning tree. Something made me look up. There, above us, were some clouds drifting by. Not many. But there were enough floating by, each a different size and shape, mostly white and pillowy. What a welcoming place for the stories we don't like, I thought, for the stories we want to get rid of, that we have pulled out of ourselves, sometimes with raw spirit-energy and great pain.

"Put them on a cloud," I suggested to these teachers. "Close your eyes, lie back, reach out and put your unwanted feelings, anxieties, guilts, problems, stories on a cloud and *let it take that stuff away, never to return.*"

They did. You too: Do that. Just step outside or open your window and look out upon the clouds drifting by. May I remind you that clouds, like wind, rain, "weather," despite state-of-the-art computer modeling, are essentially unpredictable. Each cloud is a fractal, as is each snowflake. How many snowflakes—each different and unique—does it take to make a snowfall? A koan for the Western mind! How many clouds are needed to receive, enfold, and then disappear with your burden?

That inner material, excavated from the tant'ien, placed on a cloud, returns to the implicate order, to another holographic reality that, to be sure, is part of the universe but is no longer part of yourself-in-the-world. Deliberately, through *intentioning,* you have removed it from your reality. In doing so, you have begun to transform not just yourself-in-the-world but ourselves-in-the-world, too.

Unpeeling: A Summary

Unpeeling is a serious piece of inner work. I have described some of its facets. It doesn't happen in an hour and most of the time it doesn't happen in conscious awareness *though you must want to do it.* I have been at it for years and have a long way to go as I learn my spirit and it learns itself and offers back its invitation to grand adventures in the transformation of ourselves-in-the-world. A summary of "steps" in the "exercise" may help *as long as you realize that you are invited to create your own experiencing of this inner work, and that the exercise is mainly an invitation to access points until you locate your own.*

These are all access points.

One point is to prepare yourself. This is not new. Locate the inner space, a state of beingness that is kairos where time and place disappear and you experience a detachment from the outside so that you are wholly engaged on the inside. This is very close to what Aristotle called *skole*, contemplation, that which you do for its own sake and not for the sake of something else.

A second point is to recall your *deep questioning* about your concerns, your disquietudes and tensions, and to let your body feel its pain if spirit calls for that.

A third point is about this imbalance: To bring forth, to feel, to live the imbalance, conflict, tension between spirit and social biography. Can you describe it, being as it is at that interface or juncture? Can you identify its source?

A fourth point is to recall and relive the occasions when your spirit spoke out; and in praxis within yourself or with your community of learners, reflect on what that was like in all of its specificity and concreteness.

A fifth point gets directly to the stories that constitute your social biography. Which ones does your spirit like and which ones doesn't it like? Such stories are a refinement and combination of the third and fourth points. Make a list that suits. There could be more than one. Alternatively, focus on that juncture or tension point where spirit and social biography meet. Extract or tease out those central stories. You will know it or them by the feelings evoked. At some point, so you might as well do it now, the stories are to be articulated in words despite the difficulties that our language presents in describing that experiencing.

A sixth point is about unpeeling: Peel off these stories from your persona as well as your body. As your social biography becomes leaner, the space for spirit expands. It begins to express itself. It tells you to what it holds. It begins its adventures and its endisciplining (the crux of *deep learning*). Put these inhibiting and constraining stories aside. They do your spirit no good.

Move in, about, through these access points. Locate others. Once well into unpeeling, you have truly entered onto your spirit's journey.

13

Modes of Unlearning: Unfreezing

Why Unfreezing?

Wouldn't you think that the unpeeling practices of unlearning were enough for anyone? Why unfreezing? Three reasons. First, the *method* of presenting ways of enspiriting emphasizes their diversity and multiplicity. This method of presenting parallels, of course, the method of enspiriting. It is not loose. It is disciplined. It involves substantial inner work. But there is no one, true way to enspirit, to learn spirit's disciplines, to engage in their practices. All of these ways are *access* points and *starting* points; and one or more will work for you and get you onto the enspiriting path. Once on it, *spirit will help you*. What is required is that you extend a true invitation, that you *not* play games, that you have serious concerns about yourself in the context of the world you have inherited and that you have serious concerns about the world in the context of your social biography.

Simply put, there is more than one practice for unlearning. Unpeeling is one. Unfreezing is another.

But there is a second reason. Unpeeling usually starts with *imbalance*. There is a conflict, an inner tension between your spirit and your social biography. Stories about yourself do not fit your spirit's longings, your spirit's adventures, your spirit's *reasons*. You sense that. You feel that. You go about discovering which stories those are, and unpeel them.

Unfreezing usually starts with *dissonance*. This is the conflict, the tension between the immediacy of your experiencing yourself and your world and the KBVAF that you have learned from others, that you have internalized, and that has become frozen into your social biography. Dissonance and imbalance are at opposite ends of a continuum. Basically, imbalance involves stories about yourself, dissonance involves stories about the world. But in either case, *yourself-in-the-world* and *our-selves-in-the-world* constitute opposite ends of a continuum of a reality that denies spirit's place in it. The practices of unfreezing, therefore, are not the same as those of unpeeling *though the purpose is: to remove the barriers and constraints to spirit's fullest expression so that it can create a new partnership with your social biography and vice versa, and thus initiate the transformation.*

For some, unpeeling will prove a more difficult practice; for others, unfreezing will. For some, unpeeling will get them more quickly and more deeply into the unlearning path to *deep learning*. For others, the way of unfreezing will prove more propitious. In the end, it doesn't matter. By the time you begin the practices of *deep imaging,* you will be prepared to generate images of a space where imbalance and dissonance no longer obtain. And by the time you have entered into the metadisciplines of *intentioning, discerning* and *dialogue,* you will have begun to translate those images into action.

There is a third reason. *For some, unpeeling isn't a strong enough practice to break down the walls of habit.* Some stories linger on in your social biography and won't be tossed aside even though you have truly discerned their conflict with your spirit. They have become habit, frozen into an out-of-awareness consciousness of yourself, an out-of-awareness memory of yourself, an out-of-awareness belief about who and what you are in the world. No amount of unpeeling has yet uncovered spirit. Unlearning has not proceeded far enough. Spirit still illumines, but only at a distance, surmised, perhaps sensed, a guiding light whose beam has not yet penetrated to your soul. It is still frozen out by stories of yourself-in-the-world that are set in a previously impenetrable glacier of habit. We shall want to heat it up, to melt that glacier that has separated you from your spirit. What are the qualities of the inner action of unfreezing that can generate such heat? Inner and outer conflict through *deep questioning* and *deep listening;* frustration; sometimes anger on both sides as your spirit speaks its piece to a social biography that has never listened; the friction of direct and unmediated experience rubbing against what we have been led to believe about that experience. What enspiriting practices produce those qualities? What does this journey to the space of unfreezing look like?

The Roadmap

• *The context:* As you begin this journey, you immediately enter onto the path of habit. Habit is the armor of true belief which freezes your KBVAF. It must be unfrozen. But where might that take place?

• *The territory:* Move along the road and look around. You have entered the territory of dissonance. You recall the immediacy of your experiencing in any area of your life, inner or outer, that is not at all like you were told it was going to be. All of a sudden, that road of true belief begins to shimmer and shake. Cracks appear in the armor. Habit begins to melt. An opportunity for the inner action of unfreezing arises. Seize it.

• *The inner action:* These are the practices of *disassembling* and *dismantling.* The habitual beliefs of a lifetime, almost never previously examined, are dismantled. Stories frozen in your KBVAF heat up, begin to melt away. The building blocks that have constructed your KBVAF are disassembled, taken apart. What's left?

• *The remainder:* What is left over after the disassembly are the *source materials* out of which your KBVAF has been constructed over your lifespan. These are the original molecules of *intentioning;* for along this unfreezing path to deep learning, you have moved from habit back to intention. You can now ask spirit what it intends.

• *The space for invention:* In short, you have arrived at that space where spirit and social biography invent new perspectives, new myths and understandings about ourselves-in-the-world, and new stories about yourself-in-the-world. This is the space where inner and outer transformation begin their passage into a new reality. It is the space of *deep imaging,* free of those parts of your KBVAF that have sought to put down, control, or deny your spirit.

• *The method:* Rendering the dissonance explicit. That means *talking it out.* Speak the dissonances, say what are the conflicts between the immediacy of your experiencing and what in your KBVAF denies or distorts that experiencing. You may talk to yourself in strong self-talk; to another in *dialogue;* to a piece of paper if you write it down. But unlike unpeeling, the method of unfreezing is always transparent. It always takes place in your conscious awareness, right from the start.

So you begin.

Habit: The Armor of Belief

Do you remember the *belief* questions we laid aside as we prepared for the unpeeling? They went like this:

"What are the stories about myself-in-the-world I still believe?" and "What are the stories about myself-in-the-world I no longer believe?"

In the unfreezing work, we now address these questions. Why? Because sometimes an immediate rush of success in unpeeling is followed by a lingering belief in the truth of these stories themselves. Social biography is strong. Yourself-in-the-world is a hard-won amalgam of original spirit—that which was born into you—and the embodiment of the world in you. Willy nilly, you are a carrier of the habits of the world, until you decide to unfreeze them.

We are talking about *habit*, the great glue of human society... and, more precisely, *habitual belief*. Once you have come to habit—smoking cigarettes, swearing in public, driving through stop signs, voting the Republican ticket, believing yourself a loser, always trying to win no matter what the cost, settling a conflict through violence—it's difficult to get rid of. *Conduct* we choose. *Habit* we fall into. It matters not whether the habit lies in the domain of the nation-state, the institution, the mass, or is particular to you alone.

Is the aim of unfreezing to eliminate all habits? Certainly not. Which ones? Those that get in the way of your spirit's expressing itself. How do you know which ones these are?

Has your spirit spoken up yet? Has it caught you up, even for an instant, and shaken your beliefs about yourself-in-the-world? Has it given you an inkling of its presence in the enspiriting "exercises" you have experienced?

"What a lot of hard work," you might cry. Yes indeed. But you have already done a good part of it. Have you not deep listened and deep questioned another, if not yourself, and heard *her* spirit? Move beyond the barriers of propriety and self-censorship to the untilled fields where spirit roams. Great surprises await you!

What Unfreezing Is

Unfreezing, therefore, is about disassembling habitual beliefs that stand in the way of enspiriting as well as attitudes, values, even articles of faith that you have held most dear. *Even secured or authoritative knowledge!* Does this sound familiar ... the KBVAF? These are now all open to question, perhaps even to disassembly if you are willing to let the unfreezing happen.

Like unpeeling, unfreezing is a process of what I have called the unlearning mode of *deep learning*. Disassembly is the actual practice, the inner work that only you can do for yourself. And you must do it deliberately.

What Is Disassembly?

Disassembly means to take apart that which has been assembled.

Have you ever dismantled an old clock, an old radio, an old doll, an old car, an old toy? What about an old romance, an old relationship, a past social or emotional event? I would be surprised if you hadn't done some disassembly work. Infants and young persons are always taking things apart. Disassembly is native to the mind, atavistic, picking things apart to see what makes them tick. Primate toolmakers, be they humans or chimps, do this all the time. The development of our cerebrum, our enormous outer brain, has led to and been caused by this behavior and now demands it for is own neurological health.

What to Disassemble?

Your entire panoply of consciousness that goes under the KBVAF rubric: knowledge, belief, values, attitudes and faiths. These are the mental constructs, the mental material of your neurological pathways and programs. They have become habitualized. That means they are seldom—if ever—examined to seek out and bring back into conscious awareness the conditions under which they were first acquired and learned. For example, KBVAF mediates the immediacy of your experiencing your spirit, the direct apprehension of its givenness in you, with you, to you. It subdues its piercing light in the shadows of explanation we call theology. In an era in which spirit has been isolated from the daily run of life, even denied by so many of us, the sources of the relevant KBVAF are now to be opened up and confronted. That is, if you choose to let spirit enter once more into the multiple dimensions of your life. That is why I invited you to undertake an immediate experiencing of your spirit in the exercise No. 10, *My spirit speaks out.*

What to Unfreeze?

The habitual belief that gets in the way. Without unfreezing, unpeeling may not be enough. Actions carry old flavors of belief even if the content has wafted away. The body remembers. Through the exercises on *imbalance* and *unpeeling*, you have arrived at that place in your interior journey where now a bit of push must come to a bit of shove.

Consider. To get to spirit's *deep learning,* to bypass your biography's historic barriers, some aspects of your social biography must be disassembled. Piece-by-piece, it has been built up over your lifetime. Now we shall unfreeze it, unlock it, take it apart so as to reconstitute it to something like its original state.

This is destruction, no doubt about it. How much, how little, how severe, how easy depends entirely on how imprisoned your spirit has been *and nothing else.* This is not a psychological or psychotherapeutic intervention with a "cure" in mind, or even with the honorable project of learning how to live with yourself or with what you consider your deficits. *Enspiriting is not a project designed to build your self-esteem per se or to deal with whatever range of neuroses or psychoses your upbringing has dealt you unless they get in the way of freeing up your spirit. Enspiriting is not about restoring you to functioning once again in this world. It is about transforming the world and yourself in it.* If you sense you need professional help, seek it. The damage to your psyche may have been severe and in need of repair. But for most of us, the case is simply this: *We have frozen out spirit. We have so limited the spaces in which it can express itself, in our social biography (myself-in-the-world) and in the external world (ourselves-in-the-world), that we have deformed our realities; and if by now your concerns, your troubled spirit, your imbalances and your dissonances haven't demonstrated that to you, pack it in, return the book, get your money back!*

For most of us, spirit has been close to the surface, just waiting to breathe. For most of us, the disassembly work is not a lifetime's effort; sometimes it is as little as days or weeks. I am constantly impressed at how quickly people learn and apply these disciplines of the spirit to their own case and to their action-settings. For most of us, no miracles are involved. Just good, hard, rigorous inner work within a community of learners.

One enspiritor did that hard work after her spirit did not come out upon an initial invitation through the early enspiriting exercises. Indeed, she could recall no instance of its previous expression. Her biography fought back. How well I remember her sitting alone at a table in the corridor during a coffee break, smoking a cigarette, tears welling up. "Warren," she said. "I can't do this." Earlier attempts and prior exercises had led to a few sleepless nights, to dreams, to haphazard images floating into conscious awareness *until she made a conscious decision and choice to go to her spirit and let it out.*

"This I will do," she said to herself the next day.

Then came back the sleep, the appetite, the entire engagement with her spirit.

"What do you want? Why won't you speak up? What do you want of me?" she queried her spirit.

Then she put aside the armor of her social biography, took off the fabric of her life-history and stood naked with spirit so that it could speak. All of this in a week after 40 years of believing the stories that she was unloved, unlovable, and generally incapable of leading a fully human life.

Was this a miracle "cure"? No. There was nothing to be cured. Her self-stories had imprisoned her spirit, not made her a "bad" or a "sick" person. Once let out, *it* entered into confrontation with her biography. A new negotiation began. Perhaps it will continue all of her life. But the pact will be different.

By her account, her spirit led her into kairos. Let your spirit do that for you. Try it. It won't hurt. Having entered Kairos, one week versus 40 years meant nothing to her. She had entered her space of reconstruction and emancipation wherein time stands still and place disappears. That resplendent space for spirit's breathing, loving and joyous adventuring becomes the space for your transformation if you will seize it.

Habits of the Mind

Do you remember the start-up mode of *dissonance* (Chapter Ten)? Return to it. It initiates the unlearning. It heats up the inner space where all true action takes place, for outer action—the traditional "doing something" like making policy, developing programs, implementing a decision, actualizing your intentions, etc.—stems from the inner action of the kinds described in this book. You had entered the unfreezing room as soon as you placed into juxtaposition your raw *experiencing* of life's immediacy and your *KBVAF*. They confronted each other. Did you then commence your strong self-talk? If not, return to that earlier exercise to prepare for the next one.

Let me give you a few examples shared with me by fellow-enspiritors as they entered the unfreezing room through the doorway of dissonance. The grand opera of awakening to the disasters we have perpetrated on ourselves begins with an opening chorus of "This I no longer believe...

"...I can't do it."

"...Commands, orders, regulations, policies and decisions from 'on high' are infallible."

"...Atrocities inflicted on *my* people 50 or 500 years ago warrant my inflicting atrocities on *your* people 50 or 500 years later."

"...In order to honor my parents in memory or love them in presence, I have to continue to practice the race, ethnic, class, gender, religious prejudice I learned at their knees."

"...My love for and loyalty to my spouse are strong enough to withstand 15 years of abuse."

"...Governments can solve social problems."

"...My not making first-string varsity, not becoming a cheerleader, not making the honor roll means I'm inferior to those who did."

"...Leadership is necessarily a product of charisma, luck and training rather than a gift distributed universally throughout humankind irrespective of any other social indicator."

"...Being macho and trying to screw every woman in sight is a God-given right of every male."

"...Market economics, in the name of efficiency, can justify the personal dislocations and suffering of persistently high unemployment among millions of human beings."

"...My worth as a human being requires that I be better—or better off—than somebody else."

"...Education can solve all problems and cure all evils."

"...Getting more training inevitably leads to a better job...or to any job at all."

"...Losing weight...or gaining weight...or building up pecs or buns of steel... or going on a diet of rice and beans...or switching deodorants...or moving to the all-white suburbs...is going to make me a happier person."

"...I have to flirt with males to prove my femininity."

"...The church is the only or even the main spiritline to God."

"...When my boss talks about empowering our employees, he means it."

"...Thirty minutes of 'quality time' with my kids every Saturday is what parenting is all about."

Do you see its great variety? A chorus in which each person sings her song, yet the discord is harmonious. Some KBVAFs are about outside things, some are about inside things. But they interlock like a great Gordian knot. Unlike Alexander who cut through it, we enspiritors are unloosening and unraveling it strand-by-strand until it lies disassembled before us. Indeed, we transform the very strands themselves. We discover new strands to weave the new fabric of our destiny or, as I shall put it to you in the chapters on *deep imaging* and *intentioning,* invent new fibers. We shall invite, tease, and pull out ideas, images, possibilities, alternative realities from the implicate order, from the life of the imaginal, and ground them into a new reality of yourself-in-the-world and ourselves-in-the-world.

Where Is Your Story Lodged?

Your story of dissonance may be lodged in any part of the KBVAF or all of it. Generally, the firmer it is lodged, the more likely it is that more than one element is involved. Clearly, these elements support and legitimize each other. An *attitude*, for example, when dislodged from the pack and about to be pushed back to its source, may be pulled back into the overall story by a knowledge claim or an article of faith that has served to justify the attitude. The history of racial, ethnic and religious prejudice is rife with these interlocking support mechanisms of KBVAF.[8] Each element in KBVAF defends the others. Unfreezing is a powerful way to break their iron grip on our consciousness of spirit.

This interlock among the elements is just as strong in the self-stories that freeze social biography in place as in the stories that freeze world consciousness in place. Have you not heard someone, perhaps dear to you, perhaps yourself, claim that he will never get a decent job—responsibility, meaningful work, a good paycheck—to justify or "prove" a posture of self-putdown, an attitude of giving up, all in turn bolstered by that oppressive belief that this vicious circle is inevitable?

In fact, the real crime lies in how the self-stories (about yourself-in-the-world) and the other-stories (about ourselves-in-the-world) combine within the social biography to form a nigh-impenetrable wall that surrounds the deep inner work of enspiriting described in this book. In their pioneer work, *The Hidden Injuries of Class*, sociologists Bennet and Cobb demonstrated how children from working class families accept their *teacher's* explicit admonitions that they are not college material, that they should have no expectations of pursuing an academic career and should prepare themselves for working in factories, or low-paying or non-management positions; and when in fact they grow-up, their own *self-attitudes, self-expectations, and interior beliefs* confirm what was imbedded in them in their youth: Failure, not getting ahead, not reaping the benefits or achieving a middle-class lifestyle, etc., *and blame themselves!* Their KBVAF has constituted an iron wall of self-denial within and has helped to lock in place a class system without.

Every story about yourself that you want to unfreeze because it stands in the way of your deep learning is the inner version of a larger story about the way the world works—its institutions, its belief systems, its sub-cultures, etc.—that is an integral part of the inner

---

[8] Gunnar Myrdal, the great Swedish social scientist, amply demonstrated these interlocking mechanisms in the KBVAF in his classic study of white race prejudice against blacks in *An American Dilemma*, 1944. The straightforward, no-nonsense analysis in the *Koerner Commission Report on Civil Disorders*, 1968, rediscovered this 25 years later.

story, and each—the inner story and the outer story—justifies and supports the other depending on which side of the street you're working. The two—the inner and the outer— are inextricably interwoven. They live off each other.

My point is this: Each story frozen into your KBVAF may require a different disassembling practice. Not just one will work for all such spirit-inhibiting stories. The exercise offered here is not to be slavishly followed. It seeks to provide you a number of starting points as you embark on this difficult journey to the space of unfreezing.

Getting Back to the Original Molecules: An Exercise (No. 15)

This will take some time to do. Do not rush it. The exercise has five steps or starting points, so read through it first. They are:
- Entering kairos.
- Which stories?
- Name and speak the story.
- Find the story's descriptors in you.
- Back to origins: The who, what, where, how and why questions.

The overall aim is to disassemble a story in your social biography into its component parts so that you can return to the initial situation in which that particular story was born in you in order to discover if your original intentions in the matter carry the weight they once did.

The focus is on stories that constrain spirit's expression of its true yearnings and that deny your access to spirit's essence. Are such stories frozen into your KBVAF? That is now to be queried in a deep way, continuing what you have already accomplished in *Imbalance (No. 7), Dissonance (No. 8)* and *Unpeeling (Nos. 11-13).*

1. *Entering Kairos.* One step is to locate and enter your own inner space of kairos. This is preparation, of course, but particularly crucial in *unfreezing.* The vessel of this great adventure in unlearning may soon founder on the rocky shoals of anxiety or be swamped by the great swelling waves of self-doubt. To find or create the inner space that puts you on the path of unfreezing is essential.

2. *Which Stories?* Does it matter which story you take up? Our experience suggests not. Be guided by an intuitive sense of what to work on. Your inner "computer" will discern whether it's a story that is uncovered first in attitude, belief, value, faith or knowledge.

What of the content: Does that matter? Not at the start. Some gain a quick insight into a main blocking story that has lingered on despite valiant efforts at unpeeling.

Others might want to start with an "easy" story. How would you know that it's "easy"? Your body would be less likely to tense up (a tightening in the tant'ien).

For one story that blocks out spirit leads inevitably to another. The KBVAF is all of a piece in this matter of maintaining social biography.

3. *Name and Speak the Story.* More than any other piece of inner work, speaking out the story unlocks the door to spirit's *deep learning.* The blockage has to be spoken of and about, in detail sufficiently concrete and specific that ambiguity clarifies and uncertainty disappears. This is a major contribution of dynamic psychology: knowing that *to tell a story (that blocks spirit) is to release it from its prison in your social biography so that it can be dismantled.*

That is the unfreezing, the disassembling, the dismantling. There are many ways to tell the story.

• Write it down.

• Speak it to a partner within your community of learners.

• Speak it to yourself.

Speaking or writing the story relies on words. They come out in different ways. Sometimes they stumble and halt. The flow may even stop. Other times, they tumble out, spilling all over one another. But what if the words won't come? There are other ways to begin to tell the story.

4. *Find the Story's Descriptors in You.* Descriptors locate the story within your body senses and the multiple levels of your consciousness. As these descriptors are identified and brought forth, the story begins to acquire a status in your mind that allows it to be told.

• What *color* is the story? Sit quietly by the stream of your spirit and let its color come to you. Is your story about your inability to take a risk though the outcome is attractive, what you might even have named within yourself "a lack of courage"? What color is that self-claim? What are its colors?

• What does it *sound* like? I don't mean words...*sounds!* There are an infinity of sounds throughout the world and within you. Which one—or ones—belong to your story? Deep listen for them, giving attention and being silence. What do you hear?

• Does your story evoke *smells?* Odors? In our pristine pure culture that seeks to hide or obscure or eradicate all smells—not successfully!—let these of your story come to you. Sniff them out.

• What of *pictures?* Who and what do you see in your mind's eye as the story unfolds? Suppose you seek the source of your belief about the futility of life, for example, or about the notion that the poor get what they deserve? What pictures does that claim evoke? Perhaps you can even let the pictures set the scene when notions such as these first invaded your social biography.

Of course, if your starting point lies in the dissonance between the immediacy of your experiencing and a piece of your KBVAF, do return to that experiencing in all of its concreteness and immediacy: Sights and sounds and smells and colors.

Any or all of these descriptors—color, sound, smell, picture—may begin the self-story for you, or come to it at any time in its telling. But that is not the end of it.

• *Body feelings* and *body locations*. These are primary, even foundational in any story imbedded in your social biography that closes off spirit. Where is that story in your body... literally, what part? Each element in the KBVAF has a parallel location in your body. Search for it by that kind of deep listening at which you are by now a master, emptying of mind, emptying the tant'ien so that when the body parts, the skin, bones, sinew, muscles, organs and their *interrelationships* speak out, you are there.

But what is this "speaking out"?

Listen now for the feelings—the physical sensations—by which your body tells you of its memories of this story and its sources. Sometimes, as you have already learned from your early efforts at *deep questioning*, that is pain. But not always. Listen and feel deeply and truly for the suffocating sense, for the tightness (or loose-ness), for the blockage to inner flow, for the releasing. Words, here, are inadequate to describe the ways your body locates and feels the story. Don't worry about putting these descriptors into words. That is not necessary, so long as your inner conscious-ness grasps the inner events attached to the sensings. In *dialogue*, after a while, words adequate to be shared under the gentle probing of a fellow enspiritor may come to you. If they don't, no matter.[9]

Consciousness, Clues, and Descriptors

What are these descriptors? Many things. I call them *clues* to those aspects of your KVBAF that constrain your spirit. Follow these clues to their sources. Ask your-self the "why" questions: Why this sound? Why this body location and feeling? Why this smell?

Do not seek an intellectual response. No theorizing is wanted here. No grandiose generalizations are permitted. Rather, seek to respond to the "why" question by going deeper into these modes of consciousness. Consciousness is by no means

---

[9] What of *emotions*? Why are they not included in this list of descriptors that locate in you pieces of a story that is proving difficult for you to tell (step 3)? Because emotions are not descriptors. Emotions are complex names we give to feelings in our body senses in order to render them intelligible. When I say, for example, that I am angry—an emotion—the conventional next step is to ask: Why am I angry? In this exercise—as in many other enspiriting prac-tices—the next step is to ask: *Where* am I angry? The idea is to try to locate the *feelings* of anger in my body senses and body places prior to making an interpretation of that anger, for such an interpretation is the very mediating of direct experience (e.g., of our body) that the KVBAF does that leads to dissonance. Moreover, what we aim for in this exer-cise is not an interpretation of the story but *the story itself*.

restricted to thought and to words. All of these sensings of the story's descriptors are aspects of consciousness. In the modern, rationalist era, we have sought to subdue, even eradicate these other modes of *consciousness of our being in the world. That modern rationalist project has gone hand-in-hand with excising spirit from our world.* So do I offer you, remind you, invite you to these other modes through the practices of enspiriting and the exercises designed to bring you to those practices. Even in the certainty that the self-story is eventually to be spoken, allow yourself these multiple ways of spirit's speaking.

Once I had a marvelous conversation with a cardinal; red, plump, feathery and without beads. It began when I was doing a T'ai Chi in the early morning under a great oak on the grounds of a retreat center in Ohio. At first, the cardinal just watched, his perky head looking the other way, yet all the while giving me his undivided attention. Then, in about 15 minutes, he began his whistle-song, and I knew it was for me. I quieted my energy flow circling my body and brought it back inside, and whistled back. For another ten minutes, we sang to each other. That sounding became a music of a consciousness of and with each other that put our spirits in touch.

So in these steps of dismantling the story and returning to its original molecules, do let it speak to you in its multiple ways. Your social biography is *all* of you. It is not restricted to an intellectual aspect and it is not always accessed that way. Some learn to dance by watching and copying a dancer. Some follow footsteps drawn on the floor. Some listen to the band and let its sounds guide their feet. Others feel inner rhythms in their bodies and it comes out in dance. So too with your story about what blocks your spirit. It will emerge in multiple ways.

5. *Back to Origins: The Who, What, Where, How, and Why Questions.* But now we come back to the starting points of the story. Here, become your own investigative reporter. *Who* told you this story? (Remember, the telling might not have been in words alone or even mainly.) *What* were the initial points? *Where* did you hear it and learn it, the setting and the situation? *How* was the story given to you, what medium was used? And most importantly, *why* was it laid on you and *why* did you accept it?

Each of these questions deserves a response as concrete and specific as you can make it. The focus is to seek the story's starting points. Some many be located in years so long past that memory falters. No matter. Get a "feel" for any of the starting points, a "sense" of the beginnings though its history may still escape your conscious awareness. Let your body speak out first, if that is the path.

Remember that our search is for stories (to be unpeeled and unfrozen) that block the way to spirit's expression. For most of us, this is a *few* stories, not many. The aim is not to seek cures for your problems or the world's. Stay with the exercise. *Hone in on those aspects of your social biography that are spirit-inhibiting.*

Were some of these stories delivered to you in your infancy or youth? So be it. Locate their sources—persons, relationships, events, information-inputs, indeed any aspect of the grand sweep of the immediacy of your experiencing—in the early formation of your social biography. Relive that specific formation, its feelings, sightings, sounds, touches, info-bits, the whole thing.

As that part of your KBVAF assembled, what were your intentions? What were your needs? What was your situation? Assign no blame or fault, yours or others', as the KBVAF came together, piece-by-piece. Just pry into it until the original molecules of consciousness re-emerge into body awareness, feeling awareness, intellect awareness.

And finally, the culminating question: *What now are your intentions in this matter?* You are no longer a passive recipient of some other's intentions, of some other's KBVAF, even of some other's unintentional, habitual, but highly consequential behavior. *You are an actor in your own story. To discover the script, query your spirit and let it speak to you through deep imaging.*

But What of Spirit's Own Deep Learning?

As you remember, examine, probe the origins of these spirit-inhibiting stories, they come out to greet you *where you are now*. Where is that? *In kairos*. Where you are now is an inner state of liberating your spirit by having bypassed your biography. Can you not now let your spirit speak about *its* being and doing in the world?

I asked at the beginning of the inner work on *deep learning*: "How far can each of us go in this journey to the core of spirit?"

I answered, then: "That you will discover."

Now enter the discovery phase. Much here is mystery for you *until your spirit speaks out*. Every story I hear, every story I myself tell in this book or to myself reveals a new and deeper well of spirit. It is ineffable, effervescent, luminous, re-inventive of your social biography as spirit, invited out, enters once again into yourself-in-the-world and ourselves-in-the-world.

Have you guessed? We now enter the futures room. It is empty. KBVAF has dissipated.

Spirit is engaged in its own *deep listening* with itself. It has come to trust itself, for you have removed barriers to that self-trust through bypassing your social biography.

Spirit now learns itself: Who and what it is, how it shall re-emerge in yourself- and ourselves-in-the-world and *render clear its own invitations to us and its own claims on us.*

That rendering is through the enspiriting discipline of *deep imaging.* When the invitation is true, so too are its images. Let us come to them.

14

Ways of Deep Imaging:
An Overview

Deep imaging involves a shift of perspective and action. Let's talk about that for a moment.

A Time for Moving Out

In the discipline of *deep imaging*, we shift from *uncovering spirit* to *releasing spirit*. Deep imaging is about bringing spirit back into the realm of action in a constructive, loving, transforming manner. To do that, we reverse the direction of our journey. Up to this point, the main pathway to enspiriting has pointed inward, bypassing social biography in order to get directly to the inner space where spirit dwells. Now, the focus of enspiriting shifts outward, to the world of action, person, community and organization.

This is an important strategic move because the qualities of looking inward and the effects of looking outward are quite different. Looking inward involves work that many enspiriting novices consider a private encounter with spirit, an experiencing of spirit that can't or shouldn't be shared. In this view, *deep listening* and *deep questioning*, for example, are understood solely as "technical" accompaniments to your own inner work; a new kind of "counseling" which enables your spirit to listen to and encounter itself without advice or interference except to help clarify. Our individualistic culture abets that feeling of privacy in matters of the spirit, as in almost everything else. But deep imaging, while it still involves serious inner work and may start with a focus on yourself, quickly shifts to aspects of yourself-in-the-world or ourselves-in-the-world which your spirit seeks to transform. No longer can you hide behind the protective cover of: "Enspiriting is my business and no one else's." Deep imaging engages you with other enspiritors in *dialogue* about how your stories interact, about how they influence and impact each other, indeed about how and why your spirit's quest is part and parcel of another enspiritor's quest. The disciplines of the spirit shift to a "public" mode. Perhaps at the beginning that "public" is only one or a few persons. But as spirit finds its voice and expresses it through your social biography, family, friends, colleagues, fellow-citizens, eventually even "strangers" are invited to give attention to that which you are creating, to begin their own enspiriting work, and to discover with you in what ways and for what reasons you may all be involved in creating something in common.

Transformation Time

Enspiriting is about transformation. It needn't be a big thing, although the world certainly needs a "big" transformation. It may be about a little thing, perhaps known *only to you* ... at first! But whatever the focus, *transformation means to bring into existence that which is not. Deep imaging* lies at the very beginning of transformation; it is through this discipline that new images of yourself-in-the-world and of ourselves-in-the-world are born.

Through the disciplines of the spirit, that process goes like this: The seeds of these deep images are pulled from the implicate order of other realities which we come to know through the life of the imaginal. They are conceived by your spirit in dialogue with God, with the Universal, with the Light, or however you name the transcendent which is beyond our human biography but of which a piece is lodged in each of us. They are brought into conscious awareness through the practices of deep imaging, and offered for the transformation of your world *through your action in it.*

Your initial journey from the exterior time and place of yourself-in-the-world to the interior space of spirit retraces out. But your social biography, as you knew it, and your KBVAF, as it has lodged in you, are no longer the same as they were prior to the inner work of enspiriting.

Nor is the path outward exactly the same as the path inward. The practices are quite different. In the inward movement, the practices are designed to bypass your social biography. In the outward movement, the practices are designed to bring spirit into the world through your own transformation and your *offering*—not demanding —to the rest of us to enter into a similar journey. When you make that offer, as I hope you will soon discover, *people receive it joyfully and respond with alacrity to the rigorous demands of the enspiriting disciplines. Making that offer and witnessing the application of the disciplines to the real world are the essence of the transformative leadership.*

These *practices* of deep imaging are set forth in a *grammar of imaging* in the next chapter. Many of these practices are quite ordinary. They require no great "spiritual" awakening. They are grounded in a universal human capacity *to be imaginative.*

Though many of the practices are not unusual in themselves, they are put together into a *discipline* because the deep imaging path you will traverse is full of roadblocks, potholes and traps. Unless avoided, these result in generating *false* rather than *true* images. How to distinguish between the two is a major focus of the disciplines of deep imaging and *discerning.*

Note the language here. Almost nobody in the field of *imaging* distinguishes between *true* and *false* images. Rather, the main aim in learning and practicing the skills of conventional imaging is to be effective. Bringing effective *false* images into the world is the bane of the 20th century. Millions of people have died because those false images were so effective *in getting humans to do things we might otherwise not have done*... like putting millions of human beings into ovens and gassing them to death.

How then to begin? Will a deep (if nervous) breath and an inward leap into the unknown space where true images are born be a good way to start? Are there some whistles and bells, smoke and mirrors, incantations and spells that might transport us to the realm of deep imaging? Sorry. I aim to introduce you to a set of *techniques* that constitute the craft of deep imaging. They can be readily learned.

But I must remind you that becoming skilled in these techniques is not the same as becoming *competent* in the discipline of deep imaging. To acquire competence, you must declare your intention in the matter of deep imaging: Why you want to learn and practice this amazing discipline, with what consequences for yourself-in-the-world and ourselves-in-the-world; in short, *why you want to listen to the voice of your spirit. Skill and will, ability and intention,* taken together, constitute competence. The deep imaging exercises offered here invite you to the practices incumbent to that competence.

An Introductory Exercise in Imaging (No. 16)

This introductory practice is not yet *deep imaging.* That is a piece of inner work for which serious competence is required lest we discover, *after the fact,* that what we have generated is not authentic to spirit but the result of images foreign to our spirit. The focus of this exercise is to give you a feel for imaging, to introduce you to the craft, to open the door to the futures room and see what's there.

Step One: Preparation. As usual, prepare yourself. The centering, the opening up, the yielding, the deep breathing, the creating of a space that invites quiet and the relaxing of the mind and body.

Step Two: Focus. Give attention to something that might be bothering you, not too heavy, just a nagging thing like: A little toothache and an upcoming visit to the dentist; passing the test for your driver's license scheduled for next week; getting to the bank before it closes; turning yesterday's left-overs into a tasty dish for tonight's evening meal; cleaning up your desk before you leave work.

Do you get the quality of the nag? What my wife calls: "Things to do!" A list of tasks at work, at home, at recreation that fill your daily life: Take one and focus on it, just for a moment.

Step Three: Clarity. Be clear and specific. Describe the task. The thing to do. Capture it in your mind. What is it? Perhaps *writing it down* might help. The point here is clear description.

Step Four: Imagination. Now enter your imagination. Let it run for a while.

In this step, ask: What is it like to do that task, reduce or eliminate the nag, "get at" the something you have described in specifics in step three?

Imagine it in detail, step by step. You get in your car. Can you feel the key turning in the lock? You slam the door. Hear that thump? Buckle the seatbelt. Feel that pressure on your chest, shoulder, and stomach? Put the key in the ignition and turn it. Feel the turning, hear the click, listen to the engine roar to life? Look in the rearview mirror before you turn from the curb into the street. See that truck coming down the street behind you?

...and now you're at the dentist's, the grocer's, the bank, the office desk. Stay with the last, for a moment. Now what are you doing? Picking up the papers from your desk, one by one. Hear their soft rustle? Feel that funny paper feel in your fingertips? See the words you're scanning, ah, this goes in this file, that goes in that file?

...what of the dentist's set of images? Can you inhale that special smell of the dentist's office? Do you feel your heart beating just a little faster as you wait for the inner door to open and the nurse to come out with her welcoming smile of doom?

...what about the supermarket? Do you hear the background noise and bustle in the crowd? Can you see yourself scanning the shelves?

Capture all of these images, for they are the minutiae, the *imago-bytes* in an enormous internal computer that you tap into as you bring them into your conscious awareness.

Step Five: Finish. Now you're done. The nag is gone, the task is completed. But stay in your imagination for another moment. What is it like to be finished, to have completed the task, to have excised the nag? How do you feel? Are any new images coming to you, new thoughts or feelings? *I have to drive home. Phew, I'm glad that's over. What's at work for tomorrow? After supper? Do the dishes? Then what?*

Step Six: Back to Reality. Return to the "real" world." Once again, you're reading this page and these words. A new question: What was it like to do this exercise? Was it familiar territory? *Don't you image the future, as you just did, all the time, without even being aware that you're doing it?*

You have just been "imaging," *the active voice of the imagination.* Not yet deep imaging, mind you, but still the same "technical" process and craft. We image all the time, just as we breathe all the time. Every memory is an image. Every story, written, audio, video, electronic or face-to-face, it doesn't matter: These are all images.

Dad says: "Let's go to the lake next weekend."

Without even thinking about it, and certainly not deliberately, you flash to the lake. You're there. The sound of the water lapping gently at the shore. The smell of gasoline as you start the outboard. The feel of the sun on your skin, its deep, penetrating warmth as you lie on the dock after a dip in the cool lake water. The weight and smell of the wood logs as you carry them into the cabin for an evening fire.

In a split second—actually, in a space and time too small to measure—you're there at the lake, doing and being all these things. That's imaging. And then you're back at the dinner table, stuffing mashed potatoes into your mouth, listening to your mom say: "I'll have to go shopping tonight if we're going to get an early start in the morning."

What Is Imaging? The Practice

We will return to the images conjured up in this little introductory exercise, so don't lose them. Meanwhile, be clear about imaging: It is like breathing. We all do it. It is so natural, we don't even think about it. Yet it fills a good portion of our existence. That process of imaging—the doing of it, the being of, with and in your images—constitutes the same activity as in *deep imaging. There is really nothing new to learn.* Soon, you'll be traipsing along the same imaging path...but you won't stop until you've come to the space for deep imaging, to the space wherein spirit dwells.

I want you to get clear about the imaging activity, to realize that it is yours to command, to appreciate your vast skill in imaging before we swim to the deeper water of your spirit. Let us, therefore, return to the content and process of imaging in the introductory exercise. I want to remind you about a few things in the *practice* before we go on.

1. *Images are always concrete and specific.* In the next chapter, I'll share with you the "rules" for sound imaging. But this one is so basic it deserves stating now. Imaging generates concrete and specific images. Go back to the introductory exercise and reflect on it. Weren't your images concrete and specific?

What does that mean? It means:

2. *You can see the image,* i.e., picture it. You get a picture in your mind's eye. Professional imagers call this "visualization," but I dislike the term because of the emphasis they give it, as if visualization and imaging are one and the same. They are not!

Imaging does often involve "picturing" something (e.g., the dentist's chair, the ripples from the wind on the lake, the pile of papers on your desk). But it involves a lot more. If you didn't get any picture in that introductory exercise, don't worry. At least ten percent of effective imagers never visualize at all!

What more, then, might *specific and concrete* mean?

3. *When you image, you get feelings.* Literally. Feelings of euphoria, anger, excitement, joy, envy, frustration, anxiety, fear, sadness, etc. The images come to you as feelings, in the body. You should recognize this phenomenon if you have read the chapters on *deep questioning.* So many of our concerns, disquietudes, tensions, imbalances are *felt first in the body as feelings, even as pain, long before we can talk about them.*

Do you remember the example I shared in the chapter on *deep listening* about the retired business executive who had emptied his tant'ien so that his partner's presence entered into him? He recounted *his* feelings of upset, pain, turmoil though she had not revealed to him *her* feelings in so many words. She was *imaging* her feelings. They were so strong that when he deep listened, he picked them up and felt them too. Her feelings were specific and concrete. True images. But no pictures. No smells. *Feelings.* Those two, and hundreds of other imagers with whom I've worked in the envisioning projects and workshops, attest to *coming to their images initially as feelings.*

That we may not know how or why to deal with images as feelings in policy, program and action work does not relieve us of an obligation to learn the attendant competence. Myth-makers, advertisers and charismatic leaders *constantly evoke feeling-images without consulting us. They rely on our illiteracy in feeling-images to purvey their wares.*

Technically, feeling-images are known as *meaning-feelings.* Do you ever awake in the morning with a distinct feeling which may stay with you all day? Perhaps it's a feeling of anxiety, of dread, of euphoria, of hope. You can't pin down its source, for you have forgotten the dream; but the feeling is distinct. These are examples of meaning-feelings. We get them with imaging too. For some, images come as meaning-feelings long before they come as pictures.

Which brings us to still another way of imaging that is specific and concrete.

4. *You can touch the image and it touches you.* This is a different kind of "feeling"; not about feelings as emotions but physical. Remember the feel of the cool, squishy mud between your toes as you entered the lake? That memory is an image.

How does your lover's hand feel on your arm?

When you reach out and accidentally touch the still-hot burner on the stove?

As you enter the crowded lobby of the theater or the entrance to the subway at rush hour and feel the shoulders, clothes, shoes, bodies touching, pressing, engulfing you?

These are all images. This kind of imaging, physical and sensuous, happens all the time. Often, we use it to give us a warning of a painful experience we want to avoid or a pleasurable experience we anticipate.

5. *You can hear the image.* In this way of imaging, you hear noises, sometimes voices, people actually talking, or words that you hear without a body attached. Is this what happened to Joan d'Arc? To some, God speaks directly. Yahweh spoke to Moses, according to the Old Testament. Krishna spoke to Arundja in the Bhagavad Gita. For others, our imagination creates the voice or noises long before it paints a picture. The roar of a jet's engines passing overhead. The gathering thunder, faint on the horizon, an undercover rumbling that portends the crackling whiplash of lighting as the storm approaches. Try that. Close your eyes. Can you hear that? That's imaging in concrete and specific ways.

Are those all of the ways of imaging? Not at all!

6. *You can taste the image.* Relax. Close your eyes. Bite into an apple, an onion, whatever food comes to mind. Roast turkey? Can you taste it? But it's not there. Yet it can be tasted, smelled, touched, seen. What are these? In our work with thousands of people, we have learned that images come, specifically and concretely, in this variety

of ways. As you enter into the inner space of deep imaging, allow any or all of these ways to work for you. Do not be upset if "visualization" is not your main or easiest way of imaging.

7. *You can smell the image.* Relax. Close your eyes. Now smell the bacon sizzling on the stove. Or walk down a hospital corridor and inhale that distinct hospital smell. Or mow the lawn, cut the hay. Do any of these smells come to you, real as life itself? But they are images...and you have just been imaging, have no doubt about that. Over the years, some of our best envisioners have "smelled" the future long before they heard, saw, or felt it in their imaginations.

8. *Cognitive imaging.* This is a bit different. Just as about ten percent of imagers never "picture" the image, never visualize, another ten percent image cognitively. That is, images come to them spontaneously, without premeditation, as words, isolated or strung together, sometimes as whole paragraphs. Often, we call this a "knowing," or an intuition that may come to us first as feeling images or what we sometimes call hunches. The name matters less than the fact. It is possible to image in words; but that imaging contains no logic, no train of thought, no prior analysis, no "thinking." Just the words. There is some dispute in the field about whether this is *thinking* or *imaging.* The way I've just described it, and according to many participants in futures-invention workshops which rely heavily on the imaging craft, this is as much a way of imaging as anything else. The trick here is not to fall into the trap of *thinking* your way through a problem or a concern. That's a completely different activity. In cognitive imaging, the images are words, ideas, thoughts...*but you have not been thinking.* And finally...

9. *Living your image in your body.* In effect, your body becomes your image. Your body acts it out. Children do this all the time. "Look, mommy, I'm a lion...or a kitty...or a dolphin..." Note: not *like* a lion. Just...a lion. The youngster has become her image. She feels it, knows it through her body. Just watch and listen as she roars and lopes her way around the livingroom. Skilled kindergarten and pre-school teachers invite youngsters to this imaginative bodyplay all the time. But as we grow up, imaginative bodyplay is left to the professional actors; and so most of us lose the skill...*but not the capacity!*

Once, 40 years ago, I saw the great ballerina, Markova, dance a dying swan to a scratchy record of Tchaichovsky's *Dying Swan,* an aging ballerina on an old wooden floor in the theater at Jacob's Pillow. No big crowds, no diamonds and evening clothes, no glittering lights and ballet orchestra. Just Markova, a slight, solitary figure in white...but she was a dying swan. Her fingers, her hands and wrists, her arms, her head and long neck and gracefully curving back had become a dying swan, completely and literally. We, her small audience, were anointed by her dancing that image.

This is *kinesthetic imaging.* I suspect we adults image in, with and throughout our bodies more often than we acknowledge. In our frozen culture of obeisance to the head trip, body movement and body feeling are carefully controlled and choreographed—sports, social dancing, theater and other performing arts. Even finger, hand and arm gestures that give shape to your words and carve out a universe of discourse are not acceptable, particularly in the Waspish culture, if proffered too strongly.

In summary: *Seeing, feeling as touching, feeling as "emotion," hearing, smelling, tasting, cognizing in a special way, and kinesthetic: these are the multiple ways of imaging.*

Do you get a sense, as we begin, of the infinite richness of your imaging capacity, of these possibilities for feeling, seeing, hearing, smelling, tasting, touching, even *being* your images? It is that enormous capacity of the imagination that we harness to spirit's need to express itself in *this* world, in yourself-in-the-world and ourselves-in-the-world, through *deep imaging.*

To Deep Imaging

These imaging techniques are available to just about everyone for a wide range of human endeavors. No political leader is without them. No Madison Avenue operative is without them. Likewise, no infant could grow up whole bereft of the infinite acts of the human imagination that underlie this craft. To image is to breathe, to live, to create and participate in the world.

Now note: *The craft of the human imagination is not the discipline of deep imaging,* no more than wielding a paint brush is to make a great painting. Deep imaging is *not* technique. In deep imaging, spirit expresses itself through the images it brings into the world of conscious awareness. *To deep image is to let spirit tell you what it is in such a way that you know what your spirit calls you to.* Be clear about that. It is *your* spirit calling in deep imaging, not another person's. *Your spirit calls you.* The practices of *deep listening, deep questioning, and deep learning* bring you exactly to this point in your inner journey: *What does spirit ask of me? What is its call? What does it seek to bring into the world?*

That call results, ultimately, in a transformative action by which something that was not becomes that which is. It need not be earth-shaking, though collectively, enspiritors can transform the world. It might be a little thing by anyone else's lights. No matter. The transformation is in you and with you.

That transformative action might start with a mental hunch, an inner shrug, a tension and release within, a vague feeling as spirit begins to move in you. Many initial acts of enspiriting, as you have learned by now, commence with the small thing, the twinge here or there, the discomfort in the soul that has to be dug out, the feeling of unease. By the time you come to deep imaging, however, spirit speaks out in images *which you can describe* and which call you to action *which you can name*.

Through *unpeeling* and *unfreezing*, you have moved through and beyond that which represses you spirit in your social biography. Through deep questioning, you have discovered what troubles your spirit. Through deep listening, you have learned to empty yourself of all that covers over your spirit.

Now let spirit speak through its deep imaging.

Just before you begin, a reminder that though the source of this discipline is *your spirit*, it is inextricably interwoven with the spirit of humankind.

Inhabiting the Futures Room: Who Else Is There?

The futures room is an inner space that is empty of all things except spirit. Whose? Yours, to be sure; but not yours alone. The spirit of humankind is waiting and listening to discover how *your* enspiriting will touch that of others.

What of these others? Who are they? What is their business with you? Is not your spirit *yours*, acting in, with, and of you, not some other? Who cares about the "others"? Who invited them into *your* futures room... *into your future*... *into your inner space*?

In the chapters on *dialogue*, I shall come fully to this question. But now, I want to remind you that you are never alone in the work of enspiriting. In the darkest moments of unlearning, if your social biography screams out its rage as you step past it, beclouds your consciousness as you seek to see clearly, or floods your body with the glue of desperation such that muscles, bones, tendons, cartilage and organs close down the inner avenues to spirit's release, *your spirit is not alone*.

Might enspiriting be a lonely journey? Yes, indeed, particularly if your social biography has used relationships—family, friends, lovers, colleagues—as a guise to keep you from your spirit. Starting out on your paths to spirit, you may feel lonely. But you are not alone. In your spirit space, you will discover the essential social character of spirit. That is the foundation of dialogue. It is that which invites you to a community of learners, to a community of enspiritors.

I say this to you now because many of those seeking the ways of enspiriting are at first caught up in the dynamics of their spirit interacting with their social biography —myself-in-the-world—and too readily dismiss or hide from the reality that their *own* social biography contains *all of the stories of humankind,* good, bad, and indifferent, as well as *all of the acts of humankind,* past, present and future.[10]

What we discover in *deep imaging* is that sooner or later, in a new reality called into being by spirit, both myself-in-the-world and ourselves-in-the-world walk hand-in-hand. As Rabbi Hillel said 2000 years ago: "If I am not for myself, who is for me? And when I am for myself, what am I? And if not now, when?"

Opening Doorways to the Future

You will soon discover who and what inhabits your futures room. The moment for "letting spirit out" has arrived. Now spirit is about to test out its newly won freedom. What will it say? How will it choose to enter into your world? How will it enter into *the* world—of family and friends, of neighbors and fellow-citizens, of town and city and countryside, of job and work and recreation and leisure, of politics and governance, of nations and religions, of teaching and learning, of the lakes and streams, wetlands and oceans, forests, plains, deserts and biosphere that compose our planet's ecology?

We have to ask it!

Configuring the Future: An Exercise (No. 17)

If the future is the space where the human imagination roams free, and spirit crosses into the implicate order of other realities in order to bring them forth into *this* world, *then what does spirit bring forth?* In this initial piece of *deep imaging,* extend a true invitation, without guile, without pre-meditation, without a hidden agenda.

How to do that? By now, you know the practices. You have already learned to enter kairos and come to the space of spirit. Enter again. In your futures room, time and place have disappeared, as has your social biography. All shall return in due course. But as in *deep listening,* push them aside to let spirit roam free.

What does spirit say…about anything, about everything or nothing? Set before it an empty plate, the tabula rasa of the future where everything is possible—including simple acts of loving and caring that so many of us have lost in the complexities of just surviving.

Years ago, I borrowed from the noted anthropologist and humanist, Margaret Mead, the felicitous phrase: "configure the future." It fits so well the operative question of this exercise: "What is in you about the future?"

---

[10] Anyone who has seen Peter Russel's video, *World Brain,* or read his books knows whereof I speak.

Take the future as a blank page to be filled in by that which is in you at the level of spirit. What colors, what sights and sounds, what hunches and intuitions, what feelings, what tastes and smells?

Sit quietly by the stream of your spirit as it flows through kairos and let your imagination play. Open up and relax the inside tensions. If spirit had its "druthers," how would it fill that empty page? Ask it. But have no expectations about its responses. Leave aside your biographical questions, your work questions, your relationship questions, all other questions. You have come to the space of *deep learning* where spirit learns itself and, because of the trust you have built with it, it lets you watch and wait and listen for its images to emerge.

In our experience with envisioning, what may then emerge into your multiple levels of consciousness in body and mind you cannot know until it happens. Predictions about that are useless. This practice, to which the exercise introduces you, and to which *you will always be able to return in your meditations*, is free-floating, aimless, taskless, and without focus. Dip your toe in the river as if flows by, throw a leaf on the surface of its waters and idly watch it drift out of sight, lie back on the grass by the shore and watch the clouds drifting away to the distant reaches of the universe as even that energy merges into a uniform emptiness which now spirit will configure.

Some of my fellow enspiritors have found the stream by which they sit too inviting. No longer able to stay on its shores, they step into it...or float down it...or swim with it...or find a canoe or a little skiff in which to sit, just dipping into the water occasionally with an oar.

But that is not all. As the stream carries them, they look to the shores, sometimes close by, sometimes receding as the river widens. What is on those shores? Sights and sounds, hustle and bustle, noises and energy and movement of people and things...or a quiet glade where people sit in a circle? All of these and many more images have come to our envisioning participants when they have let their spirit free to configure. Usually, enspiritors can describe what is on the shores *in great detail*, with a reality that overcomes all doubts. And if not immediately, then later on, when they return to the images to discover more concretely what is there in those "theres."

One person told me that all she heard was static; that all she saw were distant flashes of light like the heat lightning on the horizon on a hot summer's night when all else is still and waiting.

Another enspiritor tried too hard and came to a curtain, a fog, blank and gray, hanging there in front of her, which she could not get through or beyond. "Go back to it," I said. "Touch it, press your body up against it, feel its texture, just stay with it until the curtain parts or the fog lifts. When your spirit trusts, that will happen. What lies behind will emerge."

Still another found herself walking up a seemingly endless flight of stairs—no other structures present—until she came to a door that beckoned. She opened it and stepped into the universe.

One fellow, a renowned church planner, senior in the hierarchy and superbly trained in every strategic planning technique invented, came to naught...or so he said. "This exercise is too general and unfocused," he complained.

"So nothing is there?" I asked. "You came to nothing?"

"Well, not exactly," he responded. "Just a sense of floating in the sky, sort of flying fairly high up." He was upset. "Nothing is speaking to me. I don't know what I'm doing or what is happening."

He might have said: *I'm out of control.*

"Have you looked down?" I asked.

He did not understand.

"While flying in the sky...your 'sense' of that...did you look down at the ground?"

He was startled and looked at me quizzically, as if to ask: *What nonsense is this!?*

"Literally," I added. "If you're flying above the earth, look down to see what's there. Describe it. Swoop down to hear, to get close, to see, then come back up. Your spirit is soaring. Let it. Don't fight it. *This is not some sort of mystical experience. Take my words literally, turn them into your invitation. Look. Listen. Feel. Yield to what your spirit does through this imaging. Don't worry. Don't interpret. Just let the images speak to you. When you are ready for it, spirit will.*"

My friend and colleague was neither the first nor the last who had an out-of-body experience through deep imaging. But he denied the validity of his own direct experiencing of his images. He had not emptied, he had not entered kairos, he had been unable to get past his social biography.

Emptying, Waiting, and Yielding: The First Practice

After you have extended an invitation to spirit through asking these questions, *emptying, waiting, and yielding* are the key practices. Any clues about how? Of course. The mode of *deep listening* the *empty vessel way* gives us that clue. Remember the words of Chuang Chou? "The spirit is empty and waits on all things."

Each and every envisioner has told me a different story about this enspiriting discipline. The trick, of course, is to *endiscipline yourself.* Spirit will engage in its soaring or whatever, for nobody knows the *form* it will take to enter into your conscious awareness until it does. Never mind. But if you do not learn *to empty, to wait, and to yield,* it will not come by. It will take your anxiety, your not-letting-go, your task-orientation, your agenda as a sign that you have not bypassed your social biography and entered kairos, where time stands still, place disappears, and spirit alone lives in you and configures its—your—universe.

This initial exercise in *deep imaging* is a great way to come to your spirit *as it has chosen to show itself to you.* So far as I can tell from the reports of envisioners and enspiritors, these deep images show up in an infinite variety of forms and contents. That is not surprising. If you have been successful in bypassing your social biography and stepping outside the house of your culture, emptied and waiting, it would be surprising if your spirit did *not* establish signs of its presence and declare to you its unique character.

This exercise has no "time" limits. Spirit can be invited out through imaging at any time and place where you sense that deep imaging is wanted and you are ready for it. It will put you once again on the right path. This practice of *emptying, waiting, and yielding,* once well-learned, becomes a great solace in moments of stress. Return to your spirit and let it speak. In a community of learners, enspiritors alert each other that the time has come for deep imaging.

Still, spirit is more than a loose canon bashing about in the universe, undisciplined, untamed, unfocused, uncaring, doing its own thing. Its "thing" is lodged in you. *As spirit enters, it enters through, with, and in you—mind, body, feelings, history, internalized culture—even as your social biography is renegotiated. It is not accidental that spirit chose you. Why?*

Spirit now enters your world of being and doing through deep imaging. In the process, your social biography begins its transformation. Many traps await you in the journey outward, in the journey back to your "reality." The next chapter sets forth the practices and grammar of deep imaging, to keep you on a path you and your spirit have chosen.

15

The Practices of Deep Imaging

Imaging Practices and the Grammar of Imaging

Over the years, working with thousands of envisioners in non-directed imaging of the future, I have developed a set of imaging practices and formulated them into a grammar that will help to keep you honest in this piece of enspiriting work. Honesty, here, means two things:

First, that you do not force your images—and therefore your spirit—to conclusions that are not yours but someone else's.

Second, that you do not channel your imaging along a path that leads to a preconceived outcome. In *deep imaging,* you do not know where your images will take you or what is in them until you release them and they enter into your consciousness. Deep imaging always brings surprises. Welcome them. They are a mark of your spirit at work.

Integrity and ownership are essential to deep imaging. It is light years removed from the "image" complex that characterizes the public life of this century. That life, whether in politics, commerce, or the mass media, is dominated by a flood of images that seek to manipulate our KBVAF, our feelings, and our behavior. Though we characterize this century as the "Information Age," in fact most of that information comes to us through images that manipulate and interpret for us the immediacy of our experience about anything: What we should feel about it, what we should think about it, what we should do about it. We might more accurately name this the Century of False Images!

The key to these practices is to acquire competence so that no one controls your imaging process or your mental life. The human imagination is our most powerful capacity for expressing spirit. It far exceeds, I think, the rational powers that are the celebrants of this de-spiritualized age. And like human reason itself, it can be used for bad purposes as well as good. If you learn the grammar, you become at least as literate as the 20th century purveyors of trash, malfeasance, lies and, ultimately, destruction. You become competent in the practices. It is much less likely that anyone, particularly "leaders," backed by their image-making specialists, will be able to manipulate your consciousness of yourself or your world.

A friend, a well-trained and highly regarded professional, goes on regular clothes-buying sprees, throwing out high-quality, attractive and expensive year-old garments and running up a credit-card debt she can ill afford when the images of the new styles come her way. She is, literally, defenseless when it comes to her susceptibility to the well-turned image about her appearance. But so too were the followers of cult leader James Jones. His capacity for offering up images of self-esteem to replace those of self-putdown by which a racist society bolstered its institutionalized practices attracted followers who ultimately paid the price of being imaging-illiterate. Adolf Hitler and his minions orchestrated a panoply of false images so powerful that millions attempted to construct a new world order that was founded on the blood of millions of others. Another friend of mine, a senior entrepreneur whose business activity scans the globe, shares with me how his corporate and banking counterparts are caught in a web of images that celebrate status, power, wealth-accumulation and devil-take-the-hindmost, justifying the abnegation of any public responsibility whatsoever on their part.

How are these comparable? Are they? At their center, despite all of the differences in social biography, historic times, language, or culture, lies this immense imaging capacity. Simply put, *if you are not master in your own house, someone else is.* The grammar of imaging constitutes a set of practical rules that put you in charge. It is a grammar for the exercise of the imagination. It describes an inner landscape that induces a trial-and-error approach to imaging and that emphasizes an inner rehearsal prior to translating the images into action.

An Injunction for Deep Imagers

Start with yourself.

This is not an absolute rule, but focusing on concerns defined by others makes it much more difficult to release your spirit. Once you have become competent, you can place that competence at the service of a group, an organization, or a community. But even in those social settings, you must insist on being master of your own house, and you must offer true images to the group, not false ones.

This injunction is meant for enspiritors, not followers. Enspiritors are those who work together to transform their social settings (be they the immediate family or the world and anything in between) into a community of learners in *dialogue* with each other and committed to *discerning* the focus, the content, and the consequences of their collective *intentioning*. These are the *metadisciplines* of the spirit or, as my colleague Bob Luton calls them, the *community disciplines*.

This injunction lies at the heart of *deep imaging*, indeed at the center of *all* of the disciplines. Its political implications are enormous, for it places in the highest rank the *office of citizen* which then becomes the seat of legislative authority. It is not for the political leader to initiate and resolve political discourse by manipulating images of the state that appeal to an imaging-illiterate population. Rather, the citizen initiates that discourse by applying the enspiriting disciplines to the creation of settings for governance that are founded on dialogue about that which is of concern to the citizen.

The organizational implications may be at least as serious. To embrace the disciplines of the spirit is to end hierarchy. It is to enter into community with other enspiritors, whether that community is economic, social, political, religious, cultural, familial, intimate, or planetary.

What Is the Focus for Deep Imaging?

There are two strong ways to commence the *deep imaging* practices.

1. Exercise No. 17, *Configuring the Future*, is a good start-up focus. If you have already begun, follow those initial images where they take you. Apply the grammatical "rules." Induce the practices. Gradually, the first images will take on the qualities of *weight* (importance to your social biography), *occupancy* (they will tend to inhabit your conscious awareness and will not leave you alone), and *compellingness*. Spirit will shift from flitting about to announcing its readiness to enter into *dialogue* with your social biography about *what it is up to* and *what it calls you to be and to do*. These things happen when you become practiced in deep imaging.

2. That exercise is not the only way to enter this discipline. Equally valid is to use the material you generated in Exercise No. 4 (Chapter Five), *How to Start Deep Questioning*. Go through that exercise again. Gradually, as your responses to the questions unfold, you will come to a focus for deep imaging that is specific, concrete,

owned, important to you and, as you have learned to bypass your social biography, a focus that says something about what is troubling your spirit.

Does Anything Trouble Your Spirit?

Consider some possibilities. These are drawn from the ranks of enspiritors with whom I have worked. I couch them in general terms so that if one or more of them sparks your own *deep questioning*, it will not contaminate your enspiriting inquiry.

It might be that what is troubling your spirit is that it is simply unwelcome in your life or in the world. What is troubling your spirit might be a restrictive social biography that denies you your due in the world, that places self-imposed limits on your capacities and dispositions. What troubles your spirit might be its denigration in your relevant social setting of family, community, or organization, and the resulting inequities and injustices that prevail. What troubles your spirit might be intimate relationships that are false, co-dependent, denigrating or some such. What troubles your spirit might have to do with the quality of your action—or lack thereof—in your school, church, business, profession, or neighborhood, i.e., *where* you seek to do and become with other people, friends, professionals, colleagues, or fellow citizens. What troubles your spirit might have to do with the planet itself, and with all of those systems we have invented to endanger its future.

There is no concern that has not been the focus for *deep imaging*. None is too small and intimate, none is too large and public. None is politically, organizationally, socially, or culturally correct or incorrect. *Don't let anyone define your focus for you!* But in *dialogue*, through *deep listening* and deep questioning, *do* invite your fellow enspiritors to help you clarify your focus.

These two start-up exercises merge. Fly back and forth between them until you are truly on the river of deep imaging, until you are truly swimming in the stream of your spirit. As it takes you to the new spaces where spirit is adventuresome, commence the endisciplining practices—the application of these grammatical rules—that bring spirit into *its own action* in yourself-in-the-world and ourselves-in-the-world.

The Practices and the Grammar

These are of two kinds: *A grammar of validation*—four practices—that helps you in *discerning* true from false images; and *a grammar of process*—five practices—that helps in generating the images themselves. In the reality of *deep imaging*, the two intertwine. As you become competent in one, you become competent in both. Their application is synergistic as they comprise a whole that is the discipline. As you put them to work, *spirit begins self-taming under your tutelage which it will accept because through deep learning, you have bypassed those aspects of your social biography that have confined spirit . . . and so it has come to trust you. You mean it no harm.*

A Grammar of Validation

There are four rules whose purpose is to help in *discerning* true from false images. The first one has already been introduced.

Rule No. 1—*In deep imaging, always be specific and concrete.*

This means that in *deep imaging* you continually strive for specificity and concreteness in your images of the future. Images are not generalizations, theories, or abstractions. They are "of flesh and blood," to be seen, felt, tasted, heard, touched, smelled, in a word, *lived.* Though they emanate from deep within ourselves, they become palpable as they enter into our conscious awareness.

Do you see how the rule applies? Review the examples in Chapter Fourteen. Can you feel, touch, see, hear, taste, smell these images? What about the images that have begun to enter into your conscious awareness in Exercise No. 17, *Configuring the Future*? Have any of them yet achieved the qualities of specificity and concreteness? Do not force that. Always invite it by re-imaging (see Rule No. 3, below).

Rule No. 2—*Don't interpret your image. Let it speak to you in its own language.*

This means that an image conveys its meaning *in the content of the image.* If that content is ambiguous, foggy, or multi-faceted so that its meaning is not transparent, then query the image through imaging, moving deeper and deeper into its sources. Do more imaging. You're not finished yet.

Unfortunately, in the application of popular psychology to our dreamworld and to our fantasy life, interpretation has become a bit of a parlor game. The discerning of meaning is an extraordinarily complex practice which is treated in half a dozen disciplines: depth psychology, mythology, anthropology, psycho- and sociolinguistics, theology, and philosophy. But even well-trained practitioners of those disciplines are usually not grounded in the practices and discipline of deep imaging by which spirit is invited to make its impact in the world.

To help explain the primacy of this second rule, an analogy may be helpful. Consider the matter of *feelings.* When pressed by a feeling—of anger, hostility, pain, affection, joy—we often ask ourselves or are asked by another: What does that feeling mean? What is its source? Why this feeling? Those questions lead to others: How are you going to deal with that feeling? What are its effects on other persons? What are you trying to say?

That intellectual approach (i.e., about explanation) attempts to extract meanings from your feelings on the premise that *by themselves, your feelings lack some kind of substance or legitimacy,* a deficit which can be made up by removing yourself from experiencing them so that they can be analyzed.

But there is a powerful prior question: *How do you feel about your feelings?* In other words, address your feelings *in the language of feelings.*

The language of feelings, like the language of the body, is largely underdeveloped or neglected by most of us in the West. We are the products of a culture whose *lingua franca* are cognitive realities, not feeling or body realities. *So too in the language of imaging.* Let us first query our images before we try to interpret them or transfer them to some other ground of intelligibility. *Invite them to speak to us in their language.*

Here too, the practice becomes obvious and crucial. As the deep images begin to emerge, don't interpret them according to this or that perspective. Rather, *invite the images themselves to say more, i.e., do more imaging.* In deep imaging, let them speak in *their* language, not some one else's.

How can you invite that?

Rule No. 3—*When in doubt about your image, return to it, query it, and let it speak to you in its own language... that of images.*

This follows directly from Rule No. 2, but it has a wider application. Any doubts or questions about the meaning, validity, source, or implications of a deep image must be addressed by more imaging.

What if the initial images disappear? Sometimes they do. Such ephemeral images represent accidents of your spirit's history, its own trial-and-error, its own flitting about like a butterfly or hummingbird, seeking a sweet center where it can light and stay a while. Or they may have entered into your body, to rest and perhaps return later on. Do not force the issue. In their time, true images will emerge into conscious awareness when your social biography is ready to accept them and when your spirit is ready to speak them.

Vague and incomplete images need re-processing. Imaging has its own language for which I have always sought to build a grammar. When untutored in or not yet a master of that language, what is the *learning* practice? Is it not to practice a new language—of *deep imaging,* for example—*in that language* and not in some other. The old Berlitz immersion method! One doesn't learn the art and discipline of piano playing on the basketball court. So too with deep imaging. As you learn to return to your images and invite them to say more through additional or modified images, earlier doubts and questions are often resolved.

But not all the time. None of these "rules" is final, for all time. Deep question them in the actual experience of imaging. So have I extracted from the imaging experience another practice in the grammar of validation that may serve that purpose.

Rule No. 4—*Move into the image's space and live it.*

In the envisioning approach to the future, the methods call for envisioners to live in the future of that image. I call that the *future-present moment* when that image of the future comes to life in our imagination and takes on its own reality as compelling as any other.[11] But of course, this "test" applies to any deep image. Living a deep image provides for its inner testing out and rehearsal. To live it fully is to participate in that image with all your senses, as you participate in life through the direct experiencing of it: To feel it, hear it, see it, taste it, smell it, even act it out in your body. As a deep image, it gradually but inexorably takes on more of these attributes of life. At some point, *living the image compels you to transfer this inner reality in the life of the imaginal to an outer reality in the life of ourselves-in-the-world.*

On Validation: Its Indicators

The aim, here, is to validate these images as truly representative of your spirit's action. The validating act *is undertaken by spirit itself in dialogue with your social biography.* It is not yet a validation outside through external action in the world. At any point, spirit may halt its deep imaging. Only when it feels safe, or in a final extremity, desperately seeks for expression, will it resume. If your *deep learning* has borne fruit, your social biography is ready to accept spirit's venturing forth into your conscious awareness and into yourself-in-the-world. In turn, these four practices, by interweaving social biography with spirit, create a new dance in which both are partners, seeking a step that works.

Can either reject the other? Of course. When that happens, begin again. *Deep listen and deep question.* These too are disciplines of the spirit. They will not lead you astray in re-opening the space for deep learning and *deep imaging.*

The indicators for validation are simply these: *The deep images keep returning, replenishing, changing, perhaps, but at the core remain essentially the same.* As these four rules are applied and the practices undertaken, spirit's deep and true images respond in increasingly imaginative ways. That response, however, can be curtailed,

---

[11] I learned the phrase, "future-present moment," from Stuart Sandow, a colleague at the Syracuse Educational Policy Research Center in the early 1970s.

even obliterated, unless you also practice the *grammar of process*. Spirit's expressing itself through deep imaging is fragile. The dream can be killed. Many institutions and even some of your past social biography did that with success. Hence, I have always sought to encourage the imager to continue at the discipline and acquire its competence through reminding him of the following practices that I have called *the process*.

A Grammar of Process

The next five rules describe more directly the process for *deep imaging*. They guarantee nothing! *Process* refers to the language of deep imaging, *the way we learn to speak it*, not to the content of the images. The actual learning occurs in the act itself. The four plus five "rules" interact; and in the next chapter, a major exercise in deep imaging will invite you to apply and bring the grammars of process as well as validation to life.

Rule No. 5—*Empty, wait, and yield to your images. Let them flow.*

This practice is basic and essential. It can be learned but not taught. *You learn to yield through your own ministrations.* You began to practice it in Exercise No. 17.

Emptying and *waiting* are the experience of *deep listening* applied to your inner life. As the images start to arrive, do not interrupt the process. *Yielding* is a letting go of conscious restrictions, of social biography, of time and place, of the censoring apparatus inherent in your KBVAF. *Yielding* is an act of entering kairos. It produces an altered state of consciousness, not one induced by drugs but by your neurological-chemical system working to create this inner space, or more precisely, to allow it to live and flourish.

Letting your images flow refers to the way in which one image begets another. The sequence is often rapid. Interfaces between the images disappear. Each image floats on a river of movement from one to the next. As you become literate in these practices, you may learn to halt the process, capture an image, then move back into the flow as if there were no interruption.

Rule No. 6—*Do not force your images.*

This rule is lifted out of the unique characteristic of *deep imaging*; that the activity is *focused* rather than random, *deliberately undertaken* rather than spontaneous. Deep imaging is occasioned by an act of *intentioning*. You must want to do it. But you must *let it happen.* How to combine these two opposite injunctions?

Ask deep questions of your spirit. It responds in images. Yield to them, do not censor them. You have nothing to prove, only to *wait, empty, yield.*

Suppose the images don't come. Do you try harder? *NO!* Back off. Go play a game of volleyball, make love, cook dinner, take a walk. If you try harder, you will be forcing the wrong key into a lock. Eventually, the key bends or breaks. Better to withdraw and find a new key…or a new lock.

Your imaging capacity finds its sources in your multiple levels of consciousness. You cannot force imaging to take you places spirit does not choose to go. You may present a deep question, a focus of concern. You invite. You center and relax. You yield. Then, imaging takes command. As the deep imaging proceeds apace, you yield to your spirit. Now, it speaks.

In a sound practice of this discipline, the competent imager simply does not know what content will emerge into her conscious awareness until it does. Be prepared for surprises. Forcing your spirit to a focus it neither generates nor accepts defies the process. As a consequence, imaging usually ceases. You draw a blank. Emptiness or fog is generated rather than a rich flow. But if you let your images flow in response to a true question, to a deep concern, to that which is within and of you, eventually that river will turn in the direction you have previously indicated by your deep question.

Rule No. 7—*Always be prepared for new images.*

Imaging is not unlike an ever-replenishing well. It never runs dry. When invited, always another image appears. Thus, the rule reads like a Taoist text.

Whenever you continue the process and return to your images, new ones may well emerge into your conscious awareness. They may modify or alter previous ones. They may take you in new directions. Even at the point of *deep listening* for the *compelling image* (see Chapter Seventeen on Intentioning), a new image may well appear. Let it. Discover where it will take you. The life of the imaginal is richer, more dense (multi-layered), more dynamic that any other domain of human experiencing because through spirit it taps into the implacate order of alternative realities where all things are possible. We encapsulate it by placing it in categories of intelligibility and extract from it some rules and practices we call a grammar. But do not think that you can capture, reduce, or control your spirit. You can *endiscipline* it along with your social biography, which means no more than to *invite it to a discipline that hones its expression to a fine cutting edge of action in this world through you.* Indeed, the master imager knows when to leave spirit alone, when to go about the business of daily living, and when to stop imaging. She also knows when to engage the clutch that connects the processes of *deep imaging* with conscious awareness so that spirit might refresh and replenish old images with new ones.

Rule No. 8—*Shift one or more components in your image and see what happens.*

This rule is tricky and hard to apply. Nevertheless, it belongs in the practices of the discipline because we have learned, over the years, that images are often complex. The image is a *composite* image containing many elements. Each of these elements, of course, contains the entire image because of its holographic qualities. But each component is also *partial* in the larger context. An image of yourself-in-the-world, for example, may involve a host of sub-images of your KBVAF, your qualities and capacities, your various actions in your various action-settings. Deep imagers find it useful to shift or change one of these factors or sub-images as they continue to image. Why?

Imaging involves discovery. *Deep imaging* is discovery. Deliberately shifting elements of a composite image opens new vistas. When I first traveled to another country to live and work, I was convinced I would discover or fashion a "new me." I would leave the "old me" behind, perhaps forever. (A standard way of unpeeling, by the way.) And to be sure, new vistas did open up for me as the new experiences driven by a culture foreign to my KBVAF taught me things about myself and my spirit I had either never known or had hidden away. Great. *But the core remained.* When I returned home, after having been away for more than a year, the core of the "old me" was there: *Not my social biography. My spirit.*

When you evoke this practice, have no expectations. As always, surprises may be lurking around the corner of the shift. Sometimes you will be led down dwindling paths into a swamp from which nothing pristine can be drawn. Sometimes that shift will provoke new images which get closer to the mark and you can "feel it in your bones."

Rule No. 9—*Don't censor your images.*

This grammatical rule is as close to a process imperative as we have discovered. In Chapter Four (*How Do I Know When I'm Deep Questioning?*) I discussed it at length. So it will be familiar, though particularly difficult to apply. First-time imagers, no matter what we say or do, almost always do the opposite. It is the *non-judgmental* mode of *deep listening* applied to your own deep imaging.

Withhold plausibility and preference judgments about your images. Don't censor them.

One learning many of us have borrowed from depth psychology is the prevalence and the power of the censoring activity in the human psyche. Internalizing the rules, customs, conventions, and beliefs of one's society and sub-groups creates an internal mental culture—what I have called the KBVAF—that is quite determined and skilled in permitting some images to see the light of day and others not to.

Is this censoring activity inevitable? Not at all. The antidote is the kind of inner work described in this book, inner work that engages with your spirit, inner work of which *deep imaging* is one central discipline. When you catch yourself censoring your images, cease and desist.

Keep in mind two kinds of censorship that parallel the distinction between *inner action* and its action-space, and *outer action* and its action-setting. (That distinction is crucial to understanding the discipline of *intentioning*.)

One kind involves self-censorship. In this kind, you do not permit the images to enter into your conscious awareness. If they do, even if you only can glimpse them, you hurriedly cast them out, suppress them, do not pursue them, do not allow them to show their content. Thus, you abort the image before you have given it full play. You have not yet opened up your inner action space and pierced through the limits of your social biography. *Re-engage with deep learning.*

The second kind involves public censorship. Here, you will not share the image with your colleagues even though you have overcome self-censorship. In effect, you have internalized supposedly negative judgments from your partners before you have even shared with them.

Our planet and ourselves-in-the-world are in such desperate need of invention in so many of our institutional and interpersonal settings. To deprive our colleagues within the community of learners of the initial fruits of our creative and critical imagination is to doom us to a future so constrained by the cultures and the habits of the past that hope is lost and complacency and worse, despair, reign supreme.

But that is the old story. By now, you have reached the point in this great enspiriting adventure when you are ready to put together spirit's story, the story it has been hinting at throughout all of the enspiriting practices, not only in its deep images. Now is the time for you to tell that story. You have passed "Go" and collected all of the spirit-energy you may need. The next move is yours. Go to the next chapter where the invitation awaits you.

16

Story, Spirit and Voice:
An Exercise in Deep Imaging

Finding Your Voice

Spirit lives through the voice of the imagination. What does this voice sound like? Where does it come from? Whose voice is it? When we speak the phrase, "Finding your voice," or say of a person, "She found her voice," are we talking about the same thing as imagination being the voice of spirit? I think so. Since time immemorial, these questions have generated at least as many answers as the questioners. Great story-tellers, dramatists, poets, mystics, and shamans have answered. So have we all. Each and every human being seeks to find that voice which is uniquely hers because it is the voice of her spirit. Most are thwarted. Over the lifespan of our species, with its infinitely rich variations for teasing out and celebrating spirit, seldom has its voice in us been so subdued as during the last few generations. Despite the noble quest of science, the artful craft of technology, and the piercing light of human reason—the "Age of Enlightenment"—promising civility in human relations to replace the atrocious inequities of past history, we are witness to social conduct as aberrant, defamatory and destructive—perhaps more so—as any ever seen on our planet. And no skyscrapers, no Chunnels, no Mach-1-plus jets, no antibiotics, no high-tech jogging shoes, no potable water systems and populations adding 90 million babies a year to our out-of-control human ecology, no NATOs nor ECAs, no gangs of urban youth nor Third World terrorists seeking their place in the sun can fill a world empty of spirit.

If you have done this enspiriting work, you can no longer subscribe to a prevailing KBVAF of hopelessness married to addiction: That in a world composed of large, dominating "forces" and implacable institutions, swept by the tides of history and battered by random events that can snuff out a life or win a lottery, your spirit is too puny to count, its voice so subdued that your life masquerades as a piece of flotsam floating on a sea of not-mattering.

How to recover spirit's voice, and let it speak out once again is the essence of *deep imaging*. Throughout this book, I have given you examples of people in the act of making that discovery. Each is unique. The disciplines that you have learned so far, the practices that you have already undertaken have sought to carry you to the space where spirit speaks. *Now you are there, ready to release that voice.* Of what will it speak? In deep imaging, it will unearth the elements of *your story*, of *your project* in this world, of *who you are* and *what you're up to.* Spirit will speak, not to overwhelm you but to enter into a new partnership with the rest of your biography, indeed with the rest of future history that is by its very nature transformative, *bringing into existence in this "reality" that which has not been, is not now, but will be.* In short, the moment to tell spirit's story through your story is now. Bring it out of hiding and into the world for all to acknowledge. *Now is the time to find your voice—again or for the first time.*

For Whom Is This Story?

I raise this question before you begin the *deep imaging* and telling because, though you will not be the only listener, *you are the first listener.* To misunderstand this is to confuse spirit and even drive it back into hiding. In the practices of deep imaging, it speaks first to you and then, through your voice, to others.

This is what it amounts to. *First,* you will speak and deep listen to the story by and with yourself. That internal communication is the initial setting for deep imaging, a setting no different from that for dreaming, fantasizing, or musing.

As your imagination creates the story, your social biography will listen to spirit; *but it will not subdue, censor, pre-select, or seek to control in any way the images that build the story.* This injunction means, literally, that in the exercise that follows (No. 18, *Story, Voice and Spirit*), *you are both the narrator and the audience.*

For how long? Just as long as it takes for your social biography to cease its fright and let spirit speak, test out, and rehearse *in you*—not in someone else—its new life.

If you have unpeeled and unfrozen well, this might be a very short time indeed, an instant in kairos.

Second, you will speak the story—at least different pieces of it—to and with those who have, like you, learned and are practicing the disciplines of *deep listening* and *deep questioning.* At first, this will probably be a small audience, perhaps only one or a few persons in your community of learners. Seek out those who are by now prepared for being silence, for being an empathic and nurturing presence, for clarifying through non-judgmental questions. Are they not empty vessels into which you can pour the story so you too can hear it? In dialogue with them, your story is honed to a sharp, cutting edge so that its presence in the world can not be ignored.

Third, after this trial-and-error clarification and rehearsal, *the spirit in you seeks to speak out to whomever else is prepared to listen and respond.* Who is that? I call them "The public of the dialogue," the new communities of learners that are forming even as these very words are written. Someday, millions may comprise these interacting publics of the dialogue. One of my colleagues, Maire Dugan, when a graduate student at Syracuse University, came to just such an image 20 years ago: An image of a *communitas* of 5,000 to 50,000 souls dialogically linked to thousands of others, then technically very difficult but now a cup of tea literally made possible by the electronic superhighway. I can just hear the spirit of the great futurist, Betrand de Jouvenel, asking of his "surmising forum": "Do you surmise that we humans might yet learn to use these highways for other than the management of our fiscal, military, insurance, banking, manufacturing and consumer concerns?"[12] Someday, these publics of the dialogue will have multiplied. The story you are about to tell will be received throughout the planet. For now, a small group in your relevant action-setting must do.

The Dance of Spirit and Biography

In the narrative that first results from your *deep imaging,* in this first instance of its telling when you are both speaker and listener, bring into play all of the art of *deep listening* and *deep questioning* you can. Your spirit is free at last. Your biography is shorn of its spirit-repressing history. They can share the stage as dramatist and actor, as song and singer, as music and dancer, as bridge-builder and bridge. Inevitably, the deep images begin to focus on yourself-in-the-world—who am *I,* what am *I* up to? —and ourselves-in-the-world—who are *we,* what are *we* up to? The story moves back and forth between spirit and biography until a new you, a new self, a new actor-in-history is born. Wanted here are the nurturing skills of mid-wifery, not the

---

[12] One group of 23 serious futures-inventors from the Ministry of Advanced Education and Career Development in Alberta, Canada, recently gave a powerful and imaginative "yes" to that question. Write John Fisher (Devonian Building, 11160 Jasper Avenue, Edmonton, Alberta, Canada T5K 0L6) for a copy of the report on how the electronic superhighway might be used to empower learners by putting them in charge of their own learning.

aborting skills of persons driven by their histories and their cultures to nay-say that which emerges. You are about to tell a good story, one full of beauty, joy, hope, adventure, courage, risk and transformation. Who is to judge, if not you?

The dance is beginning. The partners—spirit and biography—are trying out new steps. No formal performance is yet offered—that, much later—so use all you have learned to test out and rehearse: Your body, your feelings, your questive reason, above all, your imagination.

The exercise that follows gives you a minimal framework for deep imaging. It does so by raising half-a-dozen questions of a special kind. They are designed—from experience—to help you move the narrative along—the deep imaging—in an honest way. They are not questions that give you the *content* of your images, for that is your spirit's expression and your biography's response. They are *modal* or *heuristic* questions that lead you from one part of your narrative to another, that remind you about *theme, setting, characters, plot,* that help you to build the story of your spirit and listen to its voice. In the grammar of imaging, you already possess all of the "tools," the "craft" of the storyteller's art.

Voice, Spirit and Story (Exercise No. 18): The Form of Its Expression

As this is storytelling time, let us give some initial attention to the form of its expression. Tell it first to yourself, I said; but what does that mean in practice? It means one or all of several things.

Write your story down after its images come to you so that you don't lose them. Once started, they may come fast and furious. Some take notes. Others draw pictures, jot down words, symbols, or diagrams. Whatever suits you so that you can recall the fast-flowing images. Speak it to yourself, yes, and out loud if you will, in strong and loving self-talk.

If you need a little physical space for this, close the door to your room, take a walk—my wife goes for a drive—stride among the trees or gambol beside a stream, sit on a mountainside or take a bike ride. You will be alone with your spirit, and so can literally try out *its voice in your own.* No other hears but God; and She will not interfere, for She is the one in whom *deep listening* resides. The male version is judgmental, full of sound and fury as befits the *Yawehs* of the universe. But She rocks you in Her arms as Her child as, once again, spirit is born into this world.

But speak it out loud? Do you remember Ray Bradbury's *Fahrenheit 451*? At the end, the people walked amidst the trees, each talking out loud to remember and to keep alive a piece of literature against the desolation of the book-burning time: A work of philosophy, a play, a poem, a Declaration of Independence, what have you. All were stories about how the world worked or might be made to work, be it a *Romeo and Gallate*, a *Tao Te Ching*, *The Revolt of the Masses*, or a *Little Orphan Annie*. Those talkers were neither ashamed nor embarrassed. Place yourself among them. Talk your story to yourself.

Perhaps, in your private space, you'll act it out a bit. Try a little song, a humming, or a few dance steps, shuffles, or gestures as the story begins to move within in. Remember the child in you: "I'm not *like* a lion, Mom. *I am a lion!*"

Voice, Spirit and Story: Parts and Duration

Like all stories that are of a piece, a whole that fits itself, this one has parts that eventually will merge. Each part contains the entire. Each part is a starting point. Feel free to move back and forth among them, exploring one, building another until the story sings all of its parts as one.

Does this take a long time? In kairos, an instant and forever. Can you believe that in workshop time, I have watched enspiritors begin it in 20 or 30 minutes and complete it by day's end? But they were prepared. If you have walked a true journey to this point, the enspiriting story is waiting to be told. Still, it may take a lifetime to complete.

Here are the questions, the elements. Read through them all. See where you will begin.

Voice, Spirit and Story: What Is This Story About?

Every story has a theme. What is the theme in your story? What is it about? Of course, it is about your spirit. But spirit has already spoken to you in many ways about many things. Here are some ways to discern, to sort out the sub-stories, to discover a theme or *the* theme.

1. *What troubles your spirit?* This is a good start-up question if you are discovering that your spirit is troubled. Refer back to your work in *deep questioning*. Did you get a sense of that, perhaps even a lock on it, in Exercise No. 4, *How to Start the Deep Questioning?*

There is a "technical" problem in addressing this first question: to distinguish what troubles your spirit from what troubles your biography. There are some things that bother me or are the unmet target of my energy that have nothing to do with my spirit. They may be good starting points for counseling... not for enspiriting. This has to be discerned.

For example, when I become worried about not completing a task on time, or about my children's health, or about a long trip committed to but not yet planned, I tend to overeat. Maybe I should, maybe I shouldn't. Perhaps it's a habit I can do without. But... is it my spirit speaking out?

On the other hand, when all of my relationships end up flat and unfulfilling, I might query my spirit: "What's going on here?" (But not: "What's wrong with me?") *Enspiriting assumes nothing.* Rather, deep listen, deep question, deep learn.

Go back through your inner work, to the concerns, the dissatisfactions, the pain, the dissonances and the imbalances. In that inner dialogue, did spirit say its say to you, and have you now got that focus? Perhaps this is a good place to start your *deep imaging* and to discover a theme. If so, you should be able to name it and describe it.

2. *Configuring the Future* (Exercise No. 17) may be another good starting point. Has your spirit already sounded its first notes in that exercise; if not the whole theme, perhaps its starting notes? Did your spirit, when invited to deep imaging, begin to fill the tabula rasa of the future with an image or with bits and pieces pulled by your spirit across the bridge that joins the implicate order of things to your here-and-now reality? Might you not follow these images out a bit further, seeing what else your spirit has pulled in from the imaginal domain? Look through the imaging practices in the previous chapter. Do one or two of them suggest how you could flesh out those start-up images? Might not there be lurking among them the theme, the voice of your spirit? But don't "interpret"—Rule No. 2—don't "force"— Rule No. 6—"empty, wait, and yield"—Rule No. 5—and "return to the image"— Rule No. 3. Do you understand how these practices may help you to discover the theme in this story? Here's still another way to begin, if the *theme* approach appeals to you.

3. *To what do you aspire?* Behind this question lies a deeper one: *To what does your spirit aspire?* Perhaps you have been aware of that question, even the distinction, for many years, perhaps all your life. It may be an ambition not even expressed to family and friends or in career. In that might lie the kernel of a long-sought dream that now needs announcing, first to yourself through building its story, later to others.

This question could well unfold the theme of your story. In the various exercises for *deep learning*, as restrictions, constraints, dissonances, imbalances were unpeeled and unfrozen, did something in your social biography shine through—perhaps only a faint spark or inkling—*that is your spirit seeking its destiny... the stories that you still believe, the stories that your spirit still likes, that remain after the unpeeling and the unfreezing?*

Be careful on this one. Discerning aspiration is *not* goal-setting. Spirit does not set goals. That is an activity peculiar to the Western ways of work, cultures, and need to impose cognitive structures on a civilization gone awry, out-of-control, and de-spirited. *You do not have to be a high achiever to enspirit. To the contrary, it may well get in the way and involve a heavy piece of unlearning to arrive at that space where your biography will let your spirit speak that to which it aspires.* There is an increasing number of stories about successful managers and high achievers who, in their middle years, learn to listen to their spirit and begin new, less remunerative and "low status" work that is extraordinarily fulfilling.

Sometimes, the aspiration is already voiced. Now, in this story that is aborning, spirit and biography will work together to orchestrate that tune. If so, perhaps you can now name it. It might be the theme, what your life will be about when spirit has infiltrated.

4. *Enspiriting as empowering.* Does this announce your theme? Do you remember those two exercises: No. 6—*Self-Empowering Learning,* and No. 10—*My Spirit Speaks Out? What were these about…the content?* Do some deep questioning here. I have found that these two exercises often lie at the surface of a personal ethos more lasting, more profound, more satisfying, and that may be the key to unlocking the theme of your spirit. As you recall instances of self-empowering learning and as you re-live occasions when your spirit spoke out, do listen deeply for clues that may put you on the path of your spirit's quest. I do not believe that these experiences are ever accidental though on the surface they may appear random and even be completely outside of our control. *When spirit speaks—when it barely whispers—it is never by accident.*

Some years ago I conducted workshops in Memphis on self-empowerment and the second-half-of-your-life in concert with May Maury Harding, the great futurist, one of the very few who has truly understood that *the future is a matter of learning your way into it,* not forecasting or predicting it. My lens was still clouded, so I only intuited that we were up to enspiriting work. Even then, however, I knew that self-empowerment—there is no other kind—meant *being in charge of yourself within a community of other persons who were in charge of themselves.* It did not mean having power over other persons, including having power over the conditions in which they could seek their own self-empowerment. One of the participants was the chief operating officer of a manufacturing plant, quite successful and effective in his work, doing all the things that his action-setting required of him to perform well in that traditional work organization. His career had taken that tack...*but not his spirit.* He was not in charge of himself. The workplace demanded "executive" and "leadership" behavior at which he was quite effective but which was not his voice. Finally, he came to realize that no matter how successful he might be in pursuing the executive career to the top of the multifaceted corporation within which he was a senior operating official, he would never be in charge of himself. OK. *But his spirit demanded it. It would not let go. It fought with his social biography. It challenged many aspects of his KBVAF. It even roamed through his body, creating the tensions, closing down the inner spaces, until he had a heart attack.*

Is this an old story? You bet. It is a story of hundreds of thousands of people who are what David Riessman years ago called "outer-directed" as distinguished from "inner-directed." That's another name for *enspirited.* This fellow quit the work of his so-called career. He began, close to middle-age, to work for himself in a line that put him on a path of *enabling, counseling, and facilitating others to meet certain needs rather than directing them to achieve "goals" they had never set for themselves.*

Remember that each person's story is different, and that *the most disempowering thing is to copy another's or to place yourself in a "sociological" category of the discontented, the frustrated, the co-dependent, or what have you.* If enspiriting as self-empowerment leads you to an initial response and set of images about the voice of your spirit, let that voice take you where it will through deep imaging, not through self-fulfilling prophecy.

Some Cautionary Notes

I want to say that every exercise in this book—and many more besides—may point to what the story is about when spirit finds its voice and speaks through you. You are learning to integrate spirit into a whole that is the new you. Return to them all, to your notes or pictures, to your clarifying discourse with others in your community of learners, to your memories of experiencing those exercises. The story may be lying there, waiting to be named.

Another caution: The theme may not emerge clearly at first. Don't worry. The sub-themes in my life and work often became clear only after they had been enacted. My whole life is the story of my spirit fighting through my historic biography to find its voice, declare itself without regard to the consequences for my KBVAF. In that struggle, weaknesses in my social biography have won out at least as often as its virtues. My courage has waxed and waned, a new moon sometimes slipping over so fast to its shadow that I have missed the full moon, have lost what that was all about. But then my community of learners, through *deep questioning*, remind me; and when they deep listen, I hear the inner voice once again say, *after the story has already been lived:* "So *that* is what that was about!"

You can return to *discerning* the theme whenever you want to.

The first question, then, is: "What is this story about?"

Is there another question? Of course.

What would it be like if you lived your story in your imagination, gave it the strength of your inner reality, enacted it in every way, in every sphere, in every domain, in every setting *except the exterior world that we call "the real world"*?

Voice, Spirit and Story: What Would It Be Like If ...?

This is the "fleshing-out" question, the one through which you build the body of your story. To answer it invites *deep imaging* Your responses to the question, as they unfold in the proliferation of images of *what it would be like if...* begin the transformation which, as you may by now realize, is the translation of spirit into flesh.

But the *form* of the response is quite easy, one to which you are probably well accustomed. Consider: You decide to take a vacation... a drive to Seattle. But you haven't made the decision. You haven't taken the drive. A prior question looms: *What would it be like if we took a vacation to Seattle? What would it be like if I changed careers from cutting hair to owning my own salon? What would it be like if I lost 50 pounds and could wear a size 8 again? What would it be like to be married to that woman? What would it be like if we had a healthcare system in which everybody was in charge of (empowered and competent) their own wellness and had access to appropriate services when they weren't? What would it be like if we had no guns, no youth violence, no drugs, no gangs, no unemployment among teenagers? What would it be like if the earnings disparity between CEOs and workers was in the range of ten-to-one rather than one hundred-to-one? What would it be like if...?*

There are as many *"what would it be like if"* questions as there are people. In this piece of inner work, you are invited to find your question and deep image your responses. The story is still yours, as narrator and listener. The exact form of the question, however, is determined according to the emerging theme of your story.

Consider these forms:

1. *"What would it be like if my concerns, that which troubles my spirit, were well addressed? What would be different, what would be the same?"* Describe that. Be specific and concrete. No theorizing. Live that situation in which your concern, your dissatis-

faction, your inner tension, imbalance, or pain are well addressed. *What is that like?* Can you see yourself—and others—doing and being that? Can you hear them and yourself...taste...smell...touch...feel...see, etc.? Those bring your deep imaging to its life in the imaginal. Live it. Be there!

2. *"What would it be like if a reality were reconstructed based on the deep images that came to me when I sought to reconfigure the future?"* (Exercise No. 17). Let these images come to life and live in you. Move into the time and place of a reconfigured future and discover what is there. Explore the landscape of that reality, its organizations, institutions, behaviors, values, people...*including yourself. For if you are not in that reality, where is your spirit?* What would it be like to live there, be there, work there, have a family there, go to the movies there, go bowling there? What would you read in the newspaper, see on TV, learn on the radio? How would we govern ourselves, make and consume things, treat our environment, fill our gas tanks, whatever? There are a million questions. Deep imaging responds to those that strike your fancy. This is not a sociological analysis of the future. Questions and images that "strike your fancy" are more likely to be questions and images from your spirit than those that you force...*for you own them. They are yours.*

3. *"What would it be like if my aspirations, my spirit's quest, were met?"* Straight out. You've done it. You're living in a reality in which these aspirations have been actualized. Spirit lives and is well in this world. What is that like? What would you be and do? What would others be and do: family members, colleagues, friends, strangers, etc.? What of the groups, the action-settings, the society within which you would live out these aspirations? Do you see anything new, anything different? What? Let your imaging take you there. Look around. Listen. Smell the roses. Laugh a little and see who responds to this new person in whom spirit lives.

4. *"What would it be like if my experiencing enspiriting as empowering were multiplied to a much wider range of experiencing, if it became my modus operandi, my way of life and work and thus infused spirit into who I am and what I do in this world?"* What if you felt empowered in everything you are? How would you know that? What would you look for? What would be the consequences? Again: Live that new reality in your imagination with all of the specificity and concreteness you can muster. This is not a theoretical or abstract undertaking. Deep imaging follows exactly the same mechanisms of the imagination that you rediscovered in imaging your visit to the dentist, to the grocery story, in making a delightful meal of the leftovers.

Voice, Spirit and Story: How to Respond to These Questions?

You already have the ways, the practices. They are deep *imaging*. Let your spirit speak out, placing its voice in a new reality you have begun to create; a reality still within, but not yet without.

Keep in mind that the focus is yours, not someone else's. By now, you may have entered into the sharing and clarifying *dialogue* within your community of learners; but only if your partner is prepared and competent to deep listen and deep question and *will not impose her concern, her troubled spirit, her aspirations, her mode of empowerment on you.*

The best way to ensure that the listener will be an empty vessel is for her to be silence, the first mode of *deep listening*. Later, she may be empathic, nurturing, non-judgmental. But as your story unfolds, it will often be fragile. Being silence allows your spirit's voice to be unmolested by another's.

And what of the focus? A big thing or a small, it doesn't matter as long as you are at the center of the story. This is *your* story that is unfolding, about who you have become and what you are up to as spirit voices its themes, its aspirations, its capacities as these move through and into your social biography. Your KBVAF changes. Dissonances and imbalances—those you have unearthed—smooth out or disappear.

In this journey of your spirit through the pathways of your imagination, the "dynamic" of the story comes to life, the "creative conflict" that is crucial to the story's viability. It is that part in the narrative when KBVAF must once again be confronted. KBVAF, as you remember, is the linchpin of your social biography. It holds tightly together yourself-in-the-world, the stories of yourself you have come to believe, and ourselves-in-the-world, the stories about how the world works that we have internalized to form a bastion of legitimacy within which our self-stories live and survive. You are creating a new story through deep imaging, a story in which the clues, the hints, the images of who you are and what you are up to begin to come to life as *spirit's voice in your imagination calls them out into conscious awareness.*

A Summary

The story your spirit is telling is almost complete. You have not only been *imaging* it, you have also been *deep listening* to it as your spirit's voice speaks in your imagination. Summarizing the processes and the elements may help you to stand apart from it for a moment to reflect on what is within your grasp.

• *The Theme of the Story.* What is the story about? I have suggested four areas in which your deep imaging might find its focus, four arenas for spirit's voice to take center stage. They are suggestive. Perhaps, as you review the story, you will discover a rich mix among them. They are:

1. That which troubles your spirit.

2. A future configured by deep images borrowed from the implicate order, teased out to walk across the bridge of the imagination into your conscious awareness of possibilities—"alternative futures"—that may constitute opportunities for spirit's expression.

3. Aspirations: Spirit seeking its destiny through yours.

4. A self-empowering, at whose center lies the voice of your spirit.

The idea is not to "fit" your story into one of these themes. They are different ways for you to listen closely to your spirit's voice. To discover what your spirit's story is about is a bit like trying on a new suit of clothes. Each outfit has something to offer: style, color, size, comfort, use. If you give yourself enough time—Rule No. 6, *the non-forcing rule*—one or another many begin to feel just right. So too in deep imaging: You are listening for the "fit" of the story. Is it your spirit's voice speaking . . . or someone else's?

• *The Source Material.* It's not as though you come to deep imaging untutored in the disciplines of the spirit, unfamiliar with the skills of inner work, or without any idea of what's going on. Any or all of the "exercises" you have undertaken provide rich source material for the narrative, for they are about listening for, questioning, seeking the space of spirit. Spirit may have found *its* voice—the way it speaks to you, and what it speaks about—in any aspect of this inner work of endisciplining.

• *Telling the Story.* Speak the story out loud. Do not hide from it. Speak first to yourself, then within your community of learners, eventually to the world.

• *The Dynamic of the Story.* It is the new relationship between your spirit and your social biography. A new "you," a new "self," a new "soul" is aborning. Let it. Listen for it. Nurture it but do not force it. The integration leads to a whole, not to a split. *This story is about healing . . . in you . . . in the world.* Most of your images will be about that, directly or tangentially.

• *The Flow of the Story.* Keep in mind the flow of the images—Rule No. 5, *the emptying, waiting, and yielding rule*. Different aspects of the story may emerge into conscious awareness as separate pieces. Not to worry. *The great thing about deep imaging is that it is not linear.* You are never locked in. You can always return to the image (Rule

No. 3) and replenish (Rule No. 7). Eventually, the narrative comes together and the voice of your spirit in you will be heard throughout the land.

• *Fleshing Out the Story.* Here, you *live* the story in your imagination (Rule No. 4). It comes to life in all of its specificity and concreteness (Rule No. 1). The images are palpable. You are there. It has happened. You say what it is like living that story.

• *Have We Finished?* Is the story now finished, complete? Can you go home now, rest easy? Is the enspiriting work over and now real life can begin again?

Sorry. The clue is in this last sentence. For it is in the inexorable and dynamic movement from the voice of spirit expressing itself in deep imaging to expressing itself in "real life" that the transformation takes place. Big or small, earth-shaking or self-shaking, it matters not. What matters is this:

The shift from inner realities to outer realities, from interiority to exteriority, from the implicate order of all possibilities in all universes to the explicate order of this universe, from inner action to outer action, from spirit-in-hiding to spirit-in-the-world, all finding its expression, its voice through you: That is what this book is about.

The ways of enspiriting lead to action, to being and doing. The gateway for that passage is *intentioning:* In which you search your story for an image of *that which you cannot not do and that which you cannot not be.*

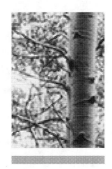

17

A Way of Intentioning

From Nouns to Verbs

The discipline of *intentioning* is difficult to master. This is so even though unlike *deep learning*, intentioning takes place in your conscious awareness. Most of the process is not hidden from you. It involves a serious, sometimes strenuous, dialogue between your spirit and your social biography. They learn how and why to act together in new ways that produce a new amalgam, a new "You."

Another source of the difficulty is that intentioning is the final bridge between the domain of the spirit and the domain of action in the world. As you are soon to discover, if you have not already, enspiriting, i.e., the enacting of the seven disciplines of the spirit, is not confined to a solely private dimension that only you have access to. On the contrary, the *inner* action of enspiriting is paralleled by its *outer* action through which we learn *what it means to take action* in a world where human action has been replaced by human behavior, and where the idea, indeed the very possibility, of *human purpose* has been replaced by the instrumental practices of efficiency, effectiveness and appropriateness.

To provide for this special emphasis on action, both inner and outer, I have concocted a bit of a strange word to capture the discipline: Intentioning. It is not found in the dictionary. *Intention* and *intentionality* are; but they are passive nouns that don't give voice to the intensely active process of coming to your intentions through a profound *dialogue* between your spirit and your social biography.[13] It is in facilitating these practices that the discipline of intentioning and its attendant competence become clear and practicable.

But that is not all. In the inner action, spirit and social biography enter into a new relationship. Through it, social biography—*yours and no one else's*—becomes the actionable channel through which spirit—*yours and no one else's*—is translated into yourself-in-the-world and ourselves-in-the-world. That translation is the very process of transformation.

While the act of intentioning requires serious inner work to re-set the social biography in harmony with spirit, ultimately, like *all* of the enspiriting disciplines, it is a *social act, indeed a political act, understood as such because its consequences play out over a field of intimates, organizations, communities, even the world.* That is why your intentions, when seriously proffered, are always queried. People don't leave you alone. "What are you up to?" people ask. "What do you mean by this? What do you intend in this matter? What are your intentions?" If a dialogue ensues because the asker is genuinely interested (for sometimes such questions are mainly a way of putting you down!), an enspiritor's response is two-fold:

1. *Judge my intentions through my actions and through their consequences for me as well as for others,* and

2. *Let me share with you my compelling image about the matter under consideration and how I came to it,* i.e., why and how I came to listen to the voice of my spirit.

The practices of intentioning involve searching for and finding a *compelling image which initiates your intentional action.* How to conduct that search is the focus of the next chapter. But before we proceed, may I remind you once again that like *deep listening* and, indeed, all of the disciplines of the spirit, intentioning is not about light and easy matters. *Much* of life involves habit, convention, daily behaviors, and the application of your KBVAF to life's events. The idea is not to make too much of it but just to let it be. *Some* of life, however, and now a rising portion of it, demands a return to and a re-learning of the disciplines of the spirit. *Deep imaging* gives you a strong sense of what your spirit has to say about those matters of concern, of disquietude, of imbalance, of injustice, of pain *and of what it would be like if they were well addressed.* So as we proceed into the *practices* of intentioning, focus on what is important to you.

The New "You"

This discipline, then, is about the movement of spirit into the world. How does

---

[13] Actually the *form* of the word intentioning is a *gerund*, i.e., giving a *noun form* to a verb, as in *writing* or *sleeping* as a noun form of the verbs *to write* or *to sleep*. Unfortunately, there is no verb form for intentioning. It means the *activity of coming to your intentions*. It is an action, has a process, involves competence, is effected through practices all of which come together under the rubric of a discipline of the spirit.

that happen in an endisciplined and deliberate way? How is spirit brought to bear on matters crucial to your dilemmas or central to the pain of ourselves-in-the-world in transformation? How does spirit's enormous energy become focused on making something good rather than bad happen, be it within your own life or in the future history of the world? How do you take the richness of the images through which your spirit speaks (the inner action) and translate them into outer action? In the stories of yourself-in-the-world and ourselves-in-the-world that are constructed by the practices of *deep imaging*, how do you locate a response to the questions, *"So what?"* *"What is my project in this world?"* *"What am I supposed to be and do that is central to and a consequence of all of this enspiriting?"*

Who is this "I"? That is the first element to be unpacked. Is it not your social biography, *now in the very dynamics of reconstitution?* Is it not the "I" who no longer fights its spirit but has learned to listen for it, to listen to it in moments of despair, of hopelessness, or of seeming ineptitude when confronted with challenges and choices for which the KBVAF no longer works? Is it not the "I" that searches the story of deep imaging for clues about this *project?* Is it not the "I" (myself-in-the-world) whom spirit transforms into a creature that has a freshness, a newness, an unexpectedness that signifies that which was not but is now? Is it not the "I" who participates in the transformation of ourselves-in-the-world through actions which were not but are now? Is it not a great invention that is the expression of the adventures your spirit calls you to, adventures deep within that perhaps no one knows but you and adventures without that show the rest of us who you truly are and what you're up to that makes a difference?

Searching for the Compelling Image

To respond to those questions about the new "you" involves an inner search. You already have most of the "tools." *Deep listening* empties you of the effluvia of an inherited past that you did not invent and need not own unless it once again becomes a matter of your *intentioning. Deep questioning* has enabled you to penetrate to the heart of the matter of your utmost concern to discover what that is. *Deep learning* has moved you beyond the demands and constraints of your social biography to the space where spirit lives *so as to invite it out.* It has disassembled your KBVAF into the original molecules of intentioning which *deep imaging* has addressed as the voice of your spirit speaking of our might-be's and could-be's and should-be's. Use these disciplines. Never neglect them as you search for *that which you cannot not be and that which you cannot not do. This is the compelling image that moves you to action.*

The idea of the compelling image came to me in the early days of the envisioning work in which participants generated images of alternative futures. But that early work had two problems. First, most participants did not free themselves from the constraints of their KBVAFs; and so their images of the future were not very fresh. Their images tended to be the same old wine captured in new wineskins: The surface stories of the images looked different, but inside there was nothing vibrant and new. We did not invite them to their deep learning. Second, the participants' imaging experiences, though personally satisfying and even exciting for many of them, led nowhere. No action ensued. Nothing much new happened that would translate their images into action. The organizations and communities with which we did this work didn't transform; most of them didn't change very much *even though their debilitating circumstances had led them to envision a new and different future in the first place.*

This is not surprising, considering that by the 1970s, the burgeoning field of futurism had developed umpteen thousand predictions, forecasts, prescriptions, prognoses, scenarios and policy recommendations by self-proclaimed futurists who fed off each other's work like sharks thrashing about around a piece of red meat. The professionals, with a few exceptions, rarely engaged in dialogue with the citizens whose futures they were claiming. Nowhere in that emerging field was there a place for action, for *citizens* to act as agents in behalf of their own futures (i.e., their very *lives*) and as persons in behalf of each others'.[14] In its search for academic legitimacy, futurism became a field of knowledge, not of action.

Then, in a marvelous conversation with Thomas F. Green (a philosopher and a professor of education at Syracuse University) in the mid-'70s on a drive through the hills of upstate New York we came to an insight that *the future is the domain of action, not of knowledge.* Put more precisely, to seek to "know" the future—as we might seek to know the past, for example, or as we might seek to nail reality to the hard wood of experiment and evidence (also a questionable task, as the quantum physicists tells us)—is a chimera. The future gives us no evidence. We can't measure it, kick it, push it around, sit on it, bring it into the laboratory, take a tape recorder to capture its grunts and groans. Then what is it? *The future is a grand act of this human imagination in which we seek to discover the grounds for acting in the present in such a way that we— you and I—can make a difference, i.e., change the future from what it otherwise would be.*

---

[14] This portrayal of *action* and its relation to the notions of *human agency* and the *personal* is informed by the keen insight of philosopher John Macmurray set forth in his celebrated Gifford Lectures on *The Form of the Personal* (1953-54), published by Faber and Faber Ltd., London, as *the Self as Agent* and *Persons in Relation*, 1957.

How could we marry the future, the realm of inquiry into our possibilities, to the present in which we live and *act*? That linking became the *envisioning project* with which I was so pleased to be a contributing member, along with thousands of others, in the work of the Futures-Invention Associates. How to connect the realm of conflicting ideas, a wide range of alternatives, a panoply of images and a retinue of dubious forecasts to the existential lives of the *do-ers* and the *done-tos*? By the linchpin of *the compelling image,* that passion for something new, concrete, specific and actionable that would make a difference—big or small—*and that would grab you and wouldn't let go.*

I made the connection between the "imagined" and the "real" by inviting envisioners to search through their images for the one—sometimes more than one—which would not leave them alone, which compelled them to take action in its behalf. But how could an "image" do that, a mere phantasm, a product of the imagination? I did not know this then. I know it now, after working with so many in 25 years of envisioning. It is not the "image" that grabs you and won't let go. God bless us, *it is your spirit speaking through the image.*

What to call this linkage, this linchpin? I sought a word that would stand for a *practice* to which people could be invited, something they could actually learn and do, an inner action of such great vibrancy and force that when properly undertaken would give direction into the future, mobility in the present, unhooking from the past.

Why not a *compelling image?* And was is that? *That which you cannot not be and cannot not do.*

But why the double negative, even more awkward than *intentioning*? In order to counter explicitly the prevailing practices of skillful leaders, skillful process facilitators and extraordinarily skillful image manipulators, who, overtly or covertly, directed other people's imaging. I wanted to lean over backwards to ensure that the *tabula rasa*—the empty plate—of the future, in that envisioning work, would be filled by its envisioners and by nobody else.

The "not not" carries with it the flavor of a gift that you cannot refuse rather than a moral imperative that you lay on someone else. The "not not" opens up the domain of transformative action invited by your spirit without recourse to the violence that we perpetrate on each other—in family relations, in neighborhoods and cities and states and countries and organizations—in the name of doing (someone else) good.

The "not not" invites you neither to moral proclamations, nor to the prejudice of one group, ethnicity, social class, denomination, moral code laying its case on the other, but to a search for the voice of spirit, yours and indeed the world's, that will transform yourself-in-the-world and ourselves-in-the-world. Making that search is the discipline of intentioning. Finding your compelling image is what constitutes *coming to your intentions.*

What is This "Action" Called for in Intentioning and Described in the Compelling Image?

Throughout the recovery of the disciplines of the spirit from their place in the limbo of a de-spiritualized world, I have said that it is important to understand that inner work is *inner action.* There is also, of course, *outer action* which is action with others. *The two are inseparable in practice, though in thinking about them we make a distinction between the inner and the outer.* In the process of moving from the realm of interiority to the realm of exteriority, we are obliged to re-discover the grounds for authentic action: *That which is true of our spirit and that which is consequential.*

Human action is part and parcel of the seven disciplines of the spirit. Unlike many ventures and forays into the place of spirit in our universe, including the time-honored domain of formal religion, enspiriting always involves inner and outer action. True action starts in its inner dimension because it requires an act of reflection, not separate from but integral to the movement of body, mind and spirit into the dimension of consequentiality.

What does this mean? All action involves (1) *an intention* to make a difference, (2) *a performance* that translates the inner into the outer manifestation, and (3) *consequences* that denote its impact on self and others. *Without consequences, there is no action.* There is, indeed, behavior; and so we may choose to speak of both animal behavior and human behavior in the same breath and to promote a science for each. But I do not understand animals to act. Absent are the reflective act I call *intentioning* and the dimension of consequentiality that are connected by the performance. Thus do we correctly speak of personal, organizational, social, or political *transformation only when enspirited persons engage in action.* Lots of things happen by virtue of fortune, fate, randomness, or so we like to think. But not transformation. If we come to, through, or out of it, it will not be by luck but by the enspiriting action of coming to our intentions.

The Politics of Intentioning

Do you recall the adage: "The road to hell is paved with good intentions"? That suggests the grave dilemma that confronts us all in formulating policies, making decisions, and taking action, whether it be private, personal or public: *how to act, what to act about, and for what purposes in such a way that we do not commit violence on, with, or to each other.* Years ago, Ralph Hambrick, now a professor of political science but then a prescient graduate student at Syracuse University, and I came to an insight as we sought to frame the future of American education in a way that would place the learner in charge of her own learning. It came out as an "American koan" that goes: *Never make a policy (recommendation) that does not directly impact on your own life.* In that lies not only the essence of what Benjamin Barber has called *Strong Democracy,* but also the intentioning discipline you are about to practice. For it is in effecting this discipline of the spirit that we discover and learn at the deepest levels of our very beingness *what it is like to come to an enspiriting action whereby spirit is translated into yourself-in-the-world without doing violence to yourself or others.*

One of the great attractions of the military experiencing war—as distinguished from being a refugee or the recipient of high-level bombing or low-level strafing—is that at the level of the small unit, the squad or platoon, the decision and action of the one not only affects all of the other members *but also oneself.* This is a key character-istic of the *civitas* when it is viewed as a self-governing community. So too in team sports. "Policy," when enacted in these circumstances, feeds back on its makers as well as its operatives. In envisioning projects on the future of citizenship, I have found it helpful to distinguish among the "policy-makers" or "decision-makers," the "do-ers" who put the policies and decisions into action, i.e., the implementors or operators, and the "done-tos" (which is most of the rest of us).

How does this "American koan" apply to intentioning? When the consequences are meted out, the categories of policy-maker, do-er and done-to collapse into a sin-gle entity of *self-governing persons.* Self-governance is the *political* equivalent of *self-empowering learning, being in charge of yourself,* and *your spirit speaking out.* Rarely do these occur in the modern arenas of government, corporations, universities or nation-al churches—which is one reason they are largely bereft of community and do not contribute to its formation.

All of the ideological talk by the free marketeers about the sacrosanct values of free enterprise, market economics and competition among producers and consumers never takes into account the essence of leadership responsibility: *Go down with your ship, like the Titanic's captain, rather than floating away with a golden parachute,i.e., accept the consequences of your actions rather than protecting yourself from them.* A corol-lary is: Don't formulate policy, make a decision, undertake an action on, to, or for others without their full and active participation even though you believe it is in their best interests. Rather, *query them* about their best interests through *deep questioning* and prepare yourself for some healthy *deep listening*. In short, invite the "clients," the "voters," the "members" and the "employees" into the practices of disciplined enspiriting so that they may take charge of their own lives in concert with fellow-enspiritors. Such advice may run counter to much organization, leadership and political theory and practice. But look where they have got us?

Keep in mind, then, that as you search for your compelling image *(and find it!)*, you are involved in a grand venture in an inhospitable world: Discovering your authentic action whereby you will make a difference to yourself—the new "I" , the agent of your spirit—in conjunction with other persons whose spirit welcomes yours as yours welcomes theirs.

18

Conducting the Search

How to Conduct the Search

Like most of the enspiriting practices I have discussed, the notion of the *search* is to be taken literally. Doesn't everybody know how to search, though some more proficiently than others? Sifting through a drawer of blouses to find just the right one? The right color, texture, design, and "feel" for the occasion? Handling ten or more ties to see which one meets the needs of your suit, your situation, your feelings about the day.

A little more difficult is searching for the trail through the mountainside forest after you have lost it. Once, following the unerring instincts of my dog and not watching where I was going, I walked off the trail with him onto a steep mountain-side at about 10,000 feet in the Colorado Rockies. By the time I had stopped day-dreaming and given attention to where I was, we were lost, slipping and sliding down through the leaves on the tilted floor of a mountain forest whose dense beauty was equalled only by my inability to see much beyond the trees that surrounded me. What was I to do? Search. Yes, but for what? No trail now existed. We were off of it, and perhaps had been for 10 or 15 minutes.

I did what I think we all do. First, I used my mind: to *think it through* as best I could, so that I could find a direction that fit my explicit perceptions of where I was, where I had been, and where I was going. Because I had just been descending a mountainside, my *idea* was not to keep going down but either to go up or sideways. But which? I used my memory not of the last 15 minutes but of when I last remembered being on the trail, and what direction that was in relation to the mountainside. All well and good, but not enough. Uncertainty still prevailed. What was great about the entire adventure was that my companion—not the dog who was still a hale-fellow-well-met with wagging tail—was quite worried, not too far distant from hysteria when confronted with being lost in the Rockies.

As a good *orientor,* I pulled out my compass and found directions. I once more looked about, discovering the direction down the mountain, up the mountain and in each of its sideways movements. Then I remembered the compass heading for our target when we had left the trailhead a few hours back, which I had checked several times during the first half hour. All well and good, but still not enough. Then I put it all into my *tant'ien,* literally emptying of worry and concern, to listen for the direction, to get my feel of it. And in a few moments, it came to me very hard and fast that we were to hike off in *this direction* and not in another. And we did. In about 15 minutes, we came upon the trail, to be sure half-a mile or so from where we had left it...but the same trail.

Now, what was all *that* about?

First, the explicit search using my conscious awareness, the left side of my brain, if you prefer, *thinking* it through.

Second, using an *external* source—in this case, my compass—that gave me direction markings or *indicators* which, though insufficient, *positioned me in that context.*

And *third,* putting it all inside, and letting my *intuition,* my *feel,* my *sense that emerged from emptying* give me a choice of action.

Conducting the search for a *compelling image* is not unlike any other search. This one is inner. Your maze is the deep images that you have already and may still be generating. You are not lost. But you do seek direction, the next steps, those in fact that when well taken constitute *coming to your intentions.*

Not much can be added here about the first practice, *thinking it through,* as you search for your compelling image except to warn you once again that thinking, by itself, can be deceptive. We can and do *argue* from any position and for any position. The proof of that is the infinite number of positions that reside in the world of debate that contain all of the issues ever dreamed of.

The third practice is getting the *sense,* the *feel,* the *intuition* that you have found your compelling image...or better put, that it has found you. *Deep listening* is essential here. It is available to every person who is prepared to evoke that discipline: *Silencing yourself, being non-judgmental, and finally, emptying*. It is the discipline most needed in exactly those moments when things go awry, when we are at sixes and sevens, or when *our direction is lost and not to be found by any other "method" we know*.

But what are you going to put into your tant'ien?

The Six Points of the Compass

What of the compass, the guide that gives your directions but doesn't find the path for you? It provides you "external" directions, not about where to go or to search but how to tell where you're going and searching. The compass is not about what to seek but about *how to tell what to seek*; not about what your intention is but about *how to discern what your intention is*. This compass gives your reflection a practical rather than a theoretical bent. Coming to your intentions is not a matter of theorizing. It is discovering that which you cannot *not* be and do that leads to—indeed, *is*—your authentic action. Here, years of experience have amply demonstrated that a *compelling image, one that is true to you in all of your totality and true to the world you have created has at least six features*. These constitute your compass readings.

The six features are:

1. *True and compelling images are always specific and concrete.*

2. *True and compelling images do no dissolve; they stay with you.*

3. *True and compelling images are owned by you.*

4. *True and compelling images unify or cement the whole story together; they are its linchpin.*

5. *True and compelling images make clear the essence of the new "you," the new amalgam of your spirit and your social biography through which spirit's voice is enacted.*

6. *True and compelling images are non-violent.*

Sift through your images. Reflect on your story. Re-enter it in your imagination and live it as actualized. What in it turns you on? What is at its center? What is it truly about? What in it compels you to action? As you conduct your search—including generating more images—these six features become your compass; not telling you where to head, but telling you what to look for to discover your intentions in the matter at hand. When all six features are revealed in your search for the *compelling image*, you will have uncovered that which your spirit asks of you, invites you to, and will support in an infinite variety ways through the never-failing reservoir of its energy.

These features are *criteria* that help sort through the deep images you have generated to find that which compels. They are also *indicators* which, if found among your
images, are evidence that your search is on the right path. They serve as your *external compass* that gives you not your *own* direction but *directions in general that you can
use to find your own direction.* And when taken all together—not just separate and linear—you can place them in your tant'ien as a *lodestone* around which coalesces your
sense, your feelings, your intuition that the search is over, *and you have come to your
intentions through the compelling image.*

Let us take each one of the six features in turn, with an example or two, so that as
you begin your search, you are clear about how these criteria, indicators and lodestone may help you.

1. *True and compelling images are always specific and concrete.*

Of course, you know this one because it is no different than Rule No.1—*In deep
imaging always be specific and concrete.* I included this "rule" in the grammar of validation, but let us now give close attention to its *practice.*

All of these criteria intermix; some slide right into each other. This one, which I
hope you already have practiced a lot, has a *pre-truth* quality to it by virtue of calling
for—enabling you to look for—the *immediacy* of the image much like, in our inner
body work, we open ourselves up to the *immediacy of experiencing that body which is
now no longer separated from us but is us.* In coming to our intentions, we are not
searching for an abstraction, a generalization, a slogan, a theory, or an ideology. By
being able to hear, feel, touch, taste, smell and picture the compelling image, you
give to it the perception of your senses and receive from it a responding *immediacy*
that is difficult to deny. And while these senses, activated in their *inner* dimension,
can deceive, that possibility is certainly not of the kind understood as false argument
or false truth claims. A pain in the stomach, for example, may indicate a number of
bodily events for which you seek additional evidence to select one possibility over
another. But the pain is *there.* So, too, in searching for a compelling image.
Specificity and concreteness reside at the level of the *beingness* of the image which
you experience in your imagination in all of its immediacy. *You live it.*

Suppose from deep imaging comes a story—a set of images—*about* a career
change, or *about* a new relationship, or *about* equal opportunity for women. These
are only abstractions. As such, they may enter our thinking and discourse as positive
goals, as good values…about which we may do nothing. They are not a matter of

intentioning because *we have not yet rendered specific and concrete what it would be like if we enacted them: Their who, what, when, where, how, and why qualities.*

The peculiarity of this criterion is just this: *Before you can sense the true quality of an image, you have to have one.* Specific and concrete images are the building blocks of your story. Coming to your intentions is not a theoretical exercise in choosing among abstract goods or moral ends. It is embracing the idea, the theme, the possibility and *discovering what it would be like to live it in your imagination in all of its concrete detail.*

Thus will your spirit invite your social biography to its new possibilities.

2. *True and compelling images do not dissolve; they stay with us.*

You also know and have practiced this one. It is an amalgam of several of the grammatical rules of imaging, particularly Rule No. 3.—*the return-to-the-image rule that goes: When in doubt about your image, return to it, query it, and let it speak to you in its own language . . . that of images.*

This is a powerful indicator that your spirit is "making you an offer you cannot refuse" if the image keeps coming back. There is back-and-forth movement here. The true and compelling image keeps entering into your conscious awareness, sometimes invited, sometimes not. On the other side, when you re-enter the image and once again live it, it does not go away. It remains there, part of the emerging story of yourself-in-the-world and ourselves-in-the-world.

In fact, the image is so solidly lodged in your imagination that you can even *build on it,* concocting other stories with this image at their core. People can try to argue you out of this image. You yourself—your KBVAF —may try to sacrifice the image on the alters of practicality and feasibility. But there it remains. It won't go away. Spirit is speaking strongly. It won't let you run away and hide among the crevices and caves of what is possible and what is probable. As my old colleague, Jack Harrison used to say: "Life becomes interesting only when you do the next impossible thing."

"And," I would add, "When spirit speaks out." Enspiriting turns the impossible into action.

Am "I"—the imager—in the true and compelling image or is it about someone or something else?

3. *True and compelling images are owned by you.*

Most compelling images, when let out of the stable to run and roam in the pastures of your life, engage with other people in the various action-settings called into play by the image. But you are at their center. You are the originator, now acting out of that *intentioning* into the world you are reconfiguring. One enspiritor brought to his envisioning a focus on changing the rewards-for-work criteria and system of his business. In a business journal, he had come across the idea of giving significant recognition for employees' careers and compensation to non-organizational, non-workplace civic and volunteer activities that involved learning new concepts and practicing new skills in the community. The idea sounded good; he began to plan about it. But soon it came into hard confrontation with his own drive which was that of a workaholic who had put building his business first among all of his life goals. So he began his inner work: What was there in this story he was imaging that was about himself? Where did his own action and responsibility lie? Where and what was his inner ground that had anything to do with inventing new criteria for employee rewards that involved work *outside* the business?

Aided by the *deep questioning* of some partners-in-dialogue, he focused his *deep imaging* until he came, finally, to the centerpiece of the whole vision: a compelling image about himself. It revealed a fundamental shift in his social biography from a workaholic boss devoted solely to making his business successful to a full human being who would involve himself more considerably with his neighbors and fellow-citizens in non-business, non-remunerative, non-"work" activities. He discovered that the idea of the story from the business journal was about himself, inviting him to a new configuration of his spirit and his social biography. His first action lay there, in himself, an *inner action,* for which designing a new system of sanctions and rewards for his employees was an *exterior action* to which he was not compelled until he discovered it inside. So he came to his intentions. So he learned to "walk the talk."

Of course, this enspiriting did not happen in half an hour. Indeed, in this case, some weeks of confrontation between his spirit and his social biography ensued before he found his compelling image and came to his intentions about himself in the matter.

Out of this kind of search comes *ownership.* But not proprietary ownership, as in owning a house or a car or a piece of property. You can invite others to share your image and come to their own ownership of it. The image may be about you in relation to others, be they intimates, associates, the whole world. But when an enspiritor says, *"I own this,"* he means: "This is *my* image. I gave birth to it. I accept its consequences. I will devote my resources to its actualization. It is my beacon, illuminating my path. It is always there for me. Though I may pack it away for an hour, a day, a month, it is still there. After a while, it pushes and pulls at me until I say: 'O.K., I'll get on with it.' I cannot deplete this image, for it is of my spirit and inexhaustible. I can rely on it. It owns me as much as I own it. *It is me!*"

But now consider the obverse.

Once I conducted a seminar with the vice-presidents and division chiefs of a national religious organization mandated to formulate overall policy for its member hospitals across the country. Many of the 20 or so participants had received postgraduate training in psychology, philosophy, human resources development, or theology. We went at it fast and furious. I thought they were truly engaging with their "intentions" toward deeply felt concerns about their total policy operation in relation to the state of wellness and healing of hundreds of thousands of persons within scores of hospitals and clinics. As we wound down the energetic imaging, a senior participant admonished us all that since the "chief" wasn't present, no one here was in a position to actualize their intentions—under discussion for three hours! "That," one of the participants and a well-known theologian explained, "is impossible without his approval."

Shades of ownership! My heart sank and my tant'ien regurgitated these indicators of incompetence (skill *and* will, ability *and* intention), fear and subalternhood. I muttered to myself, "And I thought these were grown-ups."

It is a rare organization that will state as a condition of membership or employment acts of intentioning that do not serve common or predictable purposes decided beforehand by someone else.

Discovering your ownership of a true and compelling image as a practice in *coming to your intentions* will be foreign to many of you. It is an arduous search. But... it is a delight!

4. *True and compelling images unify the story; they are its linchpin.*

Perhaps not much wants to be said about this criterion. It stands for the synergistic quality of a compelling image. The whole story from deep imaging centers around it as a hurricane centers and swirls around its eye. Without the eye, where would the hurricane be?

But here is another way to put it. The compelling image ramifies into all elements of the emerging vision. Its consequences are felt throughout. Look anywhere in the story and there you will find yourself, if not in body, certainly in spirit. Though the main theme of the image may be embodied in what *other* people do and who they are; and though they may all be affected in multiple ways unique to *them* by the compelling image: Your *presence* is felt throughout the entire story, giving it its unity, being the hub of the wheel.

You want to be a little careful here because so much of planning, social invention and policy formation relies on dissemination and replication for implementation and action.[15] *This feature is not that model.* You can not disseminate or replicate an intention. You can redesign your action-setting—invent would be a better word—to encourage *acts of intentioning* among its constituencies, be they citizens, employees, or members.

Is it then the old "center and periphery" model: Control from the center over the regional distribution points, the regional factories, the satellite units, in which orders from the "center" are understood as orders from the "top"? Not at all. A compelling image *permeates* the reality it creates as a distillation of sugar water dropped into a cup of water spreads its molecules throughout until the whole mass is homogenous.

In the practices of intentioning, what does this mean? While the *focus* or *content* of the compelling image may be unique, you are invited to search for its indicators, its consequences, its effects, its ramifications throughout its action-setting. That setting could be you alone, or it could be your organization or community involving very complex interactions. But even if it's only you, the image ramifies into *all* of you: Body, spirit, mind, feelings, KBVAF, etc. Lift any corner of that inner world and you will discover the entire image, as a hologram of that inner reality or external reality as the case may be. Visit any factory at the periphery and you will also find the center there.

Is this possible? Or is this a useless search for an aspect of a compelling image that never was and never will be? I have just described in other language, in the enspiriting vocabulary of deep imaging and intentioning, the metaphor of the "whole person," or, if you will, of the "holistic" approach to planning, to organizational transformation, to community-building and to policy formation. The whole is unified, cemented, and articulated through the compelling image that brings it all together.

Is this criterion a chimera? No. Easy to find in the search? Not at first or at least not easily. Our worlds, inner and outer, are fragmented. There are over 300 separate federally-funded programs for the child in America: her needs, her hurts, her promises. But where is the whole child? Hug your daughter, your son, your young one of blood kinship or spirit kinship. There you might find the whole child. So the fragmentation goes, with everything. That's why the KBVAF is so powerful; not only

---

[15] This "replication" approach is dear to the hearts of decision-makers in the organizational behemoths of our age, be they governmental, corporate, religious, educational, mass media. They are unwilling to allow the periphery to come to its own invention, thus ensuring that there will be little if any *ownership*. For we own and take responsibility for implementing that which we create much more than that which is created for us.

because it explains and legitimates but also because it unifies our otherwise fragmented worlds.

Search deeply. If your spirit has offered a true and compelling image, you will uncover its unifying and synergistic properties.

5. *True and compelling images make clear the essence of the new "you," the amalgam of your spirit and your social biography through which spirit's voice is expressed.*

This criterion points to the search for a new self lodged within the compelling image. It is uncovered through the disciplines of *deep learning* and deep imaging. What is that new "self"? A new personality? Does it mean the loss and require eradication of all that we have been and all that we have hoped for? Not at all. *It is that which remains when the part of the old "self" that had previously inhibited, constrained, cut off spirit has dissolved and disassembled through unlearning.* Keep this understanding at the center of your enspiriting. *This is spirit-work, not personality-fixing.* What remains is the biggest and best part of you: *Biography that now accepts spirit, that acts as the historic configuration of your spirit in action.*

This amounts to a deep healing, a bringing together of your various aspects— spirit, body, mind, feelings—that is a central characteristic of a true and compelling image. Sometimes, the indicators that are evidence for the emergence of a new "you" are not explicit. You have to dig a bit by deep questioning and *deep listening* for them in the image. Sometimes, a partner in your community of learners enters into your own inner dialogue—at your invitation!—and assists in the search by virtue of her own enspiriting competence.

This healing reduces the split among the multiple aspects of our being that are now so fragmented for so many of us, in our outer "role" as family member, citizen, breadwinner, professional, lover, group member, as well as the inner fragmentation that has left us so vulnerable to the appeals of false prophets who will "heal" us by taking on our inner burdens if we will but become their true believers.

The Indicator of Worthiness

How do you find this in your compelling image? How does your image speak to you about this healing, the bringing together of spirit and social biography in a new way? The indicator is *worthiness*. As the compelling image emerges into your conscious awareness, *you feel worthy of it* and *it feels worthy of you.*

What does this mean? There is here a marvelous reciprocity between the new image and the new reality it describes, both being of and residing in your new "you."

If I feel worthy of the compelling image, this means that the image calls out my best to match the quality of the image. It invites my excellence, my *virtue*—in the old sense of *competence* and *strength*, that which I am just very good at being and doing. If that is not the case, then my image is perhaps a design for a goal, a target, a program *that does not demand my presence in it.* It is for someone else…but I am not there and so can't possibly own it. (Do you hear in this the meaning of the policy koan discussed in the previous chapter?)

On the other side, if the image feels worthy of you, then as you live it in your imagination, it tests out the new "you" by rehearsing the performance (the action called for) and searching for its consequences. That true and compelling image is your spirit speaking out. It is not an image garnered from someone else. It is worthy of you because that which it compels of you, which it brings out in you, *is the new "you."* You match. You fit, the image and the "you." You are of a piece.

As you search for this in your compelling image, a cautionary word may be helpful. Try not to let yourself be overwhelmed by the enormity of this transformation of yourself-in-the-world, i.e., coming to your new "you," the amalgam of spirit and social biography. It may be an enormous leap. But most of the time it isn't. I believe that transformation begins in small ways. Here, the genius of the 12-step program, the adage "one step at a time," the notion, "take it day-by-day" are to be acknowledged and celebrated.

The true and compelling image does portend a shift, a change, an inner action that contains the entire transformation. The hologram of our new realities is there. Your compelling image opens up a corner of it. But the true and compelling image is not usually of a dimension that places unmeetable and insupportable demands on you and on others. Your spirit will not invite you to actions you cannot undertake. To the contrary. You have invited out spirit by way of the disciplines, all of which nurture it as part of the invitation. In turn, spirit nurtures your biography to a new state of being and doing in a loving and caring manner—as your biography, now and at last, nurtures it.

6. *True and compelling images are non-violent.*

In a world of violence whose images permeate our life experience in every possible way, is it surprising that central to the discipline of intentioning is its insistence on discovering the compelling image and the ensuing authentic action that is non-violent? Indeed, how are we to understand our world without recourse to the experience of its violence in our own lives and that of all the others about whom we read, see, or hear through the media? In discussing the search for your compelling image, I have given you criteria, indicators and suggested practices that are "value-free": They relate to competence and practice, not to content, and so might be considered "technical" attributes of the discipline. Then, suddenly, the last of these six caveats and by no means the least addresses the *content* of the compelling image rather than the *process* of coming to your intentions. What's going on here?

Now me must come to the nub of enspiriting: Why have you entered into the disciplines of the spirit in the first place? Indeed, why enspirit at all except that we humans find it difficult to avoid completely the spark, flash and hint of spirit acting in our lives however much a de-spiritualized culture pushes us in an opposite direction?

Right now, in the world we have created, enspiriting is about our transformation, its need, its possibility, its experience. I do not understand the one without the other. Enspiriting is not solely about my own salvation and devil-take-the-hindmost. It is about who we are and what we are up to on planet Earth. It is about our discovering and inventing a community of co-enspiritors who, by virtue of these disciplines, will not do violence to one another.

But now that you have become a journeyperson on the path of enspiriting, you might admonish: "Let it be, that connection. Let each of us discover our own compelling image free of a lecture on what its content must contain, whatever else may be the focus of our intentioning. By claiming non-violence as a criterion of a true and compelling image, don't you violate the non-judgmental premise of the whole enspiriting process?"

Each enspiritor will come to the content and focus of her compelling image, be it about herself in a private journey to new self-understanding, be it in a sphere or domain of human action that involves a few, hundreds, thousands, millions of others. Having undertaken your deep questioning and deep learning, you need no help from me on that score. Moreover, each enspiritor will come to his own experiencing of violence and to his own indicators and definitions of it. Coming to your intentions is not an exercise in semantics—*what is violence, after all?*—but an exercise in enspiriting.

Do commence your own reflection on this criterion by noting that characteristic of *de-spiriting* is the determination not to let spirit out, to deny its presence, and to punish (often, subtly) those whose spirit demands and finds breathing space: The whistle-blower in the Pentagon, the Martin Luther King, the abused wife who no longer stands for it, the school drop-out whose educational experience denies him his creative moments and capacities, yes, even the one who bets his fortune on building a better mousetrap.

A social biography that constrains its underlying spirit to passivity, that demands it hide away from manifestation in one's life, commits an act of violence on that spirit.

More complex is the case of the organization bereft of spirit. We have come to believe that organizational mission, goals, and behavior are not about human purposes and human projects but about organizational purposes and organizational projects. Let it be noted that organizations are human inventions. Human beings are not organizational inventions. Can human beings obsolete and dismantle their organizations when they no longer serve human purposes? Can organizations seek to render obsolete and dismantle the human being?

In the 20th century, as good a case can be made for the latter as for the former. Has the idea of the organization and the organizing principle won out? When the criteria of efficiency and effectiveness can be applied to the gassing ovens with more success than to school reform, we are in for a hard time. The former could not have occurred if the German people had been literate in the disciplines of the spirit. They were literate in everything else but that. School reform will not occur unless and until spirit—not religion, mind you—is let into the play. We cannot "reform" our schools any more than we can "reform" our prisons or our court system, "reform" our family life, "reform" healthcare. What is called for is a *transformative* process that is grounded in reclaiming our spirit as central to these and a host of other issues that defy interventions based solely on Western-type behavioral technology and social engineering. Each of these examples is a case of doing violence to some people in the name of helping others.

Is that the human condition?

Examine your images to discover if when enacted they would do violence to other people. Does your true and compelling image demand that others *not* enspirit? If so, return to deep learning and deep imaging and find out what's going on in you.

Does your true and compelling image assume that others will not also enspirit, and so you and your like-minded colleagues are the only purported inheritors of God's genius, which is to let spirit out rather than to pull it in? If so, say that to your community of learners and deep listen to their response.

Does your true and compelling image mete out social, political, economic or other consequences that deny others their enspiriting space? If so, enter their space through *empathic listening* and re-learn what that condition of life is like.

Violence exists. Our world is full of it, to self and to others. Violent images abound as the psychic manifestation of violent experience, and vice-versa. None of that is in question. This criterion is about *your spirit voicing its claims both on yourself-in-the-world and ourselves-in-the-world.* It will not deny to other spirit its due. It will not generate a true and compelling image that contains, at any level, violence towards other spirits also seeking to manifest and express themselves *through these disciplines. When understood and enacted—enspirited—with integrity, these disciplines are the safeguard against violence.* You can not engage in deep listening with your "enemy" and do him violence.

That is why so many an enspiritor, in coming to her compelling image, finds that *as central to its enactment is the offer of these self-same disciplines to others in the action-setting.* That way, the proclivities for and traditions of our doing violence to ourselves and to each other are replaced by a transformative mode of conduct in which violence is replaced by that kind of living, in family, in neighborhood, in society, among persons of different social biographies which has fidelity to the enspiriting disciplines.

To sum: Searching for and finding your compelling image provides a grand clue to your intentions about the focus of your concerns as these are translated into doing something about them, i.e., your authentic action. The six criteria for the search constitute the directions of your inner compass. They tell you what to look for but not what it is.

In effect, you have been engaging in acts of *discerning.* Indeed, the whole of enspiriting is about discerning true images from false, good intentions from bad, right actions from wrong by listening to the voice of your spirit. Discerning itself is a discipline of the spirit, with its own practices, its own competence, its special contexts. Some of these you now know. The next chapters set out the discipline itself.

19

Ways of Discerning

Why Discerning?

In the enspiriting practices, there is always the question of whether what you sense of *your* spirit is real, true and knowable. Self-delusion in matters of the spirit is a condition of humankind. But in this day and age when false prophecy and false images abound, it is doubly important to uncover a method or *methods* for making that discernment so that when your spirit speaks out in a disciplined way and calls for authentic action, you have a *grounded* sense of its *presence* and its *truth*. After all, these enspiriting practices have generally been excluded from recently certified human experience. The behavioral sciences and their social technology have not invited spirit to form a new partnership. Let's face it: Enspiriting is not part of growing up, of socialization and the school curriculum, of research and development, or finally, of daily living. Of course, spirit does erupt spontaneously in all of us. But in this book, I have set about deliberately to draw it out of hiding and into your life within a set of disciplines that frame spirit's conduct.

As if this lese majesty were not enough, I have tied the need for the re-emergence of spirit to a call for transformation. Through its disciplines, spirit frames a transformative focus in which the pain we inflict on ourselves and on others is no longer part of our conduct. The *content*, the *details,* the *design* of this transformation are yours if you will but let your spirit speak out.

Taking all of this with a grain of salt is absolutely required. In our de-spiritualized age, charlatans invite you to *their* paths and to salvage your life in return for the gift of your true belief and unquestioned conduct, *That I will not do. Instead, I now offer you still another discipline of the spirit whose purpose is exactly to help you discern the truth, the reality, and the knowability of your spirit and what it says to you.*

What Discerning Is About

Acts of *discerning* permeate the other disciplines that frame your authentic action. In the final analysis, *discerning is perceiving the new realities of transformation,* specifically those that you discover and invent through your action. But because transformation may take place over a lifetime, over centuries, or indeed within kairos as well as immediate, unexpected, and abrupt, discerning is time-free. Place no restrictions on it. Your *satori* may arrive tomorrow, if your spirit is ready. Or it may take years.

For example, discerning that my work in futures-invention and envisioning was the work of my spirit—and not mine alone—took me over a decade to realize. Early on, a few colleagues among some Sisters of Mercy pointed this out to me. But I was so caught up in technique, policy work, and problem-solving, that I was not prepared to listen. It took me years to acknowledge the deep spiritual need as well as strength in myself which others had discerned much earlier.

I say this because it is better to think of transformation as a *process* rather than as an event, a process in which the disciplines of the spirit become ingrained in the mind, the heart, the body, throughout our biography *so that we cannot act without them nor remove them from their presence and activation in us.* That state of affairs *is* transformation. *We are in the process right now and need not wait for it to begin.*

How do we know that we are in transformation? Your experience of the disciplines of the spirit surely provides you a sense of this. Can we reach further, beyond a "sense," or an "intuition" to certainty and proof? Does the discipline of discerning provide that?

Discerning as a Way of Knowing

Discerning is a way of *knowing* that leads to *judgment.* But the aim of such knowing is not to achieve certainty through proof. Such knowing is about discovery. It is about "seeing" into new realities. Saying that this discipline brings us to that inner space where the truths of our transformation are discovered places us squarely in the space of judgment but not in the space of proof. I emphasize this at the start because so many people will not move without guarantees. Ours is an age of proof. That's not what discovery is all about. In matters of the spirit, we are where we left off a few hundred years ago when enlightenment, the celebration of reason and the scientific-technological project in the West swept all before it, and transformed our way of being and doing with fantastic material consequences. *Spirit was left out.* Now we seek to bring it back in *good* ways, without inter-denominational violence, prose-lytizing, and competition, without the call for true believers and spiritual loyalty, and without the male-dominated hegemony that has characterized most of the religious institutions in the world.

To discern what is good, true, and beautiful is the focus of this discipline.

So at no point in the inner work of discerning do we find ourselves in a search for proof. To discern good intentions from bad, true images from false, and right actions from wrong ones does not set us on the road of validation but, like the entire journey of our spirit, on the path of discovery. The tests for validation are reserved for claims about what we know, not what we intend to be and do as our spirit translates into flesh. Looking for *knowing* in the sense of *proving* is an activity of the scientific enterprise that investigates the "laws of nature," of the organizational enterprise that wishes to retain its hegemony, and of the KBVAF that seeks to maintain the sanctity of received truth. To apprehend our spirit and to discern our transformation involves new practices of *knowing* different from these.

Some of these practices are ancient but not lost. They are only in need of recovery. Others, we invent to meet our de-spiritualized condition. Throughout the practices of enspiriting described in this book, you have been engaged in discerning; but there is more to it. At the heart of the discipline is a way of knowing which is *heuristic*, i.e., it furthers discovery rather than closure.

What kind of knowing is this? For example, whence comes the discerning judgment: "I *know* what I must do!"?

A Kind of Knowing That Is Discerning: A Story

During my college days in Chicago after World War II, I lived in various apartments, basements, and lofts. Like so many other students, I regularly moved from one abode to another, each autumn locating a new place via the grapevine. One year, my girlfriend—later to become my first wife—had left Chicago for New York at the same time I was in the market for a new place—room, hotplate, share-the-bath kind of thing. The wife of one couple among our married friends suggested I take up a room in an old three-story frame house about ten blocks from the University where she and her husband—also a graduate student—had a small apartment. The wife and I were a bit attracted to each other in that sleight-of-hand, sexual teasing way which people go through with nothing more in mind. No *intentioning*, here, no compelling image...but perhaps a bit of fantasizing and a lot of joking around.

I went to see the small apartment, actually no more than a room. The husband was at class. The wife met me in the downstairs hall and urged me to take it. I said I would think about it. Then I got on my bike...and a strange thing happened. I biked around the block and in the neighborhood for half-an-hour, sometimes riding off a few blocks but always returning to circle the same block. I placed the entire situation into my tant'ien—though 50 years ago I did not know I was doing that. As I biked, I pictured the room—no bath, no kitchen, but ample enough. As I brought that image (in this case, visualized) into conscious awareness and weighed the pros and cons (rent cost, eating out quite a lot, ten blocks from the University, etc.), something else was occurring internally and making its presence felt. My body began to react to whatever was happening in my tant'ien. My heart began to beat faster. A bit of a cold sweat erupted on my forehead. I felt a little sick in my stomach...uncomfortable would be more accurate. The *visual* image still contained the room-to-let, now modified by the picture of my occasionally wandering downstairs to take a meal...or a hot bath...in this couple's apartment. I continued biking. The feeling of unease and discomfort became so palpable that I had to stop pedaling and rest for a few moments at a street corner. Then it came to me *through my body* as a *meaning-feeling:* I was *not* to take that room.

Afterward, as I thought about it, I surmised that if I had taken that room, I might well have become involved with the young wife. That realization came well after the *discerning* judgment and experience, confirming it, if you will, but not initiating it. There had been no careful weighing and balancing of the moral issues or the personal consequences. Rather, my spirit had spoken through, giving me a clear and distinct *meaning-feeling*, that kind of deep image whose specificity and concreteness lies within the body and only later comes to the mind through the feelings. At no time had I visualized a dalliance with the wife.

How that happened, what happened, what kind of *knowing that was* is the focus of this chapter on discerning.

Modes of Discerning

As a discipline of the spirit, *discerning* is dense, like a multilayered cake. There are many ways of discerning. At the surface, they are not alike. Like deep learning, some of them remain invisible. All of its modes do not work for everybody. Indeed, the obverse holds. *Discerning is an exercise of the spirit; but for each person, as in the core moments of deep learning, it is different.* Each person comes to her own competence and practice. So use the one or ones that work for you and that will lead you into the underlying process.

These qualities of denseness and multiplicity in the ways of the discerning discipline set our method of explication: To tell stories about discerning that reveal different practices with the aim that you will find one or two that lead you to your own way. My aim is to describe a waterfront large and varied enough to allow your enspiriting voyage to find a safe berth. In the end, you will arrive at a kind of clarity that renders the underlying process accessible to you.

Discerning Within the Other Disciplines

You already know about and have practiced most attributes of *discerning* because each of the five disciplines of the spirit so far discussed bears its own set of discerning practices and criteria.

Deep imaging: When in doubt about the truth of your image, when it is fuzzy or vague, when its meaning is not clear from the image itself, return to it and let it speak further in its own language. Continue to image rather than analyze. If the image, when so queried, disappears from the horizon of your conscious awareness, never to return, it may well be false. It may also be unimportant. But if it stays with you, embellished or not, then you have realized in practice a major criterion for discerning true images: *the staying power of the image.*

Deep questioning: A point is reached in the dialogue with others or between your spirit and your social biography when you feel compelled to ask a question that opens up a whole new perspective because the question is basic, underlying, alternative, discombobulating. Feeling compelled to ask a question *that breaks through the grounds of propriety, certainty, or conventional understanding* is a mark that the discerning question is emerging.

Deep listening: When you have emptied so that only spirit remains in your tant-'ien to receive the other, you have entered to the very *space* of discerning and so invited your partner to her enspiriting. As you give attention and become silence, the noise from *her* social biography disappears, and she may discern her own spirit, listen to it, hear its voice call her as never before.

Deep learning: As the deep learner moves from habit back to intention through unlearning, he discerns the elements of his KBVAF that constrain his spirit. The exercises in unpeeling and unfreezing are practices in discerning.

Intentioning: Is this not all about discerning the compelling image as a practice for coming to your intentions? The criteria used in that search are applications of more generic practices in the discerning discipline.

Do these discerning practices possess a common quality? I think so. They are good examples of the *discovery* quality of *knowing* as distinguished from "proof." But if discerning is a kind of knowing that does not demand validation, then what kind of *knowing* is this? That question confronts us with the paradox of this discipline: *How to discern the ends and means of yourself-in-the-world and ourselves-in-the-world— i.e., who you are and what you're up to with other persons in an era of transformation—in contexts characterized by the uncertainty and ambiguity of transformation.*

Another Kind of Discerning Is Listening for a True Ringing

This is a practice that comes with experience. Physicians and natural healers have it, for example, if they have learned, practiced, and penetrated their art and craft over the years. So too is the *discerning* practice of an experienced farmer in *knowing* when to plant his fields and harvest his crop. A good horse trainer has this practice of discerning available to her as has any craftsperson or artist who is worthy of the term…a bridgebuilder, a cook, a parent, a teacher, a lathe operator, etc.

What is this discerning that I call a true ringing?

Once, in the Mountains of the Moon in Italy, on a two-week vacation, my first wife went searching for a piece of white marble for her work as a sculptor. A man of the people, a marble cutter, walked with her from one small piece to another broken off from the huge blocks carved out of the mountainside by these craftsmen of ancient skills—for marble has been cut from the mountains in Carrera at least since the time of ancient Rome. As the marble cutter walked from piece to piece accompanied by Jacqueline, he would rap smartly on the marble, listening then for the marble's response, a particular ringing which would signify that the piece was "sano," sound and healthy. Finally, he found one. "This piece," he said to my wife in Italian, "will hold when you cut into it. It will not crack or shatter under the strain of achieving its purpose."

As I lifted it—barely—into the trunk of the small, rented Fiat, that act of his discerning forever took lodging in my memory.

The analogy concludes: The intention, the deep question, the image must *ring true. Discerning is learning to listen for that ringing.*

But when might you do that? When your *competence is grounded in a deep and abiding experiencing of the matter at hand, be it a profession, a job, a piece of work, a subject-matter, driving an 18-wheeler or doing brain surgery.* My own work in facilitating the enspiriting forays of others is of this kind because I have been doing it for 25 years, not because of any particular "brilliance" on my part. When the true ringing occurs, don't let the neophyte or the arguer ask you to prove anything. Just make the offer of your discernment. Act out of that discerning and the ensuing action will be authentic.

But what if you are in unfamiliar territory? Then your *deep listening* comes to aid of the other who is himself listening for a true ringing. By your emptying so that all that remains in *your* tant'ien is spirit, he is encouraged to do the same. His deep listening is invited too. If he is standing on familiar ground wherein lies his special competence, then he will be invited to "rap the marble" and listen for the true ringing. A good counselor does this, for example. But perhaps that's why there are so few good ones: They don't invite in spirit to partner in the counseling.

Because listening for a *true ringing* works best when you are embedded in the "subject matter," I have searched for another way of discerning to generate that keen insight into the *truth, reality,* and *knowability* of the matter at hand which does not rely on being a master in the craft. Though I am neither a student nor a practitioner of Eastern Zen, I have discovered great parallels among the *purposes* of enspiriting in the Western modes and the ancient and contemporary practices of Taoism and Chinese and Japanese Zen. These, like passages from *Isaiah* and *Job* in the Old Testament and the dialogue between Krishna and Arjuna in the Bhagavad Gita, have illuminated my own work in coming to the enspiriting practices and the disciplines of the spirit that help to penetrate into our de-spiritualized state with an eye to emerging from it.

The Zen koan is one such practice from which I have borrowed heavily.

The Discerning Koan

The Zen koan—(two famous ones are: "What is the sound of one hand clapping?" and "All things return to the One. To what does the One return?")—in its Chinese and Japanese unfolding has been an absolutely fundamental training device and discovery experience for its practitioners to come to a direct, immediate, and intuitive *discerning* into reality. Also, its learning and practice are not partial, occasional, or momentary like so much of Western experiencing. It is of the essence.[16]

For my own enspiriting work, I have translated a few of the Zen koan's attributes into a practice of discerning that provides a glimpse into essence without the years of meditative practice that precede a Zen *satori*. You be the judge of what this glimpse enables you to see into.

I once did an educational policy seminar at North Carolina State University with a group of accomplished adult educators. When the participants had each come to their *compelling image* about the future of lifelong learning, I introduced them to the Western discerning koan as a way of checking out the *meaning* or *center* of that image. This act of inner enspiriting in the passive mode of Zen did not fit the participants' Western strengths in problem-solving and task orientation undergirded by skilled reliance on linear modes of thinking and doing. Some of them came to the discerning koan uneasily, or not at all. But others immediately found it a powerful channel to their *intentioning*. As always, my approach is to encourage envisioners to grasp their vision as a personal commitment and insight rather than as a theoretical proposition or a loose sense of "wouldn't it be nice if...," especially when their compelling images focus on an institutional or societal invention rather than a matter of private concern.

The Western discerning koan has three characteristics which I described to these adult educators.

First, it is a statement that penetrates to the heart of the compelling image—in this case, an image of lifelong learning. It cracks open the kernel and extracts its very essence.

Second, it is *spontaneous*. The statement has no logical antecedent as you quiet and empty within to let spirit speak.

Third, it is a statement that *no one else has to understand but you.* Therefore, you need not be concerned about its communicability or its intelligibility to others.

We all quieted down. Papers stopped rustling. We stopped looking at each other. We focused inward.

This has turned out to be so powerful a discerning practice that I want to share it with you as another way of discerning that complements "rapping the marble."

---

[16] For a thorough introduction for non-Zen Westerners to this powerful enspiriting method, read *The Zen Koan* by Isshu Miura and Ruth Fuller Sasaki, A Helen and Kurt Wolff Book, Harcourt, Brace and World, Inc., New York, 1965.

The Discerning Koan: (Exercise No. 19)

This is a practice that depends on your already having ascertained the *specific* focus for the *discerning*. It may indeed be a *compelling image* or a matter of concern that has already received attention given in Exercise No. 4 *(How to start the deep questioning)* or any serious response to the enspiriting practices set forth in this book or that you have come to on your own. The point is: *That has to be named.* This is not a general searching out. It is seeking to discern the essential, core *reality* of that to which you have already given some attention.

Each enspiritor will discover what kinds of items and activities in her own enspiriting fit this mode of discerning.

1. As always, prepare yourself. For this exercise, review the modes of *deep listening* and come to the final *emptying* of the tant'ien. The quiet inside usually requires you to create or go to some quiet space outside. Any distractions here absolutely abrogate this practice.

2. Name the focus. *What is it that you propose to discern about?* Write that down.

3. Place your specific focus within your tant'ien. *Image* it within: *swallow* it, *let it inhabit* or take you over completely so that your mind, feelings, body and spirit *have become that upon which you focus.*

4. Now, when you're ready, *close off all thought. Yield. Wait.*

5. What comes to you…a few words…a picture…sounds, colors, music, shapes…capture and, if possible, write down. If the first arrivals are not words, place them back in your tant'ien with a quiet, quizzical, loving invitation: *Thanks. Will you give me a few words that stand for the essence?*

6. Continue until something happens that constitutes the essential reality and truth of that which you seek to know.

7. *Is that intelligible?* Yes, to you. *The flash of meaning is there.* Is it intelligible to anyone else? Probably not. In any event, you'll never find out because under no circumstances do you communicate your koan about the essence of your focus to anyone else. Just pack it away, get on with your work—including enspiriting—and give yourself an inward smile.

What if nothing happens? O.K. Have you given yourself enough "time"? As you learn to move into kairos, have no fear of missing the target. Over the years, we have learned that as the neophyte enspiritor practices this, as well as other, ways of discerning, she begins with offering herself plenty of "minutes"—15, 30, an hour, etc. —but sooner or later learns to transpose from the place and time of the here-and-now to that other state which is the inner space for discerning.

Discerning Is Standing Apart from and Questioning Popular Truths and Cultural Myths

True ringing is a generic mode of *discerning*, one that has been with us since time immemorial. I include it in the enspiriting disciplines for those whose enspiriting craft has already brought them to this point of competence and because we always seek a *true ringing* when listening to the voice of our spirit. A discerning koan is also generic—i.e., "culture" free—but is applicable in just the opposite case, when experience and craft are absent but the need is there.

This next mode of discerning is quite different, for its focus is already given and is one peculiar to our transformative era. How are we to discern the truths and the realities of our transformation, whether within the biography or without?

Here, we search out the false questions in our culture, however firmly they may be implanted in our KBVAF. Here, we also seek to discern true questions that place us on transformative ground. The discipline of *deep questioning* is as central to this mode of discerning as *deep listening* is to the mode of true ringing. Reviewing your work in *Exercise No. 8 (an exercise in dissonance)* would give you a leg up in this mode of discerning. How did you discern the dissonance between a social truth, for example, and your direct and immediate experiencing?

Each age, of course, lifts up its own central questions. These frame an era's realities. What is included and what is not? Where do they come from? Are they not embedded in the history of that age, their roots sometimes dug into the soil of earlier centuries out of which that culture has grown? For example, in our Industrial Age have come questions about progress, improvement, change, and success. Such questions were not raised in the pre-industrial eras, at least not by the commonfolk. Now, they are commonplace. Moreover, most of our questions are *instrumental*. They are not about human purposes. We assume we know these. Assumptions about human purposes are lodged deeply within the KBVAF. We seldom tease them out. Yet we must do that, for something about how we understand what it means to be human has led us astray.

What kinds of questions are we likely to ask from the standpoint of living solely within our culture and civilization, incompetent to stand apart and discover another ground on which to stand to ask who and what we are. They are likely to be *how to* questions, such as:

How to succeed without really trying...many versions.

How to succeed by really trying...many versions.

How to lift myself up by my own bootstraps...many versions.

How to feel good about myself...many versions.

How to win at any cost...at no cost...and at every cost in between.

How to pretend it doesn't matter.

How to protect, affirm, advance your vital interests, for yourself, your country, your religious group, your business, your ethnic group, etc. (This question accepts the prevailing notion that human beings as individuals and in their groups are best understood as collections of interests.)

How to make transportation and communication faster, more efficient, more effective, etc.

This is a very small sample. These questions don't go very deep, but they are illustrative of our age's questions. They fit into our collective KBVAF.

Old Myths and New, Old Questions and New: An Exercise in Discerning (No. 20)

This *discerning* exercise has two parts. The first part is about uncovering popular truths and cultural myths of our times. The second part is about transformation. In both parts, we seek to tease out the basic questions. It often helps to develop these questions within a community of learners, be it two persons or 20. Each person brings to the exercise a perspective gained from living and sharpened by the competence of *deep questioning.* It also helps to do this exercise with children and youth, in conversation at the supper table or in a relaxing atmosphere where no one is thinking "exercise." Their perspective is not yet fully molded, the KBVAF not yet locked in place. Their innocence may give you an insight you once had but have since buried in order to conform.

PART A (Exercise No. 20): Popular questions and myths that fit the world we (I) live in.

    1. What is the question? _____

       What is it about? _____

    2. What is the question? _____

       What is it about? _____

       And so forth... _____

PART B (Exercise No. 20`): Questions from our transformation.

Here, the idea is to discern the deficits of our age's culture by pulling away from the popular or main questions and prevailing myths to name the questions *that have not yet been asked, that have been avoided, or are not part of popular discourse.* To do this, you must distance yourself from your prevailing, collective KBVAF. On what ground will you stand? Such questions are prompted by your spirit, so the competence of deep questioning and *deep listening* come into play.

Here is an example just to get you going, one that has emerged into Western consciousness in the last 25 or 30 years, though in other times and places other peoples have raised and answered it.

Are we human beings stewards over the environment or partners with it?

What are some others? What are the new questions yet to be asked? What are the questions that arise from our being in transformation, be it yourself-in-the-world or ourselves-in-the-world?

1. _____

_____

2. _____

_____etc.

Now reflect on the questions from Part A of this exercise. Do they not enable us to hide from or excuse what we do to each other and to our world? Do they not let us put on our best face, the powder and rouge of a culture that accepts premises such as that deprivation, suffering, and injustice are God-decreed, or are inevitable, or are the necessary cost of doing business?

If our age's questions have not led to an uncovering of spirit but rather to its suppression, then how are we to discover what deep questions to ask? *Accept neither your age's questions nor its answers.* While that rule of thumb is an incomplete response, it is an extraordinarily powerful starting point for discerning what questions to ask.

I have already suggested that the generating of questions both for Part A and Part B of this exercise be undertaken within your community of learners. I have also suggested that you invite young persons into the *dialogue.* Still another helpmate is to *invite those who are marginalized—living at the margins of majoritarian society—to ask their questions. You do some deep listening.*

The discipline of discerning applies not only to deep questioning but indeed to all of the other disciplines of the spirit *for which it is a corrective.* It might be an image of the future or the past, an appetite or a need shifting towards an intention, a sense that a lesson once learned is the wrong lesson about a wrong naming. Whatever their application, acts of discerning the truth often rest on *posing alternatives to what is popularly or habitually offered.* Prompted by their spirit, great scientists and humanists do this in the name of discovery all the time. We ordinary folks better initiate and practice the discerning discipline across the waterfront of our issues, our deficits, our discomforts and disquietudes, our pain. Shall we? That question gives us transformation's problematique.

A Summary

What have we learned about the discipline of *discerning*?

• That we want to ask about the *truth, reality,* and *knowability* of the enspiriting disciplines.

• That in this day and age, discerning focuses on *transformation*, both within and without.

• That the discipline involves a way of *knowing* that is heuristic, discovering and judgmental but requires neither proof nor certainty.

• That the practices of all of the other disciplines of the spirit involve their own discerning modes in which you have already engaged.

• That discerning is listening for a *true ringing*; but what kind of *knowing* is that?

• That the discerning koan may reveal something about an innermost core of *truth* and the *reality* when you already have a solid focus.

• That in this day and age, a central activity of discerning is to tease out new questions about ourselves-in-the-world.

Is that all? Can we tie these together and move on? Of course. For it turns out that the discipline of discerning is best understood as *process* rather than *event*; and that we have yet to uncover that underlying process, which is the focus of Chapter Twenty.

20

Discerning as Process

Discerning as Process

Can we uncover the process of *discerning*? Certainly in part and to a level that gives us some additional discerning practices. In describing the process, I move it along from part to part, from the beginning through the middle to the end. Truly, though, I don't think that's the way discerning actually works. Like the other disciplines of the spirit, enter it through your own insight and experience, enter into whatever part of the process that speaks to the disposition of your spirit, and you will have gained entrance to the entire discipline.

The sequence I propose to follow is this:
- A start-up mode of interior imbalance.
- Another start-up mode of external conflict.
- Meaning-feelings as a testing ground.
- Deception as a lever for digging deeper.
- Planting the seeds.
- Stretching the inner space; returning to the original.
- An intuition of feelings.

A Start-Up Mode for Discerning: Interior Imbalance

A great starting point for the *discerning* of spirit and its voice (however that is expressed) occurs when the binding together of wholeness and the synergy of a human being is stretched beyond its breaking point; when the integrity begins to disintegrate; when the wholeness begins to tear apart; when the motor energy of the spirit begins to run roughly, to vibrate unevenly as if it were going out of tune. These are warning shots across the bow. That interior imbalance sometimes becomes immediately palpable, as in the story I related of a discerning during my college days. Other times, the imbalance takes longer to notice if the spirit has been buried by your social biography. The mode of imbalance described in Chapter Nine is a direct experience of this starting point.

What is this imbalance? Wherein does it lie? We feel its effects. What are its sources? How are we to discern these?

Another Start-Up Mode for Discerning: External Conflict

The condition of external conflict has much in common with that of internal imbalance. The questions are the same, though the initial focus of attention is different. At the interior level, *discerning* focuses on sources of discomfort and pain within ourselves; at the exterior level, discerning focuses on sources of discomfort and pain among ourselves and others. But even then, in the more conventional conflicts among persons, groups, organizations, interests, nations, a wholeness, an integrity, a *harmony that is always there in principle* has been torn asunder. The parts bump up against each other, sometimes with great force and physical violence; sometimes more gently if a sense of the loss of the whole still exists.

The key to discerning the external conflict is the same as discerning the internal imbalance: Locating *your* part in it, coming to *own* that, not placing blame on the *other* but asking the deep questions of your social biography in *both cases*. With the interior imbalance, it is *yourself-in-the-world* of which I speak. In the external conflict, the actors are *ourselves-in-the-world*. But in both domains, the discerning is about that aspect of social biography with which spirit has begun to engage. Coming to own—i.e., in this sense of recognizing and acknowledging—the social biography part of the imbalance or conflict is the result of these start-up modes of discerning. Many of the practices of the disciplines of *deep questioning* and *deep learning* are integral to this part of the discerning process.

Easier said than done? Of course. So we re-engage with the disciplines of the spirit, those of us who are ready; and by *our witness* make an offering to the other or to our spirit that invites *dialogue* with the other-in-conflict or between spirit and social biography. Although this book is not about conflict-resolution, I have no doubt that the enspiriting disciplines, all of them, create a way of being and doing that in its essence is *healing*.

But perhaps we get ahead of ourselves in laying out the discerning process that may start either way. For the acts of enspiriting, even as we are practicing them, generate many false starts.

The First Inkling of Deception

We discern because we deceive, not always advertently. The deceptions are by self and to self, by others and to others. Is enspiriting the antidote? Not always. Acts of enspiriting are sometimes complex. Sometimes, these enspiriting acts are deceiving. Sometimes spirit is involved in the deception! How can that be? Who is deceiving whom?

Note now that at its surface, the interior move of enspiriting may cover over a social biography out of kilter. I think there are contemporary modes of spirituality as well as some experiences in formal religion that cover spirit smoothly rather than dig deep to *uncover* it. Like the skin of a shiny red apple, the spiritual story may carry all before it *in a surface way.* Have you not purchased such an apple only to discover much to your annoyance that when cut open the apple is rotten? Have you not experienced that? Slicing into a fruit pulsating with ripeness and temptation only to discover the soft brown of disintegration? Have you not started a great friendship or love affair to be caught up one day by the painful discovery that the relationship is running rough because either or both of you acted out an intemperate need rather than a worthy feeling?

Self-deception and other-deception go hand-in-hand with *discerning*. One is the occasion for the other. But deception by spirit, deception of itself: What could that possibly mean? Among other things, that enspiriting is no panacea. It is a constant searching, a constant trying-out, a constant offer and re-offer. That holds for the discipline of discerning as for all of the other disciplines of the spirit.

How might we get closer to the kernel, get beneath deception, closer to the truths and the realities that enspiriting demands?

Enter the Meaning-Feeling Mode of Discerning

The *discerning* process often involves the emergence of a *meaning-feeling*. Of all of the practices of *deep imaging*, this one is most central to discerning. Here, the inner imbalance translates into a *meaning-feeling* that stands for the state of your interiority, not in a mental way but in a feeling way that I have described as a sense of discomfort, unease, tension, disquietude. That meaning-feeling creates a strong question: *What's going on here?* The meaning-feeling is the sensed manifestation of a quagmire of ourselves-in-the-world, the uncertainty, the ambiguity, the amorphous quality of our having entered into a transformation throughout the world *and in our very selves* shorn of directions, frameworks, guidelines because those lodged in our KBVAF *are false by virtue of our having denied spirit a partnership for too long.*

External conflict is also well served by the *meaning-feeling* mode of discerning. When that kind of image emerges, it points to underlying sources of the conflict that are so often hidden in slogans that obfuscate in the hope of denying the conflict in the first place.

Do you see, once again, the parallel between the interiority of imbalance and the exteriority of conflict? In either case, a hard nut to be cracked by discerning in the meaning-feeling way that a deception has been perpetrated by myself-in-the-world or ourselves-in-the-world to *preserve the imbalance, the tension, the conflict, the pain that in these cases are the emotional glue of the KBVAF.* And we enjoy it! The gnashing of teeth, the shouting of epithets, the shaking of fists and the shooting of guns involve body, feeling, mind and spirit wrapped into an impassioned synergy, a feeling of being-at-one-with-yourself that drowns the pain of interior imbalance and external conflict. Spirit is also party to that *unless the disciplines of the spirit are practiced.*

Some among us will then seek desperately to falsify matters of the spirit to cover up the interior imbalance and the external conflict. In the mid-East, for example, the Arab-Israeli conundrum is sloganeered by fierce appeals to a Moslem or Hebrew faith, as if that were a source of the conflict rather than, indeed, a potentially binding glue. Hence the need for discerning. Hence, *depth* and *inner action* as the location and practices of these disciplines. We tend too easily and too swiftly to construct false edifices to our spirit, to turn to cures that are worse than the disease, to erect grave social theories, to utter theological pronunciamentos, to formulate interventions and action-plans, to construct social policies *none of which rest on the ground of our spirit.*

Beware the temptation of self-certainty, the shiny surface of that juicy red apple. *Argue powerfully but listen deeply.* Discerning is a special kind of inner work that cuts to the quick. It hurts, not so much the other as yourself.

Deception here is a matter of our spirit moving hesitantly and not yet truly into ourselves-in-the-world. It has yet to find its voice. Do not view spirit as omnipotent. View it as a loving, creative, joyful, extraordinarily powerful manifestation of spirit energy in the universe, birthed into our flesh but enduring in times and places of which our three-score-and-ten on this planet are as a pebble on the shores of the oceans, a speck in the sands of the deserts, a flitting spark in the infinite horizons of the stars overhead. Nevertheless, when it is enfleshed, it will erupt and it will participate in nefarious practices unless the invitation is to its own endisciplining.

When invited through these disciplines, spirit begins a *dialogue* with our social biography, hesitant, not fully trusting, poking around here and there. But its seeds will be planted.

Planting the Seeds

Each act of the spirit is a seed planted in the soil of ourselves-in-the-world. Images of our possibilities generated in *deep imaging* are such seeds. Will they grow? Are the seeds well planted in a bed of *hope* well cultivated by *courage,* now to be nurtured by the healing rain of *deep listening* and the warming sun of *deep learning* so that the blossom of our transformation springs forth through deep imaging, breaking through the encrusted soil of tradition to proclaim the brilliance of its foliage and of its many colors in *the possibility of a shared vision that does not deny us our uniqueness while permitting us our community?*

Spirit may sow its seeds on unprepared soil and retreat. Which seeds will grow, which seeds will die? The struggle is not uncontested. From time to time, each of us disputes with spirit: A Jacob wrestling with the Angel of Yahweh; an adolescent so disempowered by the false images of her times and condition that she rejects the loving arms of Sancta Sophia, Mother of Wisdom, to seek her self-esteem in an undiscerned pregnancy; a high achiever mounting her career to ride the path of power, accumulation, prestige, all the emoluments of an acquisitive society and an ego desperate for self-aggrandizement even while her spirit rests uneasily in her tant'ien and occasionally reminds her body with the twinge of a pre-ulcerative cramp or an uneasy sleep of anxiety that all is not well with the way she has chosen to create herself-in-the-world.

The Core of Discerning

So we come to the essence of the *discerning* discipline in which we seek the truth, the reality, the knowability of spirit in all of the ambiguous, uncertain, indeed unknowable context of transformation *to which spirit calls us in the first place.* It is the *problematique* of discerning which, unlike the other disciplines, is occasioned by its own deception. How? By discerning that...

• Spirit can deceive itself if, by virtue of its historic suppression, it springs forth untutored and undisciplined into a world that will receive its energy and its passion, but not its promise. That promise is why the disciplines of the spirit, long ago uncovered in ancient lands and traditions, are now recaptured and offered anew. (Spirit deceiving itself is the focus of the next chapter, Discerning About Discerning.)

• Spirit can deceive social biography, be it myself-in-the-world or ourselves-in-the-world, by virtue of forays into the world *prior to the deep learning by spirit of itself.* The practices of unlearning must go very deep indeed to remove the constraining aspects of KBVAF so as to give spirit space to confront itself and discover what it is up to and bring it forth through a *compelling image.*

• Social biography may deceive spirit by enticing it out with false promises and hopes, then capturing it and placing it in the service of ideology, institutional hegemony, organizational dominion, or personal avarice.

When spirit first speaks out—a cry, a twinge a murmur, even a shout—each of us seeks a clue that more is at stake here than an accidental alignment of occasion with intention. What ripens within? What calls forth discerning? "What's going on here?" asks the troubled youth, biking back and forth around the core of an unrecognized inner conflict until his inner space, deep listening all the while, sends forth the meaning-feeling that is his discerning.

Stretching the Inner Space; Returning to the Original

Is this ground on which we tread too soft? Have I led you into a quicksand with no syllogism to hold on to, no hard rules presented in a manual for the neophyte who wants to play the enspiriting game? Yes, it is quicksand of delusions, false starts, wrong significations, sweet feelings that do us in, "deep" questions that get us to where we wanted to go in the first place (self-fulfilling prophecy!), visions of a future that recapitulates somebody else's past unworthy of you, listening "deeply" in a way that is marked down on the sheet of good deeds by the counseling that ensues rather than the emptying to receive the other's spirit.

Where is the solid ground? What of *intuition?*

There can be, and often is, a *first reaction, the flash of an instant—no more!—*when the truth of the matter is revealed concurrently with the provocation. Leaping blindly is the negative side; but sometimes what we call *a leap of faith,* unreflected, born from within, is prompted by the spirit that carries all before it in an initial foray. We are saved by a *discerning* act of spirit that wields the occasion and the intention into a flash of awareness like a bolt of lightning and a peal of thunder so close that we know the strike and smell the smoke in the same instant.

Yes, sometimes we are saved by our spirit making the discernment despite ourselves-in-the-world. But don't count on it unless you are long and well-tutored in the disciplines. Spontaneous acts of discerning work when they do, but can not be called out deliberately. In the time of travail which accompanies the early stages of transformation, the flashing wit of instant discerning often is of little avail. We want to *stretch* the discerning moment by creating space within that slows down, pulls back, and captures the outward occasions before they disappear from the screen. Once again, we seek our inner kairos.

Discerning complexity and deception are not simple matters where spirit is involved. The spirit will be invited to examine itself, to engage in a reflexive act as in *deep learning*, wherein social biography is not involved at all. *That clearly is the key, whereby deception is removed and spirit comes to know itself, its truths, its realities and these become visible.* That happens in the space we call kairos. Here, the implicate order and the explicate order of all realities come together to create a milieu within which spirit discerns.

But when you seek that quiet, "stretched out" inner space, look at what you're up against.

Fighting the Tyranny of Time Revisited

A characteristic of modern cultures is the fleetingness of events and the superficiality of experiences. Today's fad is deposited on yesterday's ash-heap as payment for tomorrow's provocation of the senses. Today's plane crash becomes yesterday's tenement fire as the sounds of gunshots from tomorrow's terrorist attack pepper the wet ink of the AM newspaper or the blurred images of the six o'clock news. There is little *discerning* here, hardly time for noticing anything much less giving it attention.

Were we able to stretch the space for discerning, we would deep question sloganeered truths, deep image alternatives and deep listen far beneath the surface of territorial games, ideological rivalries, cultural hegemonies, and the ego-needs characteristic of acts of ruling as distinguished from acts of governing.

Discerning requires a moment stretched beyond its instant. It requires the vast expansion of consciousness to overleap the conventional fences of time, place and past history. It invites disconnecting the future from the past so that we can free the former's possibilities from the limits of the latter's certainties. It is an action undertaken first within an inner space where it reverberates, breaking all conventional boundaries set by the social biography, where it tingles and penetrates all levels of consciousness, where it can be savored and replenished before it—discerning—is transposed into the outer world of judgment, choice, and decision.

Where is this space to be found . . . or invented? What is this space . . . time? Often, we enter the *space* of kairos through the time and place of the moment evaporated by its inadequacy. "Take your time, child," admonishes the loving grandparent gently, when the child presses her nose against the glass case full of the unfathomable splendor of chocolates, hard candies, sweets beyond compare. Time and place have disappeared. Neither the authority of the clock nor the cold hard of the glass mean anything. The candy and the child are present to each other. Inside their space works a yearning wonderment to which, in fact, the candy eaten five minutes later can do no justice.

In an external world characterized by this fleetingness of experience and the inexorable demands of "real" time, batch time, innovative time, response time, conflict-resolution time, and decision time, acts of discerning are an anathema. For they require transposing attention from externalities to begin stretching the inner space.

What is that like? How to do it?

Is the slow motion of moving pictures a case in point? Does that not provide a savoring, a repeated tasting, a seeing with a different eye and for a different purpose? Slow motion, by pulling apart the connective tissue of ordinary time, opens up another reality, a new perspective. A searching out is now possible, and so invited. A tempo of stretching out, of repetition, of on-goingness creates still another inner milieu for discerning. Indeed, in *deep imaging* and *deep questioning*, discerning is initiated by the *return*—to the original image, to the earlier question to discover if it remains, disappears, or changes.

Like a rubber band, stretching the inner space allows for the return to the original. Sometimes, of course, the original act of enspiriting, whatever its domain and its disciplines, carries all before it, storming the barricades of doubt and uncertainty. Nothing need be added. The blossom has opened and borne its fruit. But when a true ringing is absent, when the feel is not quite right, you must open the entire inner space for all of the disciplines to work together.

Do you realize now that all of the disciplines of the spirit, acting together, in concert, not torn apart and categorized to frame a book about them, are the mode of discerning, its process, its practices, its sources?

Discerning as the Intuition of Feelings

To summarize to this point: Initial acts of enspiriting—the active voice of spirit—may be tentative, wary, or misplaced, not yet properly prepared for by the crafts of inner work. Quite rightly do we question their truth, their reality, their knowability. Such acts settle on inhospitable soil. The unease, the tension, the imbalance are the interior signals that the inner work is not yet done, indeed may have to begin. Stretching that inner space, returning to the initial practices of each discipline reconstitute the inner work of enspiriting. Are my images false? Have I got the wrong question? With whom shall I deep listen and when? What have I learned over my life that I must now unlearn?

Are these "thought-questions"? Are these to be unpacked by the processes of thinking? So far, I have skipped over the thinking mode of *discerning*. I have reminded you throughout this book that the thinking activity is more suspect that we are trained to believe. When queried about the validity of final ends, even the great thinker Aristotle is alleged to have said, "Only fools try to prove that which is self-evident." Human purposes are revealed by a process of discerning that goes far beyond a thinking activity, though it is included.

Thinking serves too many masters. Is *critical* thinking an antidote to the essential instrumentality of thinking? Bereft of the skills of critical thinking, we are without control over our destiny. But relying solely on the skills of critical thinking, we can not discover our destiny.

In searching for our compelling image, for example, or in querying the validity of our KBVAF, is thinking involved?

In discerning, a movement takes place, back and forth, among the inner competence of the spirit. Use reason when it serves to reveal rather than to hide. It certainly can help in the *sorting out* part of the process, when confusion, doubt, self-obfuscation reign in the early stages of enspiriting in any of the disciplines. It is central to *deep questioning*. Thinking...mentation...analysis...the cognitive activities and skills, *in a time of transformation*, uncover questions but not answers. No acts play us more false than those of the intellect in providing answers. You can *argue* for or against any kind of position. Intellect serves any master. How often does the so-called hard ground of familiarity, empirical validation, or statistical correlation edge inexorably toward the sinkholes of ideology, value-dispute, obfuscation, and the passion of certain righteousness when ourselves-in-the-world are queried.

This back and forth movement is the interaction of the disciplines of the spirit. Enspiriting engages with ourselves-in-the-world through feeling, thinking, and imaging as it searches for its proper mode. One prompts the other. One transforms into the other. Seek the *fit* of these disciplines, how you will arrange them, how you will intermix them. I myself feel that *deep listening* as a discipline of self-focused inner work and early discerning are fond sisters, walking hand-in-hand through the tangled underbrush where spirit first meets ourselves-in-the-world.

Feelings play us false less often than *thinking* or even *imaging*. A male-oriented culture emphasizes the thinking activity as a way of approaching the world and therefore of discerning. I myself have had to work very hard to move beyond that mode to that of *feelings;* and it is mostly women who have helped me. I have a long way to go, but I know that feelings of unease and imbalance, whether within or without, are true signals. Feeling them is knowing them. As doubt arises in early enspiriting and you call upon yourself to begin the discerning, query your feelings. What are they about? What has occasioned them? How do you feel about them...your feelings? What do they express when listened to deeply?

In the obfuscation of our times, false images abound. And uncritical thinking is the byword of the non-historical mind that lives only in the present. Living only in the present is not the same as the idea of *presence* and the fact of *being present,* as we shall discover in the chapters on *dialogue*. So living only in the present is to deny that the past and the future live in us, and so it is to deny spirit. All critical thinking involves a memory of the future as well as the past. And the body remembers, too, perhaps better. Feelings are the way our body engages with itself and with the world. They provide the solid ground on which to stand as you move into the discerning discipline. No syllogism can replace the intuitive sense—the feelings—that an initial set of claims, an initial foray to interiority, an initial enspiriting are just "not right."

But you can't stop there. Discerning's process is a spiral open at both ends, the input side and the output side. That spiral is a structure that permits acts of discerning to feed back on themselves so that, as in deep learning, spirit learns to discern itself.

How that is possible, what it is like, and how you can participate in spirit's discerning itself is the focus of the next chapter.

21

Discerning About Discerning

Cracking the Nut

How do we pierce the dilemma engendered by false starts, ambiguous offerings of the spirit, tentative engagements with external realities that may lead us astray? After all, as *discerning* is a discipline of the spirit, is it not also subject to misapplication or to the vagaries of an untutored faculty? How could this be? I mean, after all, if we can't trust our spirit in this matter of discerning, who or what can we trust? I think this is the nut to crack.

The problem here is threefold:

First, how do you learn to invite out spirit to engage with yourself-in-the-world?

Second, who is the "you" that extends the invitation? Is it the same "you" that does the discerning?

Third, how do you learn to trust your spirit?

Discerning as Invitation

The how, what, and why of inviting out spirit are all of a piece. Spirit demands entrance into our realities, ourselves-in-the-world. Look to your own inner experience and that recounted to you by friends and colleagues if you doubt that demand. While we may not "demand," we certainly invite, because recourse to all of the other modalities of "fixing" things in ourselves and in the world have come up far short of what we know to be our potential.

Yet there is a certain peculiarity in the abstract idea of "spirit" as an entity or object which we can "invite." We should be a unity of body, mind, feeling, and spirit that proclaims our oneness, our indivisibility, our wholeness. But because that unity has fragmented in the modern world, we have come to think of ourselves as separate entities, each one in contrast to, often in competition with, other parts of ourselves. These distinctions among spirit, feelings, body, and mind are not just analytic; we *feel* them, we *name* them, and *we act out of that fragmented reality.*

So, for example, a Nazi concentration camp guard might participate in horrendous acts during his on-duty hours, and become a model, loving husband and father at home. So the loving parent can admonish his children to play together, to work together on a joint project, to learn to share and collaborate even while he prides himself on beating the brains out of his business competition. So too, the church-goer makes his weekly peace with God but, during the rest of the week, gives no more attention to God's call to him than he does to the sound of the traffic outside his office window or shop door.

In these initial stages of enspiriting, one "part" of our fragmented self makes an invitation to another "part" of our fragmented self. The social biography, out of a great need that it itself may find difficult to comprehend, extends the invitation, usually in the form of a poorly articulated cry for help. Each of us makes that invitation—or plea—to spirit to her internal status. Many can't extend the invitation at all—for example, persons in despair or the ultra-rationalists who fear anything that can't be analyzed.

But for those who are ready to extend it, the invitation has many sources. Does yours start with a question that pries open an entrenched institution of which you are a bored member or a suffering victim? Are you intrigued by the possibility of emptying the tant'ien so you can undertake a new kind of listening? Have you been astonished by the images that flood your dreams, your fantasies, your waking moments unbidden but forcefully pressing you to consider realities alternative to the commonplace truths about how the world works...or how you work? Is your curiosity still unhaltered despite years of being schooled in the rules of what to learn and what not to learn?

Does it matter if you couch your invitation in the practices of one discipline rather than another? Not at all. No matter where you start, all of the disciplines eventually weave into a new fabric that clothes your person in an aura of spirit that can no longer be concealed. *But you have to make the invitation*—not someone else—for it is your spirit that waits in silence, deep within your being, for those acts of yielding that tease it out.

In the time of early childhood, spirit springs out before it has been suppressed by parents afraid of or unaccustomed to their own enspiriting or by teachers for whom *deep learning* and *deep imaging* are the very activities with which they will not deal. Our youngsters show us what deep learning and *deep questioning* can do. That terrifies most of us. Our youngsters ask questions about themselves-in-the-world, about justice, about sexuality, about human relations, about Mother Earth and all of her creatures, about birth and death, about *spirit itself that is of them*, questions for which each age gives partial answers. But children move forward, inventing theirs, propelled by their recently enfleshed spirit... until we tell them to STOP.

Then there is that long hiatus between childhood and old age. For most of us, spirit sinks into the caverns of our souls, into itself, hiding in the tant'ien and biding its time. That is when the invitation must be deliberately and lovingly extended as a response to those initial forays of the enspiriting soul, the inner stirrings, the discomfort, the pain, the imbalance when ourselves-in-the-world begins—or continues—the process of disintegration that always accompanies transformation.

But as you become practiced in the disciplines, you need not wait for unease, discomfort, tension, imbalance. As you become familiar with your inner territory, spirit shows up in many ways, sometimes playfully, sometimes painfully; and as moments of joy surge towards ecstasy, as moments of terror at the oblivion beyond turn into the welcoming comfort of spirit engaging with spirit in other spheres of existence, you have learned to yield to the spirit in you and let it speak.

That yielding is what invitation to enspiriting is all about.

Do you remember the three questions ? First, how do you learn to invite out your spirit to engage with yourself-in-the-world in the first place? Second, who is the "you" that makes the invitation and does the discerning? Third, how do you learn to trust your spirit?

The second question must now be addressed. We must probe the "nature" of spirit a bit more. For if we are separate from spirit, as the purveyor of the invitation would suggest, we are also not completely just ourselves-in-the-world. Were that the case, we would be captured. We would be useless as agents of transformation. There would be no hope.

Who are we that give ourselves the name "enspiritor," the one who enspirits, the one who is in the discipline along with spirit? Does the discerner stand outside or inside this conundrum?

Who Is the "You" in the Acts of Discerning?

Isn't this an odd question? It rings out in a funny way, abrupt, prior, the answer already assumed lest we could not do the enspiriting in the first place, lest the disciplines be empty phantasms conjured up by a wizard. There is, after all, a certain solidity and safety in acknowledging that when all is said and done, each of us is who we are..." a rose is a rose is a rose." Why not just leave the question at its existential best?

Were it the case that ourselves-in-the-world could continue on a stable trendline into the future, so too could your "you" be satisfied with itself. But the transformation of ourselves-in-the-world is otherwise because it starts within each of us. *Discerning* that transformation so that we are *agents in its behalf* rather than bystanders requires a fulcrum on which to set the discerning levers of discovery and judgment. As we transform ourselves-in-the-world through a synergy of inner work with outer work unified through the seven disciplines, spirit must review the methods and products of *these very disciplines because, like social biography with which it has newly joined, spirit itself needs disciplining and tutoring as well as welcoming and experimenting.*

That is the meaning of the question: Who is the "you" in acts of discerning?

Can, then, spirit review, examine, listen, judge, assess, discern *itself?*

Where Is the "You"?

For spirit to discern its own action is for spirit to engage in a reflexive act whose need and possibility must be built into its primary disciplines of *deep listening, deep questioning, deep learning,* and *deep imaging.* The meta disciplines of *intentioning, discerning,* and *dialogue* must be somehow located in the four primary disciplines...or somewhere else.

But where is that "somewhere else"? Is it the tant'ien which I have named as the abode of spirit, its house, so to speak, in your body? Tant'ien is lodging and not act. It provides space within which your feelings, your hopes and your vital life energy can themselves act. Recall the discussion in Chapter Seventeen (Ways of Intentioning) as I remind you that central to my approach to the disciplines of the spirit is the movement from noun to verb, from spirit—what and where is that—*to the acts of enspiriting,* from experience to *experiencing,* from image to *imaging,* from intention to *intentioning.*

The question, where is the "there" implied in "somewhere else," is falsely posed. Our aim is not to search for a place located in a "you." It is to search for an act, or a series of acts that I have called *process*.

Discerning as a Reflexive Act of the Spirit

The Old Testament Jew in me admonishes that we shall be known—judged, discerned—by our acts. So too is spirit discovered and discerned in and by the acts of enspiriting in *deep imaging, intentioning,* etc. As I have already pointed out, *discerning* interacts with and is an integral faculty of all the other disciplines. It is a special virtue of enspiriting that *spirit acts on itself. The "you" in the acts of discerning is the enspiriting itself.* It is not the protocols of external or objective research, and certainly not the biases of ourselves-in-the-world that stand in such desperate need of transformation and so are very shaky ground on which to set any fulcrum of judgment.

We have a language problem here, because reflexive acts conjoin that which we have split apart. We'll start simply.

In the first instance, spirit discerning itself means that subject and object are the same. Have we any experience in this reflexive state? Of course. I shave myself. He scratched himself. She empowered herself. At its root, discerning is a reflexive act, spirit acting on itself to perceive its truths and its realities in an age of transformation.

Its movements are not unlike the self-corrective adjustments of a pole vaulter in mid-air, shifting his weight, shifting his balance, re-aligning his muscles, body, position, inner circuitry in the very act of vaulting...or skiing...or long-jumping... or walking a tightrope...or enspiriting. As it becomes proficient in its disciplines, spirit moves among them, adjusting, modifying its questions, its images, its intentions, etc., *deep listening* to them all to generate its truths and realities through the authentic action, inner and outer, it undertakes within the new "you" of spirit and social biography dancing to a new tune.

The Open-Ended Spiral of Discerning

An analogy may be helpful here. Image an open-ended spiral, connecting a deep-within space where spirit lives to an external space in the world as we think we know it, a manifestation of our collective KBVAF. These reflexive acts of *discerning* occur at any point within the circuitry of that spiral where spirit seeks its own truths and realities, whether prompted by itself or by the social biography that also lives within the spiral.

At the bottom point of the spiral, call it the innermost, are entry points for spirit itself, ways that it can creep in tentatively, carefully, self-protectingly because it has been shut out for so long. What is this "spiral"? Is it not the *disciplines* themselves, which spirit tries out as it is met by the social biography coming in?

Had enough? Consider then that this spiral is permeable at all points along its length open to a universe, indeed all of the universes that ever were, are, or shall be. This is *the implicate order* in which spirit is born and to which it returns, bringing back and forth the images of the possibilities that are the raw material of our transformation.

Spirit and social biography meet and begin their negotiations within the you that is this spiral itself. Both parts, both open ends, exist... *and each knows the other*, however much anyone of us may deny that based on the conventional wisdom lodged in our KBVAF. If you seek an account of this relationship of spirit and social biography flashing back and forth on this spiral of self-discerning, read up on quantum mechanics. That account of reality rests very much on a similar description in another vocabulary for which "evidence" itself is a problematique deeply embedded in the account. There are more than one account or theory which seek to explain and articulate quantum reality.[17]

This spiral is a dynamic circuitry of interrelationships among various levels of consciousness and expressions of the spirit, evidence for which stems from the experience of people within these acts of enspiriting as they have shared them with me and with each other. The discerning spiral of the spirit is neither time nor place. Its nature is movement, juxtaposition, process.

What then is the "you" in the you? Is it not this dynamic, interactive process of interiority, the open-ended spiral that provides the moving perspective of the reflective act of discerning? Spirit *becomes present to itself*, discerning the truths and the realities of its own acts of enspiriting as it engages with ourselves-in-the-world through the circuitry in which social biography is also immanently present.

---

[17] For a description of eight views of reality that are held by different prominent physicists and mathematicians, see Nick Herbert's *Quantum Reality, Beyond the New Physics*, Anchor Press/Doubleday, Garden City, New York, 1985. Among these eight accounts, two reverberate closely with my understanding of enspiriting. One Herbert calls Quantum Reality #3: "Reality is an undivided wholeness... that in spite of its obvious partitions and boundaries, the world in actuality is a seamless and inseparable whole." (p. 18). The other, Herbert calls Quantum Reality #4: "The many-worlds interpretation. (Reality consists of a steadily increasing number of parallel universes.)" (p. 19). Though Herbert's book is written for the lay person, I don't pretend to understand all or very much of the multiple accounts of reality occasioned by the work of Werner Heisenberg, Max Planck, Neils Bohr, and all the rest of the great "reality" physicists of the first half of the twentieth century. But note that the opening sentence of my Chapter Nineteen is: "In the enspiriting practices, there is always the question of whether what you see, hear, feel, and sense of *your* spirit is true, real, knowable." That question is, *in principle*, no different than the question of "What is reality" raised by quantum physicists. Their work has been occasioned by deep problems that have ensued as a result of seeking to *measure* the quanta that the particle physicists have uncovered since the smashing of the atom. In enspiriting, we do not *measure*, at least in a quantitative way. But we do seek to *know the truth and reality of our immediate experiencing of spirit through the practices of enspiriting*. On what other ground can we stand?

I offer the analogy of the inner spiral of spirit-energy that constitutes the seven disciplines. Whatever you come to, and even if you seek a "final" answer and do not find one, do not let such intellectual inquiry rob you of the profound experiencing of your spirit at work in you and, through you, in the world.

But What Is Knowable?

Does this account of the inner work of spirit *discerning* itself sound ephemeral? Where is the solid ground on which to stand, to place the fulcrum so as to move the world as Archimedes asked, or as God calls us to do? How solid is this ground of "inner circuitry," the open-ended spiral of enspiriting into which everything feeds? Can you grab it, stand on it, kick it? Not at all. Ultimately and finally, can it be regressed into a hard diamond of immutable reality, the essential you, your spirit? Of course. But what is that? Have we at last come to it? Then what and where is it beyond this spiral analogy?

My response? *"Spirit" is a craft of inner action. We know spirit by its action in us and in the world, and we come to that action through a set of practices I have named the disciplines of the spirit:* Never at rest; always awaiting their moment; in process; in quest; in venture because ourselves-in-the-world stands in such dire need of transformation.

This spiral is not a place. It is not a physical mechanism. It is energy, exactly of the kind which Neils Bohr discovered held together the particles whipping around the nucleus of an atom. There is nothing there but energy, configured into wave-motion or particle-motion *depending on what you're looking for.* So too is spirit, a diamond of energy glowing and sparkling and unquenchable.

Thus, the "you" in the discerning process *is the interaction itself, the complex interaction of spirit meeting with yourself-in-the-world.* At any moment, the focus of the interaction may shift toward one or the other end of the spiral. As spirit enlivens and engages, it is buffeted by the externalities of ourselves-in-the-world: the Pharisees against whom the Rabbi Jesus proclaimed his call for justice, love, and a return to Yahweh's commandments; the historic American institutions and habits of racial prejudice against which John Douglas, Thaddeus White, Red Cloud, Martin Luther King and innumerable others enspirited, seeking their authentic action in a world of institutions and behaviors supported by a KBVAF that tried its mightiest to deny them that authentic action of their spirit; the British colonial system of oppression and hegemony through which the Mahatma marched to the sea to make salt and for which Northern Ireland, God bless it, still seeks a like spirit. And spirit's invasion of ourselves-in-the-world is manifest in the countless millions of daily occasions of intimacy when we humans engage directly with the injustices and heal the pains in the lives of those we love, live with, work with, our neighbors and friends too.

Discerning as Trusting Your Spirit

My third question is: "How do you learn to trust your spirit?"

A little review may be helpful. Sometimes, spirit emerges surprisingly quickly. Sometimes it emerges with surprises! Sometimes invitation—yielding—and reflection through the disciplines may take a lifetime before its voice is heard. No matter. But what is to be trusted? How and why is it to be trusted?

Often do I invite my colleagues in enspiriting to a *praxis* of the experiencing question: *"What is it like to do this?"* rather than attempting to provide a theoretical account.

Return to the image, I might suggest, and see if it still lives. Let it speak to you in its own language of images. Let your feelings speak to you in their own language rather than relying solely on the explanatory or judgmental gestures of psychology. Trusting means becoming used to. At the start, with little or no experiencing of spirit to build on, the cases are still too unique and unfamiliar. "Where did *this* question come from?" you might ask yourself as the process of *deep questioning* begins. Certainly in *deep imaging*, an image may come into your conscious awareness whose content, whose direction, whose promise take you completely by surprise. Some with whom I've worked have looked askance at the notion of *deep listening*. Yet each, exploring in her own way how to empty of feelings, values, judgments, past expectations, etc., has descended to her tant'ien to discover that quietness of an inner space in which spirit lives, and has received the other's "words" without judgment ... returning then to her conventional world of consciousness awed, half-afraid, and only half-believing. What have I uncovered? What am I to believe? What is happening that lets me hear the other's unspoken words, to gather in the other's unspoken thoughts and feelings, to feel her spirit present in me?

Is not this trust of your spirit no more than a burgeoning *familiarity* with the ways your spirit works, the ways its announces itself to you? This is a practical question. Spirit expresses a uniqueness coincident with its very essence for which personality, character and social biography are only resemblances. Disposition is no doubt closer to the ways of your spirit.

So let your spirit become familiar to you. Let it show itself in its own way, within the modes and styles it chooses. Later, as it learns to enact the practices of these disciplines with competence, you may come to trust how it will manifest itself. After all, a mechanic—now, with fuel-injection engines and computers, a technical engineer—

opens the hood of your car to be confronted with familiar space, a territory of motor parts of *which he has an internal map he knows how to read*. More, he trusts his own capacity, part experience, part knowledge, part instinct. Use that last word, "instinct," to cover the trusting part. A great diagnostic physician—my father was one by all accounts—goes beyond the tests, the probes, the machines, the chemistry, using these but going beyond them to a realm of instinct, hunch, intuition, feelings. These are loose words, not rigorous concepts. Yet are they not language for acknowledging the successful linkage of inner and outer ways of work, for trusting that along the inner circuitry of the spiral, spirit and social biography have found a way of partnering?

Trusting is a word we use to describe the familiar which may later turn into the habitual and the expected. I expect my spirit to engage forcefully when I am confronted with injustice...and it does. I trust my spirit to discern its right action if I give it the space. I trust my spirit to yield up the images and feelings that give direction and concreteness to my *intentioning* when my rational calculations do me false or provide no clear answer to a moral dilemma or to a difficult choice. Learn the deep listening craft and your spirit will speak to you. Learn to empty out the social biography that has monopolized your "you," so you can hear the inner voices speak. Then listen deeply. Those voices do not lie. They do not dissimulate. But you must await their moment. You can not force them. They speak in the time of kairos.

"Spirit is empty and waits on all things."

In Sum, the Process of Discerning

- Readiness.
- Preparation.
- Identifying the focus, the need for *discerning*.
- Deep, inward movement to get onto the spiral.
- An altered state which engages us completely.
- Waiting, quieting, yielding, listening.
- Spirit speaks its discernment.

1. *Readiness*. Are you ready for an act of discerning? Is the need, the disquietude, the imbalance, the conflict *there*, felt, known, intuited? Rest, and let it search you out.

2. *Preparation*. The first stage blends into the second. Do you know how to prepare yourself? It is no different from preparation for entering any of the practices of the disciplines.

3. *Identifying the focus.* Of course, this comes at the beginning phase of any of the primary disciplines. At some point in enspiriting, spirit's energy comes into clearer focus: a special question, an enduring concern, a deep pain, a compelling image, etc.

4. *Inward movement.* This always occurs, a sinking, a yielding to, an entering into the realms of other consciousnesses that move deeply back and forth along the inner spiral, going to its open ends and seeing what's there, jumping about as the cork of our cognition bobs back and forth on the surface.

5. *An altered state.* So difficult for the Western intellect to deal with and comprehend. But as we enter into this process of discerning and *become the process itself,* the different aspects of ourselves, the divided and fragmented persons, become whole again, a ground on which we can stand forever and a day.

6. *Waiting, quieting, listening.* This is the space where kairos breathes. A second, an eternity, it doesn't matter. Guilt, anxiety, task, or the kettle boiling over: These have disappeared into the haze on the horizon. We tremble with anticipation. Will the lion roar, the eagle soar, the mouse whisper, the buffalo speak? We are on the *medicine wheel circle of learning.*

7. *The discerning.* The act occurs. When you return from kairos, the truths, the realities, the knowability of transformation, big or small, of yourself-in-the-world or ourselves-in-the-world, has illumined who you are and what you're up to, your authentic action, your project in the world.

22

On Dialogue

The Sociability of Spirit

Most enspiriting practices, because of their emphasis on *inner work*, are undertaken by the individual person. In some religious cultures, ancient and contemporary, enspiriting is seen as a *social* act in which the spirit, both interior *and* universal, moves through the body of the community as it moves through the body of the person. In the Judaic-Christian Western mode of *congregation*, enspiriting is understood to be a communal act, though my own experience with a number of denominations is that *community* of any kind is often absent. To take two distant examples, the *Sufi* whirling dance which generates an ecstatic altered state within which spirit enters is more than an individual act, as we have come to understand that in the West. And participation in the *medicine wheel* or the *sweat lodge* among the plains tribes of North America is a communal act in which, while one may be spoken to and so gain insight from the Great Spirit, the entire community benefits from the enspiriting experience of the one and the one from the collective enspiriting of all.

It is not easy for us to understand that *while spirit's life and expression in each of us is unique, its fullest and most authentic action takes place in acts of community with other enspiritors.* Yet that understanding and its translation into practices of enspiriting as *being and doing together* is at the crux of this seventh discipline.

Dialogue, then, is a discipline of the spirit in its *communal* aspect, by which I mean *unifying, sharing, transcending—though still celebrating—the uniqueness of your spirit by uncovering its social form and inventing its social space.* But as we are mostly bereft of community in this age of rank individualism, large organization, and mass society, spirit seeks new and special ways to express its sociability. These ways are the seventh discipline, and they are enacted in a social space which, years ago, I named a *community of learners.*

We are called by our spirit to learn our way into community, not as an ideological, a political, or a policy act, not as a social movement or a religious upsurge, but as the very essence of enspiriting. Spirit does not live in the individual alone. It is most alive when two or more persons join their spirits to form a new *locus for enspiriting.*

Until now, I have postponed a formal discussion of this discipline. But a critical reader and *all* enspiriting practitioners must have already realized that in the very first discipline offered, that of *deep listening, two persons*—and soon on, more—*undertake those practices together.* One becomes silence while the other speaks. One gives attention while the other holds forth. One seeks to be empathic and enter into the other's *presence* while the other describes her images, her concerns, her disequilibrium, etc. One is non-judgmental while the other offers her judgments. One re-enters the space to nurture the images, the ideas, the risks that the other takes. And, finally, one empties of all *but her spirit* as the other's spirit enters her tant'ien and speaks out.

From an action and practice perspective, I could easily have initiated your introduction to the disciplines of the spirit through dialogue. For this is the supreme act of spirit *in which the joint work of spirit and social biography , in their inner dialogue with which by now you are so familiar, transpose into an outer dialogue with other enspiritors who are not only experiencing their own inner action but are also experiencing yours . . . and vice versa.*

Then why have I waited to present the discipline and practices of dialogue to the final rather than the early chapters of this book? Two reasons, each of which is germane to the discipline itself.

The Method of Analysis

Aristotle said that the *method of analysis* and the *method of action* are not the same. So too, would I add, the methods of presentation of analysis—in books, for example, lectures, or Congressional hearings, etc.—and the methods of action are not the same.

Enspiriting is action of the spirit. Understanding, analysis, critique come afterward, through *praxis.* They are not prior to acts of enspiriting. Knowledge does not lead to action, though it can correct it. Rather, action leads to practical knowledge, i.e., reflecting on who we are and what we do in specific and concrete settings. *Reading this book is not enspiriting. Reading this book is not practicing the disciplines of the spirit. Reading this book is not becoming competent in their practice.* Reading this book is an intellectual enterprise, cognitive, analytic, linear, explanatory and descriptive. When you enspirit, you will immediately understand these differences (if you have not already). In my thinking about how to invite you to your enspiriting, it has proven easier to describe and present the first four *operational* disciplines and then to carry through to the *meta*disciplines of *intentioning, discerning,* and *dialogue* in that sequence. But that is not how it works in practice. For example, when invited to and then practicing deep listening early on in your enspiriting work, some intentioning is involved, however vague or ill-formed. Otherwise, you might not do it, for deep listening is a strange and provocative way of communicating compared to conventional standards of discourse. Not looking at the other person when she is talking to you? What kind of nonsense is that? Being silence? How is *that* communicating? So even at first blush, spirit's intentioning is involved, as some blinders in the social biography and some habits of communication defended in your KBVAF are disengaged. Yet we do not unpack the discipline of intentioning for another hundred pages or so. In short, the action is there before the analysis; and dialogue begins at the start of enspiriting and is, like discerning, part and parcel of the other disciplines.

The Absence of Community

But there is a second reason. I have couched the starting points of enspiriting in the inner work of a person rather than a community of persons because *most of us don't belong to such and find it foreign to our experience.* Most other enspiriting practices world-wide, be they a *Yoga asana,* a *Zen meditation,* a *T'ai Chi form (action)* or a *Christian prayer,* are also lodged in an individual's inner work. But if I were to stipulate that in order for you to enspirit, you must first enter into community with other persons, I suspect you would look askance at that injunction, throw up your hands, and exclaim: *Why, how, where?*

Why you enter into or build community, where you enter into or locate it, and how you might do that as a matter of your intentioning are the *operational questions of entering into transformation.* For if we do not learn to do that on this planet, I think we are lost. But having said that, I have not chosen to lay on you that trip. Rather, I have spoken to the Western, and particularly Anglo, proclivity for celebrating the individual as the locus of action, responsibility, ownership, initiative, risk-taking, courage, choice and decision: All characteristics of the enspiriting mode translated back into a commonly understood vocabulary of individualism.

But now, having said that, I invite you to enter into dialogue with your fellow enspiritors, if you have not already done so, and to read on for a clearer understanding of the discipline and its very special conditions and practices which, when brought to fruition, bring you right smack into the space of transformation of yourself-in-the-world and ourselves-in-the-world.

What Is Dialogue—and What Is It Not?

I think that most of us understand *dialogue* as a verbal exchange between persons. This exchange takes place through conversation. It is about some matter of importance to each. The conversation, then, is not idle chitchat, but of substance. What are its outcomes? The exchange may produce an insight into a truth where previously there was obscurity or confusion, (e.g., Socratic). Or, the conversation moves the parties toward agreement where previously there was conflict (e.g., some forms of conflict resolution). Or, the conversation generates a sharing of ideas and practices where previously there was insularity, (e.g. a research conference or seminar, or teamwork).

This conventional understanding of dialogue is quite reasonable. Its occasions are matters of importance. The competence constitutes the art of conversation. The consequences can be found in mutual insight, agreement, the sharing of ideas, even common action.

Is this understanding adequate? Not anymore, and certainly not in the practices and disciplines of the spirit. Why not? By now, you know the litany. Ourselves-in-the-world is rending and tearing, sometimes at the most intimate and private domains of yourself/myself-in-the-world and certainly within the social, even planetary domains of ourselves-in-the-world. A transformation has begun. Each of us in our own way, expanding the boundaries of our external action, pushing against the limits of our internal action, is called upon to participate in dialogue as an agent of transformation.

You may not choose to do so. But if you enspirit, you can't help yourself. Acts of the spirit are not solitary, insular, provincial, or alone. In the final analysis, you will or do find yourself unable to enspirit without other persons who are also enspiriting.

Dialogue is the discipline of the spirit in which the inner work of the one is transposed into the outer work of the two or the many who seek, who practice, and who enter into a community of persons grounded in the mutuality and reciprocity of their spirit through the vehicle of constituting themselves as a *community of learners.* Dialogue is the connective tissue that enables each and all of us to enspirit together (i.e, practice and actualize the disciplines) about that which troubles the spirit of any one or all of us. It is the *enspiriting mode of compassion,* whether that be for self, for others, for the world. Its connective tissue is fragile because its practices, not unlike the other ways of enspiriting, have to be tried, tested, rehearsed (for most of us) and learned within a general social climate that does not always welcome them.

How dialogue can be undertaken, under what conditions, and with what consequences for and application in the *community of learners* is the focus of these last chapters.

Conditions for Dialogue

What we want to do first is to name and set forth the *conditions* of *dialogue* in whose absence that fragile connective tissue is seldom generated and often torn apart.

One such condition is to understand the *sociability of spirit* and the creation of *social space* for dialogue to take place.

Another condition is to understand the *intimacy* that characterizes that social space.

A third condition is to understand the nature and fact of *presence,* a state of being that underlies dialogue as a foundation.

When we have these conditions in hand, we can then deal directly with the act of *turning toward* through which the connective tissue of dialogue is established. This is the *practice* in which the *community of learners* is initially formed (though in *deep listening,* as you by now know, the physical act is turning away, not looking at the talker, your fellow enspiritor, just so that the *turning toward* of the spirit can be actualized).

Modes of Dialogue

As I understand the discipline, *dialogue* has three modes.

One mode, most familiar, is *external.* Most often, we undertake dialogue in this way, with the other in which presence is mutual. That is, my presence to and with you is entirely reciprocated by your presence to and with me. We have become an "our" presence, transcending an "I" and a "Thou" to become a "We." Here, the inner work of each is bridged by an outer work that I call a *turning toward.*

A second mode is *internal*. It is dialogue within, the name of the inner action that encompasses social biography and spirit in conflict, working together, forming a new "I," and spirit acting reflexively upon itself that I have identified as the core of the discipline of *discerning*.

The third dialogue—I scarcely want to call it a "mode"—is with God. As this is not a religious tract or a theological dissertation, I will have little to say about this except to alert you to Her presence, by whatever name you choose to call or *not* call, that *always* accompanies you on the journey of your spirit.

In these modes, the essential practice of dialogue is *praxis*. *Praxis* is reflection by members of a *community of learners* on their enspiriting experience. Modes of dialogue and its *praxis* are the focus of the last chapter.

The Lack of Social Space for Enspiriting Together

Much of what I have written so far about the disciplines of the spirit could be understood in the sense of individuation: That the disciplines practiced by the individual person as agent in behalf of her spirit find their expression and purpose also so located. As I have said, that is a partial and therefore wrong reading of spirit. Yet persons still tend to ground the life of the spirit in the individual—even in the presence of God!—because there is no other ground for us to acknowledge. Family? Of course, except that we have come to understand its demise, its change, and its deficits in a sociological way rather than as a matter of a family learning how and why to enspirit together about their situation. School? Naturally, except that rarely is it understood as a community of learners seeking to help each other to their *deep learning*. The corporation? The subterfuges of community are resplendent in the false manipulation of information and image to get employees to bond themselves to corporate purposes. But where is the healing, the nurturing, the enspiriting, the compassion characteristic of a *community of learners* (as distinguished from good spirits and boosterism)? Recently, I conducted some envisioning sessions with middle management and senior technical people in a transnational corporation. Over half of them identified *issues of the spirit* and *issues of community* as central to the future of their company. Of course, their insights were ignored by corporate policy-makers because to translate them into internal organizational changes would have required, among other things, a vast, hierarchical, largely impersonal organization employing tens of thousands to transform itself into many *communities of learners;* and that is understood as neither the practice nor the purpose of the typical business organization. It is ironic that *unless that institution learns how and why to do so, its likelihood of survival into the next century is not very great.*

And last but not least, what of the congregation? There certainly we should find a community of spirit among the parishioners, right? Most often, wrong. Members may worship together in the same liturgy; but like the corporation, the religious setting is designed for an individual approach to God, for a forgiveness of individual—but not group or societal—sins, for a redress of individual—but not collective—grievances, and for relief from an individual—but not social—guilt and anxiety, the two major motivating forces in the Western world. For example, *as a nation,* the German people have been as unable to deal *in community* with each other and with the Jews, Gypsies, the handicapped and the other groups decimated by that holocaust just as the North American peoples *in community* with each other and with the Native Americans have been unable to deal with their conduct in 400 years of holocaust, one that still obtains because the White Faces in both Canada and the United States having stolen from the Native Peoples not only their land but also their spirit, *and still do.*

In a modern world bereft of community, the sociability of spirit still goes unrecognized. In the contemporary world of mass institutions and a popular, mass culture, so many of us consider matters of the spirit to be a *private* concern. How then might we best invent the space for spirit's embracing of other spirits in *dialogue*?

Creating the Social Space: the Community of Learners

In enspiriting work, we have needed to create a social space which allows for the possibility of an enspiriting community without forcing it and without enticing people into it under false pretenses. That invention emerged in the formation of the *community of learners,* a fundamental practice of envisioning the future in projects, workshops and seminars I began in the fall of 1970.

How, I asked—the typical *instrumental* question—would envisioners, invited to image the future of their concerns well-addressed, within organizational or community-based projects and in graduate schools and continuing education seminars, *share* that material?

Quickly, I came to a prior question: *Why* would they *want* to do that?

As the process and practices of envisioning the future—first called *inventing* the future—evolved in those early years, four responses to those two questions were uncovered.

First, the possibility and desirability of shared vision, a task for *dialogue*.

Second, the likelihood of self-deception—a task for *discerning*.

Third, the need for clarification—a task for discerning.

Fourth, the search by most futures-envisioners for justice and community, though the search showed up not in bold generalizations or in a theoretical perspective but as specific and concrete images of justice and community come to life within their own, relevant action-settings, from the prison to the corporation, from the school to the planet, from the local congregation to the professional group, and from the neighborhood to the nation-state—a task, as it turned out, for dialogue.

The Possibility of Shared Vision

It soon became obvious that within any given group of enspiritors—if they focus on the future, I call them *envisioners*—be they ten or ten thousand, there existed both significant *differences* and significant *commonalities* in their images. We sought to fashion a set of practices whereby each envisioner could maintain the *uniqueness* of her own concerns and images while allowing for *common vision* to be discovered. We invited envisioners to seek a shared vision *in an honest way:* not by coercion, herding, manipulation, withholding relevant information or by directed imaging—a method, by the way, which professional imagers love to use with imaging illiterates. How then? By inviting envisioners to view each other's images of the future or concerns about the future with an eye to commonalities. In a number of community-based projects in the United States and in Canada, 100 citizen-leaders might generate 100—or more—unique images of the future. They would then reduce that spread to about ten scenarios whose proponents *could maintain the integrity of their individual images while at the same time generating a commonly-held future which represented their collective intentioning.* Whatever your perspective—wave theory or particle theory—*both* uniqueness and commonality were sought, were celebrated, and were discerned. The practices were dialogical: Envisioners deep listened, deep questioned, and deep imaged *together.* And because that is enspiriting work, they began to learn and to practice the discipline of *dialogue.*

In short, these envisioners in hundreds of projects and workshops around the world sought to help each other to their mutual learning about what was inside each of them—*their spirit speaking out!*—about the future that *bonded* them as well as *separated* them—a *community of learners!*

The Likelihood of Self-Deception

This likelihood of self-deception and the *discerning* practices that serve as its antidote have already been discussed. What may not be obvious, however, in a culture caught between the Scylla of individualism and the Charibdis of homogenization—e.g., the popular KBVAF, political correctness, don't rock the boat—is that many people, when invited to such enspiriting practices as *deep imaging* and *intentioning* find themselves on very shaky ground, unnerved by the invitation and highly suspicious. Why? Because they do not believe the invitation, the invitor, or the sponsor. And, they may be afraid of their own responses. In one community-based project, in the first sessions attended by the chief elected official and the chief local government administrator, citizens questioned them severely about the integrity of the project. Four years later, it turns out they were at least partially right in being suspicious, for the social inventions and policy recommendations they made have not been enacted, and the administration is once again running scared of what at least some of its citizen-leaders have envisioned and intended.

Two litanies generate a powerful song of refusal: *What is the (your) hidden agenda? What, make myself vulnerable?*

But we are all game-players. Learning to adhere, to follow, to participate, to pretend are social behaviors in which most of us are reasonably competent. So we begin the *deep listening* and deep imaging, even if we are hesitant. We keep to ourselves our doubts, our suspicions and our reservations. Social survival, after all, is quite appealing … except, perhaps, in the time of our transformation when it is very unclear who and what will survive.

This suspicion has many consequences. In the enspiriting disciplines, *self-censorship* and the self-imposed criteria of *feasibility* and *practicality* are substantial barriers to doing the deep inner work. A result is that envisioners—or enspiritors engaged in any other activities that invite the enspiriting work—often deceive themselves and others about what their spirit calls them to. Spirit itself, if invited out for the first time, may participate in its own deception.

While we might all wish to think that the discipline of discerning is self-effecting, that the corrective mechanism is automatically built into the enspiriting practices, such efficacy is not my experience. *We need help in discerning the deceptions and the omissions.* We need help in coming to the heart of our concern, the sources of our pain, the viability and compellingness of our images, the quality and intent of our ensuing outer action that makes it authentic.

We are a suspicious people. Toward the end of the 20th century, as we look back and as we consider our present predicaments, who wouldn't be? I can't count the number of times we have been lied to, manipulated, withheld from, by persons in positions of leadership—political, organizational, media, etc. In all of the so-popular "leadership training" programs with which I have been associated or know about, self-integrity and other-integrity of the kind built-in to these disciplines of the spirit are sadly lacking and, in many cases, deprecated. "That's not how you win." "That's not how you lead." "That's neither effective nor efficient."

So when the invitation comes your way, why should you respond honestly? The habit is not there. Deception is the mode of response, often unwittingly, most often by yourself of yourself.

But we learned that as two persons began to *share* in the practices of deep listening and *deep questioning,* even at first by such simplistic devices as *being silence* and *giving attention,* they began to trust each other, i.e., know what to expect from the other because she was engaged in the same activity and seeking also to learn, to test out, and to apply the same practices. *A community of learners* was emerging by virtue of that sharing of new ways of work in which each person confronted the same sorts of doubts, confusion, misunderstandings in the practices. How and why do I deep listen, deep question, or deep image? That sharing, then, gave each permission to address the possibility of self-deception in a *loving, nurturing, yet rigorous way.* As each person learned about her own inner life, coming finally to her spirit by bypassing her social biography, *she learned about the other in a way that would help herself and would help the other.*

In short, they generated a provisional set of *common understandings* about *common practices* rendered intelligible by a new *universe of discourse* which are all considered central—though by no means sufficient—to the formation and maintenance of community

This is a mutuality of learning that we come to in dialogue, and a matter of vulnerability and presence that I will discuss shortly. But in our schooling experience, indeed in our broader socialization into social norms and behaviors, what is fostered is not this mutuality of learning that is a fundamental quality of a *community of learners.* What is fostered is competition, advantage, getting ahead the fastest, as well as social, gender, class and ethnic discrimination.

This possibility of deception had to be confronted, not by admonition but by invitation to all fellow-enspiritors to help each other through that morass.

What absolutely amazed me—though now I think I understand it—is that they did! And still do 25 years later!

The Need for Clarification

Actually, this need surfaced in the very first graduate school seminar, "Inventing the Future of Education" at Syracuse University in the fall of 1970. I had not yet named the practices and grammatical "rules" in the literacy of imaging. Instead, I gave attention to setting long-term (20-year) goals, a very special kind of imaging that often does a disservice to enspiriting if undertaken too soon because of a misplaced concern for practicality and feasibility while the images are still aborning.

An invitation to specificity and concreteness as criteria of sound work was always made; but, in those early years, many envisioners in organizations and communities set goals that were so *over-generalized* that no one could discern what it would be like if those goals were achieved and thus could not specify what to do *in the present*— i.e., authentic action—to begin the movement toward and into a future illuminated by these over-generalized goals, like: "All children will have equal access to sound education." Like: "Education will be redesigned to enable all learners to achieve their full human potential." Like: "School policy will be set by a participatory approach that involves parents, students, members of the community-at-large, teachers, administrators and members of the board." Like: "Schooling will be understood as an integral part of lifelong learning rather than as terminal."

Do these sound familiar? We are still framing our educational reform activities in similar language 25 years later and still not getting there. Why? Because the over-generalized and abstract nature of these long-term goal statements serves to (a) *hide conflict (for who could disagree?)*, and to (b) *relieve us of the difficult and even transformative work involved in their actualization.*

What is missing? Clarity. Specificity and concreteness. Actionability. Ownership. Compellingness.

How to get it?

Ask envisioners hard questions that will help them clarify and stipulate *what they're up to* (the matter of *intentioning*) *without attacking them or their images, without putting them on the defensive.*

We all had to learn to do that, I not least of all (and I'm still working at it!). What might prepare the way and place two or three, or even an entire group of envisioners into the domain of non-judgment? *Being silence* and *giving attention.* Just *listening* ...and not retorting. Even 25 years later, these are considered a strange form of *dialogue,* a communication aberration, *until the enspiritors actually do it.* Then, it's like falling off a log.

Is that all? Not quite. Enter *empathy* and *nurturing.* Not only are these modes of clarification. They are also modes of *community* because they introduce the possibility of sharing spirit. Being in community always involves sharing something central to its formation, not peripheral. For example, a communistic community shares its means and modes of production, what we in the so-called capitalist societies call *property.* Many Utopian communities of the 19th century in England, Germany, and the United States sought to do just that without the totalitarian overlay of the old Soviet Union. In a *community of learners,* what is shared are the disciplines and practices of enspiriting. By undertaking these ways, the talker/imager/goal-setter intuits that while her own work may be clarified and, indeed, even challenged by her partner's *deep questioning,* her colleague is offering support and compassion at the levels of feeling, body and spirit.

In every possible setting—religious, educational, governmental, research, professional, business, neighborhood—we found that these forms and practices of communal relationships had to be learned by most people *learning together* and building their *community of learners* as the social space for dialogue.

The Search for Justice and Community

How might envisioners/enspiritors *share* the substantive images and concerns that emerged from their inner work? *Why* would they want to do that? These are the two historical (and still operative) questions that started us on the formation of a *community of learners* and brought us to the uncovering of a seventh discipline of the spirit I have named *dialogue.*

What has happened is this: The majority of the goals, the images, the intentions and the actions of literally thousands of envisioners in every possible action-setting have been oriented toward a search for community and a search for justice. The concerns, the disequilibriums, the pain that these people have felt and enunciated are also about the lack, the absence, the deterioration of justice and community in their lives, be that their *inner* and even private lives, or in their *outer* lives; that is, the various publics and organizations of which they are members and in which they participate.

I do not offer this conclusion from a theoretical or ideological perspective. Practitioners of the art of envisioning and the practices of enspiriting all couch that search in the specificity and concreteness of their life stories, their life hopes, their life disappointments, and lodge the search in their relevant action-settings.

What is this search?

In the community focus: "How are we best to live together, work together, be together, love together, raise our kids together, be professionals together, be prisoners together, learn together, teach together?" That question is translated into the most practical foci you can imagine. If you have done this work, you must find it in your own concerns, imaging and intentioning, not because you seek to answer a generalized question but because its *lack*—that of community—plagues our lives like locusts ravishing a beautiful, green, lush, promising harvest that will be our community when we have come to it through our transformation.

In the justice focus: "What do we owe to each other by virtue of being human, of being children of God, of existing on the same planet, of being members of the same family, same business corporation, same ethnic group, same professional group, same country? " This too is an ancient question and there is not one situation I can think of or imagine at any time or place on our planet when it has not been asked *and answered*. Once again, envisioners have not engaged in a scholarly debate about the nature of justice, a debate that goes back as far as recorded history and to which the great philosophers, leaders, cosmologists, prophets of ancient times (Aristotle and Plato, Confucius and Lao Tse, Moses and Amos, Erasmus and Meister Eckhardt, to name a prominent few among many) have made a contribution which still sets the terms of the debate. But when the child says to mommy or daddy or sibling: "That's not *fair*," she has entered into the greatest conundrum of our species, and will never be out of it so long as she lives.

Would and should these twin foci of envisioning justice and community, found everywhere in this work, be *built in* to the very way we do this work of enspiriting together, into the very process and practices? I surmised that without grounding our quest in the enspiriting realities of what we were doing together, we are playing a game, doing a simulation, avoiding the stark realization that *justice and community start at home, with myself and with others in my here-and-now*. What does that imply? That our *ways of work in envisioning and in enspiriting might adhere to the same quest of our spirit that we unveil through our deep imaging*.

"Walking the talk" is the modern parlance. So the practices of sharing, of clarifying, of nurturing, of asking hard questions, of enabling each other to come to her best work—*even when there are substantial disagreements!*—are expressions in actuality of these two generic and universal domains of human enterprise. We must put into practice these considerations and see what happens.

Seeing what happens—what are its consequences—is the focus of the dialogical work of *praxis*, the *sina qua non* of dialogue. I shall take that up in the next chapter. But in fact what happened is this: As we—the envisioners, the enspiritors—have done our work, we have begun to learn that what we do together is not only forming ourselves into a *community of learners*. *It is also a harbinger of our very transformation.* That is, in the enspiriting we are learning not only how and why to enspirit. We are also learning new *ways of being and doing together,* ways that are still largely unacceptable or hazardous or threatening to many people *until they actually do the work.* In that work, through the *community of learners,* they are testing out new forms, new structures, new intelligibilities and, most importantly, new practices that are, in small but actual measure, *being in transformation.* Dialogue is that mutuality of enspiriting that gets us there.

So it turns out that the *community of learners* is a precursor for the invention of dialogical institutions and social practices across the spectrum of a new reality that we—our spirit—have already begun to practice. Those spaces for dialogue are inherent in deep questioning, deep listening, deep imaging, and deep learning. Why inherent? By the fact of *presence.* Properly understood and practiced, not as an intellectual exercise only or primarily, *community of learners comprises persons who are present to each other in spirit. Presence is the bedrock of dialogue and the foundation on which such a community is constructed.*

In dialogue, the spirit flourishes mightily and sweetly, sometimes ecstatically, sometimes painfully. In enspiriting with the other, spirit comes to the full flowering of its deep learning and its intentioning. In dialogue, spirit achieves its fullest expression. It finds its home, drawn out of the recesses where it has hidden so long, invited out by the presence of the other who extends by her presence an invitation which cannot be refused. *Presence is a way of naming the poetry of the spirit. That metaphor carries all that spirit is.*

But what is presence?

Presence as Intimacy

As previously discussed, *dialogue* is generally understood to mean an exchange through conversation between two or more persons at the level of ideas. Thus, the ideal of the Socratic dialogue has come down to us as a model of cool, dispassionate reason applied searchingly to the illumination of propositions about what is and what is not. Heat, anger, passion, the joyous embrace are generally regarded as having no place in dialogue.

While dialogue certainly includes the juxtaposition of opposing ideas, particularly if *deep questioning* moves them to a more revealing ground, it is *presence as intimacy* that calls out spirit in all the ways we are able to understand that intimacy: Parent with child in the fullness of listening to child fashion her world in dialogue with Teddy, or with God[18]; or the child's dialogue with Mommy about why Daddy beats her; or lover with lover in the close interpenetration of spirit with flesh; or wife and husband together in the intimacy of the daily rituals of living and, occasionally, brought to their presence to each other by the ways trauma invades their family and their home; two friends testing their loyalty to the openness, frankness, non-judgment, and acceptance that distinguishes their relationship from the chit-chat and self-congratulations of acquaintances and social friends.

Of course, these examples suggest stories where dialogue is operative through its expression in presence. We all know of too many cases where the same events breed different stories. It is a discipline of the spirit, after all; and when spirit is not present, which means not released, the intimacy is of a different kind, and the relationship often tears apart.

What is it like when spirit is present? How would we know that? Of course, throughout these chapters, I have offered you the condition for and the practice of emancipating *your* spirit. What of the other's?

Stories of Presence, Past and Future

If presence is that kind of space characterized by intimacy that enables the spirit of one to engage with the spirit of another, what could that possibly mean?

One way I learned this was not in the presence of human spirit, but spirit of another kind.

Once, I did a T'ai Chi beneath the majesty of a looming slate granite cliff near Kotor on the Western shore of old Yugoslavia where the mountains come down in a steep drop to the Adriatic sea. A group of us were off from work, having a picnic in a meadow after a two-hour drive down the coast from Dubrovnik. I had been doing a seminar at the Postgraduate Institute on envisioning the future of education, a seminar, by the way, that for most of the participants was a failure because they were unable to emancipate their spirit from the confines of themselves-in-the-world that

---

[18] For a remarkable account of how youngsters engage in *their* dialogues with God, do read Robert Coles, *The Spiritual Life of Children*, Houghton Mifflin Company, Boston, 1990.

demanded they first be authorized by their governments before they could join the envisioning.

As the picnic continued, we talked with an Albanian youth from Macedonia about the ethnic hatreds and prejudices that prevailed among the people of that part of the world.[19] But I was inexorably drawn to this granite mountain that came straight down to the end of the meadow. It loomed at my back and drew me to it even as we picnicked together and told stories. I walked a hundred yards to its face, clearly not aware of what I was doing or why. Then I began my T'ai Chi on the grass not five yards from the mountain's face that rose abruptly from the flat. Oh, how the spirit of the mountain was present to me and I to it as the dance of the T'ai Chi moved my spirit energy out from my tant'ien to flow through my fingertips into that granite cliff. My body, that space, the cliff were imbued with the joining of spirit. Presence was there: That space where the mountain's spirit and mine intertwined; and as I write this, I can still *feel* it in me.

What account is that? What of *human* spirit?

Presence is in kairos, time- and place-free. The *immediacy of intimacy* is most often its occasion. But in kairos, earthly forms are of no moment.

It was no more than five years later that I gingerly approached the giant spruce ten centuries old in the rain forest just off the road from Portland to the Oregon coast of the Pacific Ocean. What an ancient it was, a giant living through the ages. My approach was not casual. My spirit tiptoed. My heart beat faster as, arching my head upwards, I sighted its canopy way above, 200 or more feet from the ground, gentling the forest and now me, telling me it was all right to approach, yes, even to lean up against that enormous trunk, 15 feet in diameter, lean up to it, stretch out my arms as I embraced it flattened against its bark, *her skin,* and joined my spirit with her ancient one.

We were present...but what of human beings? Mountain spirit and tree spirit have traveled the ancient eons and go into the future uninterrupted. But we humans, in flesh and in spirit, are volatile, changeable, sprightly, fragile, and different from one another. When we have become present as spirit, a great uncovering has taken place that sends the omnipotence of time, place, culture, and social biography spinning away into the void. What is left? That is very frightening to most of us. Too strong, too heavy, beyond our cognition except perhaps through poetry, music, drama, dance, and chant that move us to the space of spirit. So "art" is the great medium of the

---

[19] That was 1976. That youngster—perhaps 12 or 14 years old—provided us a chilling, yet matter-of-fact account of ancient hatreds that, 15 years later, erupted into the diabolic violence of ethnic cleansing. Would *deep learning* and *deep listening* in dialogue among them have offered an alternative to these internicine wars?

spirit. It is the universal way of enspiriting for all of us in our scientific, technological, analytic, linear, and pragmatic world.

In transformation, we shall invent and come to many spaces where each person in her inner *dialogue,* the one between her spirit and social biography, provides a healing witness to the others by her presence as they also reconstitute themselves-in-the-world. Whatever its institutional or social/political/economic/cultural form, these will be the spaces of dialogue.

In short, presence is a space where spirit will out *both* to you in your own internal dance of intimacy between your social biography and your spirit and with the other whose spirit becomes present to you as yours does to hers.

Learning to create and witness that space is the discipline of dialogue; and its practices are the other disciplines of the spirit come alive in that space.

23

The Act of Dialogue:
Modes and *Praxis*

Groupness

I have said that the discipline of *dialogue* is, to my way of experiencing and thinking, the fullest expression of spirit and the coming together of all of the other enspiriting disciplines and practices. Without dialogue, there is no enspiriting. With dialogue, spirit invariably has opportunity to emerge from its insularity in each person, often in hiding, and express its essential sociability.

But are these any more than banal reflections of the kind that emanate in such grand generalizations, to wit: "The human being is a *social* animal"? Well, who or what isn't part of a social milieu and a group perspective? Why call a number of individual mountains a range, a multitude of individual trees a forest, an uncountable number of individual specks of sand a desert, an infinity of individual star systems a galaxy, 400 million plus individual worshippers of a certain liturgy Catholics, white people—all individuals! —caucasians?

Our perspective—the questions we ask and the lens we use to filter in and out the answers, our KBVAF—determines what we look for and see. Trees or forest? as the saying goes. But my contention about spirit's sociability, expressed in the intimacy of presence as the basis for dialogue is not offered because of my predilections. To the contrary, people who know me also know that I am a rank individualist, that being part of a group of like-minded thinkers and doers, much less a community, has always proved an anathema to my spirit *ever since I can remember;* and I have had to work very hard at being in community with anyone. Nevertheless, when the invitation is from another spirit, mine will out; and the enormous strength of my social biography is as a plaything in the hands of that enspiriting. No, the sociability of spirit *is spirit itself* and not perspective. So dialogue is the endisciplining of that sociability, not an accident or peripheral add-on, and certainly not the product of an agenda that is only mine.

But how might you test out this claim in enspiriting practice? How might you come to understand this discipline as the *peak* enspiriting experience, as Maslow might say, or as the *ego-transcending* experience of enspiriting, as Assagiolo might say?[20]

The testing is achieved by giving attention to *three modes of dialogue,* and to the penultimate act of dialogue that I call *praxis,* borrowing that word from the ancient Greeks who did not confuse the domains of theory and practice by giving to the former a primacy and a priority over the latter as we moderns have done. We have reified theory as the domain of the absolute and the universal, rather than giving prior attention to who we are and what we do with each other in practice (i.e. action, doing). As you will see, *praxis* in dialogue is a way of reflecting on who we are and what we do when we enspirit.

First, the *Act* of Dialogue: *A Turning Toward*

The conditions for *dialogue* have been named: Coming to understand the sociability of spirit; seeking and creating the social space which enables intimacy; understanding what it means to be present. But what of the *act* of dialogue? It is the act that I call *turning toward.*

First, as to its literal meaning. Turning from back to front, facing each other, breast to breast, loin to loin, nose to nose, we turn our bodies toward each other as the initial *physical* act of turning toward. This act signals the readiness for dialogue and is the offering through which dialogue is established *if reciprocated.* Keep in mind, now, what this is: *The soft body parts present themselves.* The spine, the back, the vertebrae, the rib cage are furthest away, pointing in opposite directions. This is a powerful gesture of trust not very different from when an animal turns on its back to offer up its vulnerability, its throat exposed, to have its belly scratched.

This is a literal, physical expression. No doubt, we can extrapolate from it to various metaphors and behaviors to describe the vulnerability of turning towards consequential

---

[20] These are two very famous Western psychologists who, though coming at it from quite different places, nevertheless argued persuasively for a hierarchy of psychological states that culminated in the person's being able to move beyond his body, his ego, even his societal place to a special state that, in my language, is the space where spirit flourishes.

to spirit as well as to body. What else, then, does this act of turning toward construe? Is it not an opening up, removing as much as possible the covers that enclose spirit so that it can be present to the other? The barriers, social as well as physical and biographical, may vary from one culture to another as Edward T. Hall pointed out so forcefully in his comparative studies of time and contiguity in different cultures. Social space is not uniform and its configurations may well have to be invented differently in one or another culture.[21] But the sociability of spirit is everywhere when we let it express itself in dialogue. So the initial turning toward varies from culture to culture and, of course, from person to person as different kinds of physical presences are established and different kinds of protective social habits are discarded. Because we have learned so much about body language as strongly expressive of human judgment, we have come to the practice of *looking away* in *deep listening* just so that body language does not interfere with spirit's dialogue in deep listening.

In all of the possible ways of turning toward, literally and figuratively, here is what is said: "I am here. I am present. I am ready. Are you here? Are your present? Are you ready?"

When the response is affirmative, though it may not be given verbally, then is created by this mutual turning toward the *concrete spiritual tissue* that is dialogue. Do you understand why I say how far short of this realization and act falls the notion that dialogue is defined as the exchange of ideas through conversation?

Though turning toward is the essential *act* of dialogue, it is actualized in all of the disciplines.

But what happens when the response is not affirmative? Not every offer is accepted. Whatever the mix of disciplines, and whether the turning toward is with *another or within* (wherein spirit and social biography finally learn to turn toward each other), dialogue is established when, through the turning toward, being present becomes concrete and specific. That turning toward by the one gives a signal to the other. Will you reciprocate?

No forecasts can be made as to that response. Expect nothing. Hope for everything. The acts of enspiriting of which I speak throughout this book are too deep to be programmed by the psychological, the educational, the policy mind even if one should want to try. So spirit lives whatever is done to the flesh.

---

[21] When I was Peace Corps director in then-Eastern Nigeria 30 years ago, the Federal Minister of Economic Development and I met for the first time at the small, local airport in Enugu, then capital of Eastern Nigeria. We had previously heard of each other. To my discombobulation, when we met, he not only shook my hand but drew me close to him—six to twelve inches—and discoursed with me for 15 minutes while I was close enough to see the pores in his face and smell the perspiration of his body in that overheated clime. But let me tell you, within a few minutes my embarrassment at being held so close to him in that greatly foreshortened physical space was dissipated by the enormous power of his presence, not only his words and our words, but his very *beingness* which I now surmise was his ability to project his spirit into our encounter and to create a social space for our dialogue *that I have never had with another political or any other kind of leader in the West*—and I have met many—except, of course, John F. Kennedy, who in my one meeting with him accidentally in a corridor of the White House, our both turning the same corner from different directions, projected his spirit too, as we talked for a few minutes.

But then how can you establish dialogue, and with whom? Of course, it's a two-way street that grows into a *multilogue* when enough of us are competent in its practice. (Remember? Both will and skill, intention and ability.) One or the other may be the first to turn toward. Its initiation may well be constituted by listening deeply and non-judgmentally but very much empathically to the clues the other gives that she is turning toward.

Do you see this crucial difference? At issue is not always when *you* want to initiate dialogue. What of the other, be it spirit inside or potential fellow-enspiritor outside? What if the other, however tentatively and frightened, however self-protecting, *begins to turn toward you?* Are you ready? Can you hear the signals? Have you become empty? Can you accept the extraordinary power of the presence of her spirit in you?

Vulnerability: The Indicator of the Dialogical Act

If you are ready, the other tentatively moves into her own vulnerability and invites you to yours. Depending on the new "I" that signifies the newly formed relationship between spirit and social biography, that vulnerability may be expressed in many different ways and degrees. If you are not ready, she may turn away and withdraw her offer. The notion of vulnerability, often used to describe the mystery of presence, means that the spirit hidden inside the recesses of the tant'ien, protected by all the accouterments of one's social biography, *is beginning to show itself to the other.*

What is this vulnerability, this state of being vulnerable?

First, you are invaded by the presence of the other, by her spirit. It mingles with yours whatever be the modes of that expression, be it in images of the future, pains from the past, deep questions about ourselves-in-the-world, the wrenching of learning from habit back to intention, the movement of the other's spirit into your own inner feedback spiral of *discerning.* The palpable presence of her spirit may be overwhelming to your social biography and, ultimately, to the mental culture, the KBVAF, that legitimates and renders intelligible yourself-in-the-world.

Second, to be vulnerable is to be surprised. Simply put, in true dialogue, we don't know what to expect. Always, we are surprised. So...we shy away from it. Signals go out. Don't get too heavy. This is none of your business. I'm not ready for it. Let's get something to eat. The baby is crying. The world's coming to an end. This is neither the time nor place (meaning, of course, the *space)* for it.

Third, to be vulnerable is to face and to allow for the possibility of being hurt. That possibility is often stated by persons who shy away from *dialogue.* But what is hurt? Never spirit. It can be frightened. It can run away and hide once again because it knows your social biography is not yet ready for it. That is an inner conflict whose resolution is a matter for inner work of the kind described in this book. But I don't think spirit can be hurt. In its matter form, it is a hard diamond, an essence, as Almaas says, that is untouchable. *But your social biography certainly can be hurt.*

Vulnerability is a consequence of turning toward not in theory but only in specific contexts; that is, with fellow enspiritors with whom you dialogue. That determines what dialogue is about. That, in turn, determines the limits of your vulnerability.

Dialogue with the Other

This is the mode by which dialogue is popularly known. Even if understood by most people only partially, nevertheless *dialogue* is understood as the exchange and, in that sense, as a social act.

Who is the other in dialogue? *Anyone and everyone who is ready...though not necessarily competent as an enspiritor.* Can it be more than one? Of course. We seek to discover, we seek to invent a *community of learners* in which we are present to one another when that counts. And *when that counts,* we are in dialogue. Two or more, but how many more? You say, certainly not a thousand, much less a billion, etc. I don't know. (Recently, on TV worldwide, perhaps two billion viewers watched the Oscar ceremony of March 1994. Well, that's not dialogue. Of course not. But the *Internet* technology is there, or soon will be, whereby everybody in the world who cares to can be in touch with everybody else in the world who cares.)

What will they talk about? Aside from the myriad conveniences that fill the craw of a consumer-oriented world culture, *what will they talk about? Will they enter into dialogue about that which troubles their spirit, about that which pains them, about their hopes, their dreams, their visions couched in images they can share? Will they learn to deep listen and deep question, taking nothing for granted and everything as possible? Will this emerging "electronic superhighway" turn out to be no different from other, more primitive vehicles for cultural aggrandizement, financial hegemony, and the technology-sharing of the new media itself? Or will it turn out to enable a new kind of intimacy, presence, and vulnerability among those who choose to practice their enspiriting within its media requirements?* I suspect responses to these questions are forthcoming in the electronic networks now burgeoning across the globe. One project in Canada, the *Cultural Leadership Development Project* sponsored by the Center for Cultural Management at the University of Waterloo is developing at least a partial response by linking together cultural leaders and participants across that vast land, from Dawson City to Toronto, from Vancouver to Baddeck in Nova Scotia...for their focus is *cultural transformation as we have been talking about it throughout this book, and their method is learning their way into it through envisioning.*[22]

Two or more? A thousand or a million? I don't know. The study and advent of mass psychology, especially in this century, asserts the likelihood of its impossibility. Be wary of a chorus of "yeas" because they are bred by the master imager, the master manipulator through mass communication. But when that happens, with a thousand or a million or a billion, *in every case those persons are not in charge of themselves and are untutored in the disciplines of the spirit.*

When we come to be in charge of ourselves, fully capable of enspiriting in these multiple ways with each other about ourselves-in-the-world, I for one am certainly not going to say that dialogue cannot happen among the many present to each other in a *community of learners* that enables uniqueness to flourish in community and without hegemony.

Let us invent it. Start with yourself as I have with myself, move to the other, *invite in not the masses but the multitudes.* If the advent of the computer can handle the infinity of data bits, who is to say that spirit can not handle an infinity of enspiriting acts?

Dialogue Within

This is the mode of *dialogue* carried on within, between social biography with itself, between social biography with spirit, and between spirit with itself in the disciplines especially of *deep learning* and dialogue. Is this more difficult than dialogue with the other? For some, yes, for some, no. A great deal depends on that aspect of your social biography that understands the nature of *its* issues and *its* proclivities as *private* rather than *public*. Many with whom I have worked begin at the so-called "private" level, uninterested in or undiscerning of the world "out there" that has so formidably influenced the nature of their inner, private life. Associated with the notion of "privacy," a deep concept that goes back to the founding of Greek and Roman society and philosophy, are the ideas of intimacy, authenticity, transcendence, and a psychic inner life not to be made accessible except to the closest of family and friends.[23]

---

[22] To learn more about this project, query Donna Cardinal, the project's director and, more, a master envisioning facilitator with whom I have worked closely for years...and a feisty enspiritor as well. She can be reached by phone (403) 435-3278, by fax (403) 434-3078, and on Compuserve 73004,2444.

[23] In *The Fall of Public Man* (Vintage Books, 1978), social philosopher Richard Sennet has this to say: "Modern ideas about the psychology of...private life are confused. Few people would today claim that their psychic life arises by spontaneous generation, independent of social conditions and environmental influences. Nevertheless, the psyche is treated as though it has an inner life of its own. This psychic life is seen as so precious and so delicate that it will wither if exposed to the harsh realities of the social world, and will flower only to the extent that it is isolated and protected. Each person's self has become his principal burden; to know oneself has become an end, instead of a means through which one knows the world. And precisely because we are so self-absorbed, it is extremely difficult for us to

Yet I do not dismiss the inner dialogue, but celebrate it *as long as it does not stop there*. Many persons talk to themselves. What is that? I call it strong talk. Often, it is an uneasy spirit trying to engage with yourself-in-the-world about the pain, the feelings, the events, the interrelationships which are aspects of the injustices in which you—and we all—participate, whether you are victim, perpetrator, or pretend to be an innocent bystander.

But some of us have hidden from our spirit and so can not engage it in dialogue. Spirit is not present to us. The intimacy of inner work through a *deep imaging* or a *deep questioning* is absent, not essayed, unpracticed, without precedent. *Then the dialogue with the other must begin first.* That invites the activity of the mentor: The one who not only teaches and enskills the other; much more, the one whose spirit through that outer work of dialogue lovingly given becomes present to the other's spirit and thus lends hope and courage for her to *learn to mind her own business,* i.e., the emancipation of her spirit: to learn the practices of enspiriting, that is, to learn *her* practices, for each expression is unique. In the course of that learning, the mode of the internal dialogue becomes possible.

The mentor, then, is the one who is listening deeply, whose spirit understands that the moment is ripe for invitation, for nurturing, for teasing out the other's spirit. That is the special competence of *turning toward* when the offering of dialogue is to receive, without judgment, the first tentative steps of presence, of intimacy, of vulnerability, of surprise. Often, this mentor's offering to receive is hidden in the protocols of enskilling, of teaching and facilitating, of transferring knowledge and the how-to-do-its of literacy training, basketball coaching, violin preparation, research for the doctorate, learning how to milk a cow or stow hay in the barn, or pull the figure out of the clay or stone rather than to put it in. That focus matters not at all in the mentoring of dialogue though it matters totally to its focus or subject-matter. For true mentoring, be it by a school teacher, a role-model, a parent, a friend, a lover, an

---

[23] *(continued)*

arrive at a private principle, to give any clear account to ourselves or to others of what our personalities are. The reason is that the more privatized the psyche, the less it is stimulated and the more difficult it is for us to feel or express feeling." (p.4.).

I should add that to this extent, the more difficult it is to feel compassion and to be present with the other. Of course, *psyche* is not *spirit,* as I have used the latter. Nevertheless, in a de-spiritualized culture, psyche and therefore psychology have come to replace that which throughout the generations we have come to know as spirit. But dialogue is no closer to psychological counseling of any kind than deep imaging of the future is to strategic planning or deep learning is to education.

Also crucial to unpacking and deflating the *privacy* interpretation of enspiriting is the conflation of the notions of the private, the personal, and the public in modern and even popular discourse. Hannah Arendt's *The Human Condition* (The University of Chicago Press, 1958) lays bare essential historical and philosophical arguments in clarifying their meaning; and her great insights support my own conviction that central to our era of transformation is the problematique not of *governments* (world governments, the U.N., national, provincial, state, local, etc.) but of *governance,* i.e., how shall we learn to govern ourselves on this planet with justice and in community of the kind which permits us our uniqueness, privately, personally, and publically while at the same time facilitating our giving attention to the world in which we live—the public domain—and from which we derive much of our social biography. But that issue, whether of *external governance* or *internal governance* is conjoined by the strong relationship and indeed continuum between the inner work and the outer work, the inner action and the outer action of the spirit, of which *dialogue* is its discipline.

editor, a coach or counselor—we have so many names for it—enables the one to commence the dialogue with the other. And that leads, sooner or later, to the emancipation of the dialogue within, the *discerning* acts through which *we discover the truth of our own transformation within the transformation of ourselves-in-the-world.*

Does dialogue stop there? Of course not.

Dialogue with God

This is the transcendent mode of *dialogue.* I do not mean to belittle it by labeling and categorizing. All modes of dialogue flow, the one into the others. Nor do I have much to say about this because I want to honor the infinite variety of its expression, going far beyond though including the religions invented by human beings and institutionalized into the churches of the world, be they cathedrals, temples, mosques, medicine wheel circles, or protecting the spirits of ancestors housed in the Igbo's Achi tree.

When you and God enter into dialogue, you know it. When your spirit mingles with God's, you know it. When She puts her loving arms around you and heals, you know it. When She says, "*In my name,* what are you up to?" you know it... and tremble. When She announces herself in a spring rain, a newborn calf, an ecstatic dance of Sufi or Hassid, an ancient emptiness that is the Way, a joining of universal consciousness, you know it. When you worship in your community and engage its liturgy until something bursts in you and your tears heal, She is present. When you move from polite chitchat to strong talk to *deep questioning* to the hermeneutic dialogue in which we unpack the most powerful of ideas, and you look around the room at your colleagues and discover that what has transpired is beyond your collective erudition, that somehow She has been present in the inquiry without ever being named, you know that too.

And when you come to the end of your lived life and mete out your measure on the scale of justice, having done what you have done and been what you have been, She welcomes your spirit back to its home with Her, perhaps for a rest, perhaps to send you off again on another journey into ourselves-in-the-world, to participate once again in the transformation of which we are all about.

This is the third dialogue. As you learn and practice the disciplines of the spirit, you will find it, giving it a name that befits you. She will find you. Both, now, deep in dialogue about the transformation that is upon us.

Dialogue as *Praxis*

We must, of course, end on a practice, an enspiriting action that is immanent to the enspiriting discipline of *dialogue*. It is *praxis*, a dialogical action in which fellow-enspiritors visit together for a few minutes, perhaps for an hour or more, to inquire into what they have been doing *with an eye to improving it*. Practice, from this Greek word, was understood not only as a doing, an action, but also a habitual way of doing things that could be learned and that could, under the proper tutelage, be made better. I have applied the idea to our work in enspiriting because the experience shows quite clearly that at the beginning of enspiriting, there are serious questions, even doubts, in the minds of the enspiritors about *what they are doing and how well they are doing it.*

If you were to seek to improve in the practices of enspiriting that I have set forth in these pages, how would you go about doing it? Wouldn't you look at your practice, at what you had actually been and done? Wouldn't that reflection hold true for the *inner work* as well as the *outer work*? Over the years, we have sought ways to help enspiritors raise questions of the kind that (1) lead to improved competence and (2) lead to *ownership* of the entire enspiriting project of disciplines, practices, and entering transformation. I have put these questions and the ensuing dialogical process into the form of an "exercise." You may begin to engage in dialogue with fellow-enspiritors just about as early in the enspiriting practices as you choose. You can practice at *praxis*, and you may do a *praxis* on *praxis* until you feel your competence in this discipline enables you to enter into *praxis* on any occasion of importance to you.

The exercise consists, simply enough, of three questions.

An Exercise in Praxis (No. 21)

The first question. This question opens up all sorts of feelings, concerns, issues about an enspiriting practice, (for example the various modes of *deep listening*), by inviting enspiritors to *re-experience the practice and to reflect together on its nature*. It is: "*What is it like to do this practice or practices*, e.g. *deep listening* or *deep imaging*, etc.?"

It is possible for an enspiritor to engage in this *dialogue* solely with herself at the inner level. But it is very difficult and usually is not undertaken in that individual mode of inner dialogue until the enspiritor is pretty good at it. In addition, by sharing her experience with other enspiritors who are also commencing the work, the enspiritor receives all kinds of provocative insights from the others and at the same time realizes that indeed he is in the same boat, trying to stay afloat and row as the swells threaten to capsize the whole thing. That *communal* realization, based even on this initial dialogical sharing, is the harbinger of forming a *community of learners.*

Some caveats may be helpful.

1. Gather in *praxis* groups of a size that allows every member to speak. We have found that half a dozen is a good number.

2. Remember, this is not a "theoretical" discussion. The question is posed in such a way that it encourages each enspiritor to delve deeply into the experience itself, at all levels of her being, very much including body, feelings, and spirit, as well as mind. Still, some like—in fact, are habituated to by an educational system, particularly at the University level—to engage in theoretical or abstract inquiry instead of just plain digging into the experience and addressing the question of what is it like to do this. Sometimes, one enspiritor has to pull another enspiritor back into that more precise and focused inquiry about *practice.*

3. Give yourself a common focus, and one that is not too complex. By this, I mean that if you are doing a *praxis* on *deep questioning,* don't include a focus on *deep learning.* By shifting back and forth among different disciplines in this dialogue, enspiritors are falsely encouraged, once again, to "rise above" the mundane question of what it is like. That question, however, invites you to penetrate to the very heart of the enspiriting practice at the level of the immediacy of the experiencing.

4. *Non-judgmental listening* is an absolute requisite here. Don't cut off an enspiritor trying to figure out from his experience what this is all about by pooh-poohing his offering and substituting yours as the truth.

5. Remind each other that there is no one way to do a practice. Each spirit and each social biography seeks its way. Thus, if the dialogue works well, each will learn from all and all will learn from each: The style of a *community of learners.* That doesn't mean you can't ask hard questions, particularly if you sense that your colleague is staying at a level of superficiality or if you sense that perhaps she is deceiving herself because the practice in question has moved her too fast and too far into the realm of spirit, and, simply put, she can't handle it. Many times, I have seen enspiritors in the envisioning projects engage in *praxis;* and as the dialogue got deeper, literally burst into tears when what she or a colleague were offering suddenly penetrated to the heart of her inner predicament. This happens in deep learning and *intentioning* particularly. In both disciplines, the complex and often conflicted relationship between social biography and spirit can no longer be mitigated by a *surface adherence to the*

skills of the enspiriting practices while avoiding the issues of competence. (Remember: *skill plus will, ability plus intention*).

The second question. This one invites enspiritors to a *praxis* about *naming*, about *vocabulary*, and about *jargon*. It is: *"When you are doing this practice (named and specific), what are you (actually) doing?"*

Why invite enspiritors to consider this question? Because it is the case that in the enspiriting work, some are suspicious of new words, like deep listening or intentioning. In this day and age, a great deal of language is used to obfuscate, to deceive, and to avoid *naming the experience for what it is.* Thus, a company discharges its employees when profit margins erode, and calls it "downsizing." So a missile whose warhead can turn 100,000 human beings to ashes is called a "peacemaker." So killing civilians as an inadvertent consequence of a bombing attack on a military target is called "collateral damage."

Language- and image-manipulators abound. In something as precious and as crucial as spirit and its emancipation, particularly in an age that denigrates spirit as an actor in history and dismisses the possibility of its play in the fields of ourselves-in-the-world, inviting people to their enspiriting and naming the practices by using old words in new ways, or by inventing new words invariably breeds serious questioning about that *naming*. "Why," some first-time enspiritors have asked, "Do you append the word 'deep' to listening, to questioning, and to learning? After all, these are activities in which we engage all the time. What's so special that they need a jargon to encapsulate their meaning?"

In fact, such questions must be addressed up front. *Praxis* dialogue renders that likely. For in this second question, we invite enspiritors to move beyond vocabulary to the immediacy of the experiencing to discover what it is that they do (and be) when they do it. The question invites a translation between experiencing a practice and reflecting on it. The question invites enspiritors into the core of our *beingness in this world and spirit's place in it,* for that core is always *mediated* by the human condition of assigning *meanings* to it *or letting others do it for you.* So, for example, one of the most critical penetrations of the overwhelming hegemony of television is that it assigns *meanings to ourselves-in-the-world*—who we are and what we do—without our participation in giving birth to those *meanings*. This is not a simplistic argument against violence on T.V. as the most preferred form of conflict management, i.e., *kill them.* Our evening news, for example, tells us not only what to acknowledge in the myriad "newsworthy" events—though again, much newsworthiness has to do with documenting violence in "real" life rather than just in movies. It also assigns to those events their meaning. It manufactures our KBVAF.

Is there an antidote? I know of none, and fear that the birth of the electronic superhighway will exacerbate this curse rather than offering alternatives. But in our enspiriting work, the *naming* of a practice must eventually be accompanied by the enspiritors getting beneath the naming and finding their own language to mediate the experiencing and share it with other enspiritors who are also bemused.

This second question, then, invites enspiritors to move through the experiencing of the practice (the first question), and beyond the question of *naming* to the issue of *ownership. We have learned that in dialoging about this second question, enspiritors come to an ownership of the practice in question. It is theirs. They have accepted proactively the naming or given it another. They know what they're up to, not only the how of it but also the meaning of it within their own experiencing.*

Praxis is such an emancipating and at the same time penetrating kind of action. Imagine if, prior to all of the efforts at school reform over the years, teachers were invited to sit together and do *praxis* on what they were doing and being in class. What is it like to teach? When you teach, what are you doing? Broaden the questions from the so-called "teaching" focus to their being and doing within the multiple systems of education in which they participate and whose names they accept: The political system of their classroom, their school building, their school district, their state education department and legislature, the NEA, etc.; the teaching-and-learning materials system in which they have little say; the management systems in which they also participate as professional or technical employees, etc.

Praxis, as we have come to understand it, *is the single most powerful way for anybody to reflect on their experience with a view to owning it, discarding it, improving at it or changing it. Praxis in enspiriting, within a community of learners, is the single most powerful way for enspiritors to do the same.*

But this leads us, inevitably, to the third question which by now you have no doubt uncovered.

The third question. Eventually, of course, we must move from practice to purpose. Eventually, we must re-enter the space of our spirit and ourselves-in-the-world to ask: *"Why are we doing this (the enspiriting, the specific practice)?"*

Dialoguers might start by addressing this question in the context of the specific discipline and one of its modes or practices. Why deep listen? When would you do that?

But not only, under what conditions? Also, Why? Why would you deep listen with anybody? For what purposes? What does it do for you? What does it do for the other?

All of the other aspects of the *praxis* raised by the first two questions emerge into this last dialogue. But now, something else is added: direct (but loving) assault on the reasons for enspiriting in the first place. At first, the dialogue may focus on the purposes of the specific discipline or practice. But later, perhaps even when a larger group of enspiritors gathers to reflect on their experiencing, the *supreme* and *final*— or is it the *originating*—question becomes fodder for their collective spirit to chew on. *What are we about? Why do we do this? What are we up to? How might we bring spirit back into ourselves-in-the-world? With what consequences?*

So the dialogue proceeds in a *community of learners.*

A Transformative Liturgy

Is there anything in the work of the spirit we do together that invites celebration and worship? Celebration signifies something out of the ordinary, perhaps occasional, wherein we share together the importance of the event or experience and *the importance of the persons with whom we are celebrating.* Worship has to do with honoring the sacred, giving it homage, perhaps God if that is your naming, perhaps an experiencing that carries its own transcendence.

Every group of enspiritors with whom I have worked comes to this moment, sometimes several times throughout the experience, sometimes at its end. I'm not talking only about thanking each other, though that, too, is an exceptional action among people who, most of them, have been going to conferences, workshops, seminars, gatherings all their lives to pick up the latest information, the latest skills, the latest knowledge, and to network. They are so habituated to these forms of interaction that they have nothing to thank each other for.

What then is a liturgy that fits enspiriting?

Because enspiriting is transformative, inner or outer, we search for new liturgies. Let that search occur and aid it. Become its enspiritor and inventor along with your colleagues.

A couple of years ago, I worked with about 40 folks in a three-day envisioning workshop to which each participant had brought her own focus. Many of them were teachers. Some were human resource development professionals, counselors, psychologists. Some were management experts, some were envisioning facilitators with whom I had worked before. Several were administrative or political executives in local or provincial government. They came for lots of reasons, ostensibly to understand and experience envisioning as a form of leadership and policy; but, of course, each of them had her own reasons that gradually surfaced in her work and in her *praxis*.

Under the aegis of envisioning, we enspirited. Not all of the practices, but perhaps half of them; lots of emphasis on *deep listening, deep imaging,* and *intentioning,* particularly culminating in each one discovering her compelling image, and then joining others to form into self-selected groups to build a "scenario" that represented the intentioning input of each member.

It was a long, arduous, endisciplined experience. Some participants objected to the discipline. They just wanted to take notes and be "objective" observers, picking up as many tricks along the way as they could, believing that this was mainly a skills-demonstration experience of the kind that proliferates across the frontiers of Western human technology. But it was not that. By the last day, those who had arrived with that in mind realized how much they had missed of their own enspiriting.

Here's how we ended. On the third and last day, at about 2:30 p.m., we gathered our chairs in a large circle. Each group—in envisioning, they are called "scenario teams" or "intentioning groups," averaging four to eight members—made its *offering* by entering the center of the circle and giving to the rest of us, through words, through song, through drama, through symbolic gestures acts that not all of us could understand in a literal way but could apprehend at the level of spirit, the fruits of their envisioning, the fruits of their enspiriting together.

The last group, as I remember, did not "perform" at the center. Rather, they maintained their chairs and lit a candle. Then, the candle was passed from one person to the next, sitting right alongside. As the candle was passed, its receiver sat quietly, closed her eyes, held the candle, and let her spirit sing to her inside. You know, to pass the candle from one to another took over an hour. We all sat in silence, some watching outward, some looking inward. Absolute silence reigned. *Being silence together.*

Then, when the candle was passed around the circle, we continued to sit together without words. *What a dialogue of the spirit.* Our medicine wheel had brought our spirit to life within that communal event. For another half an hour, silence. Then it was getting toward 5:00 PM. A few of us got up and, again without a word, went to those with whom we had become particularly close, either by virtue of loving conflict or by virtue of finding a fellow-enspiritor. Then a few quiet words were exchanged, an embrace given and received, a forgiving or a loving, all within the sharing of spirit. Then we went on our way.

Toward the very end, a woman came up to me. She was short—certainly less than five feet—in her 50s or 60s—wearing steel-framed glasses, her face creased by her travails, her black hair still hanging off her shoulders in a sheen of a once-beautiful embracing of her head and neck. We had not talked once during those three days. She was not a great talker. She was a great listener.

She moved to me and held out her arms as if she were holding a heavy weight that she wanted to offer me, so that instead of reaching up to put her arms around my neck—which she couldn't reach in any event—she held them waist high. And I put my arms on her shoulders.

And she spoke. Not thank you. Not this was great. Not parting pleasantries.

She said, " I have hope again."

That's all.

Her eyes glistened and tears etched the feeling of my spirit on my cheeks.

We held each other for another moment or two, in silence. Then we parted, she to her Native space, I to mine. Spirit had come out and blessed us.

References

Barber, Benjamin. *Strong Democracy: Participatory Politics for a New Age*. Berkeley: University of California Press, 1984.

Coles, Robert. *The Spiritual Life of Children*. Boston: Houghton Mifflin Co., 1990.

Gabor, Dennis. *Inventing the Future*. New York: Knopf, 1964.

Gendlin, Eugene T. *Focusing*. New York: Everest House, 1978.

Herbert, Nick. *Quantum Reality: Beyond the New Physics*. Garden City, New York: Anchor Press/Doubleday, 1985.

Kovel, Joel: *History and Spirit: An Inquiry into the Philosophy of Liberation*. Boston: Beacon Press, 1991.

Macmurray, John. *The Self as Agent*. London: Faber and Faber Ltd., 1957.

Macmurray, John. *Persons in Relation*. London: Faber and Faber Ltd., 1961.

Miura, Isshu, Ruth Fuller, and Sasaki, *The Zen Koan*. New York: Harcourt, Brace & World, Inc., 1965.

Myrdal, Gunnar with the assistance of Richard Sterner and Arnold Rose. *An American Dilemma: The Negro Problem and Modern Democracy*. New York: Harper & Brothers Publishers, 1944.

Sandburg, Carl. *Abraham Lincoln. The Prairie Years and the War Years*. One-Volume Edition. New York: Harcourt, Brace and Co., 1954.

Sennet and Cobb, *The Hidden Injuries of Class*. New York: Knopf, 1972.

Watkins, Mary. *Waking Dreams*. Dallas, Texas: Spring Publications, Inc., 1994.

Watson, Burton, translator. *The Complete Works of Chuang Tzu*. New York: Columbia University Press, 1968.

Wilbur, Ken. *Eye to Eye: The Quest for a New Paradigm*. Boston & Shaftsbury: Shambhala, 1990.

To Fellow Enspiritors

Some of you may wish to continue and deepen your exploration of your spirit; how you may learn to listen to its voice more readily; how you may re-enter into the negotiation between your spirit and your social biography; how you invite it to emerge more powerfully into your life, your community, and your organization.

We invite you to continue this work of enspiriting with us, in short workshops and seminars, and in longer residential programs held by invitation in various locations in many parts of the world. We have developed special workshop and training materials for *enspiriting* as well as for *envisioning* to assist you in your explorations.

If you are interested in more information about *enspiriting*, photocopy the form provided on page 277, fill in the information requested, then mail or fax your information to us. For your convenience you may also call **The Enspiriting Institute** directly at our toll free number, 1-800-303-484-9739; when asked, enter the four-digit code 2439.

To Trainers, Facilitators
and Professionals

Some of you may wish to participate in the growing cadre of fellow enspiritors who have learned and so offer the disciplines and competencies of *enspiriting* in professional contexts, within organizations, communities, and a variety of action-settings.

The Enspiriting Institute will prepare you for your professional enspiriting activities by offering residential preparation programs. These will enable you to use our materials and exercises specially designed for a variety of enspiriting and envisioning contexts and situations: with business, government, civic, professional, community, and affinity groups.

This work takes very special skills as well as an intentioning spirit. Our preparation helps you to discover how and why you choose to do enspiriting with other people; how to use and apply our materials and exercises; how to collaborate in the difficult design and facilitation decisions that maintain the integrity and honesty of the enspiriting work.

For more information photocopy the following form, fill in the information requested, then mail or fax your information to us. Or call us, toll free, at **The Enspiriting Institute,** 1-800-303-484-9739; when asked, enter the four-digit code 2439. We will enter into immediate dialogue with you about your aspirations and when and where the next preparation programs will be held.

For more information
please photocopy this form,
fill in the information,
and mail or fax to:

The Enspiriting Institute
of the Futures-Invention Associates International
PO Box 260466
Highlands Ranch, CO 80126-0466
1-800-484-9739, code 2439
FAX 303-773-1431

Name: _____

Address: _____

City: _____

State/Prov.: _____

Zip/Postal code: _____ Country: _____

Phone: (home) _____ (work) _____

FAX: _____

Organization: _____

(Please indicate your areas of interest).

_____ I am interested in further *Enspiriting* work for myself.

_____ I am interested in the preparation programs to prepare myself to do *Enspiriting* work with other people.

Would you like to help organize a workshop or residential program in your area?
Yes _____   No _____

Other: _____